THE RECORD SOCIETY OF LANCASHIRE AND CHESHIRE

FOUNDED TO TRANSCRIBE AND PUBLISH
ORIGINAL DOCUMENTS RELATING TO THE TWO COUNTIES

VOLUME CXXXV

The Society wishes to acknowledge with gratitude the support
given towards publication by
Kirby Archives Trust
Lancashire County Council

© Record Society of Lancashire and Cheshire
Janet D. Martin

ISBN 0 902593 38 2

Produced by Sutton Publishing Limited, Stroud, Gloucestershire
Printed in Great Britain
by
Book Craft, Midsomer Norton.

COUNCIL AND OFFICERS FOR THE YEAR 1997

President

Professor A. Harding, B.Litt., M.A., F.S.A., F.R.Hist.S.

Hon. Council Secretary

Dorothy J. Clayton, M.A., Ph.D., A.L.A., F.R. Hist. S., c/o John Rylands University Library of Manchester, Oxford Road, Manchester, M13 9PP

Hon. Membership Secretary

Maureen Patch, B.A., D.A.A., c/o Manchester County Record Office, 56 Marshall Street, Manchester, M4 5FU

Hon. Treasurer

B. W. Quintrell, M.A., Ph.D., F.R.Hist.S., c/o School of History, Liverpool University, 8 Abercromby Square, Liverpool, L69 3BX

Hon. General Editor

Philip Morgan, B.A., Ph.D., F.R.Hist.S., Department of History, The University, Keele, ST5 5BG

Other Members of Council

Elizabeth A. Danbury, B.A.	D.A. Stoker, B.A., M.Ar.Ad.
B. Jackson, M.A., D.A.A.	J.R. Studd, B.A., Ph.D., F.R.Hist.S.
Jennifer I. Kermode, B.A., Ph.D.	A.T. Thacker, M.A., D.Phil., F.R.Hist.S.
P. McNiven, M.A., Ph.D., F.R.Hist.S.	T.J. Thornton, M.A., D.Phil.
J.R.H. Pepler, M.A., D.A.A.	T.J. Wyke, B.A.
C.B. Phillips, B.A., Ph.D.	

Clement Taylor (1688–1742).

The Account Book of Clement Taylor of Finsthwaite, 1712–1753

Edited by

Janet D. Martin

PRINTED FOR THE SOCIETY
1997

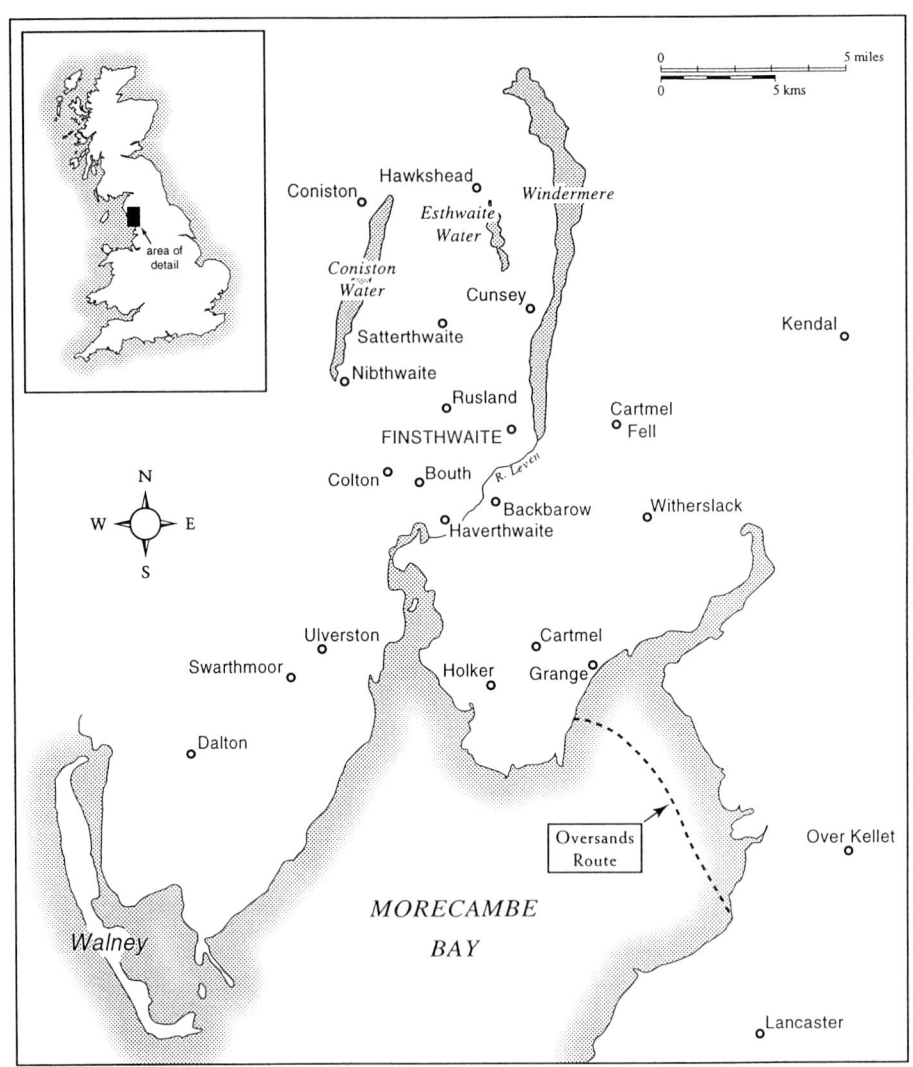

Finsthwaite in its setting.

CONTENTS

Preface ix

Abbreviations x

Figures, Maps and Illustrations x

Introduction xii

The Account Book of Clement Taylor 1

Appendix: John Hathornthwaite's Will 221

Biographical Index 224

Glossary 244

Bibliography 253

Index 255

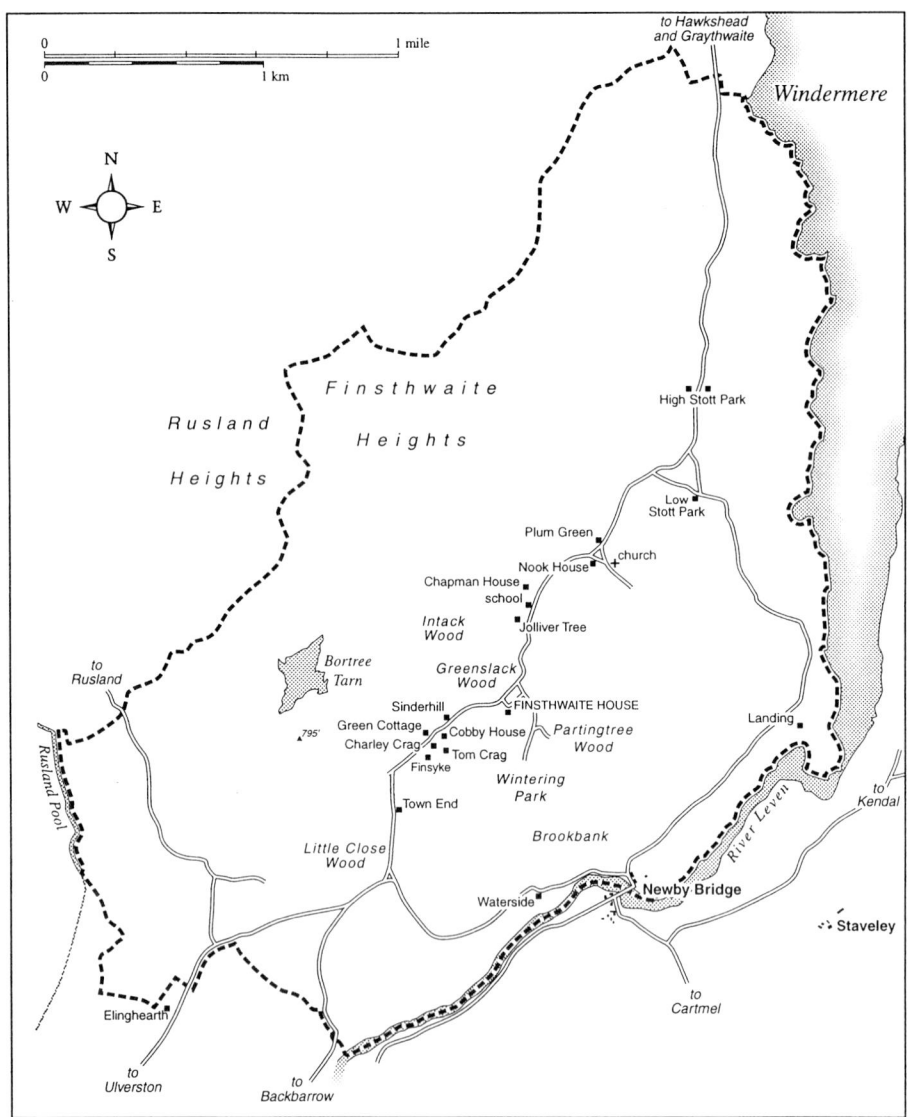

Finsthwaite in the eighteenth century showing the principal places mentioned in the text.

PREFACE

Many friends and colleagues have helped in the preparation of this book. In particular I should like to thank the staff of the Lancashire Record Office and its former archivist, Ken Hall, for easing my path in so many ways, and those at the Cumbria Record Office in Barrow-in-Furness and in Kendal, especially Richard Hall, for their cooperation and advice. Dr Philip Morgan, the Society's General Editor, has borne the deficiencies of my elderly word-processor with friendly forbearance and has helped both the book and its editor through the press with unfailing good humour. Blake Tyson freely shared his wisdom in architectural matters, and I have benefited over many years from the friendship and learning of Susan Denyer. It gives me especial pleasure to thank Claire Mary Chaplin of Finsthwaite House for permission to publish the manuscript and to reproduce the frontispiece, and her husband John for his time and trouble in discussing the development of the house with me. My daughter Sophia has suffered Clement Taylor and his affairs for many years and I am deeply grateful for her patience and her help, both practical and intellectual. My greatest debt, as ever, is to my husband, Geoffrey Martin, without whose generous support this book would never have been completed.

Janet D. Martin
Finsthwaite, 1997

ABBREVIATIONS

CRO	Cumbria Record Office
LRO	Lancashire Record Office
PRO	Public Record Office
CWAAS	Cumberland and Westmorland Antiquarian and Archaeological Society
CW1	CWAAS *Transactions,* 1st series
CW2	CWAAS *Transactions,* 2nd series
Note	In the footnotes to both introduction and text cross-references as e.g. see p. 27 are to pages of the orginal MS. Cross-references as e.g. see 27 are to pages in this volume.

FIGURES, MAPS AND ILLUSTRATIONS

FIGURES

1 The genealogy of Clement Taylor	xi

MAPS

1 Finsthwaite in its setting	vi
2 Finsthwaite in the eighteenth century	viii

ILLUSTRATIONS

1 Clement Taylor (1688–1742)	iv
2 Finsthwaite House from the south-east	xxii
3 The old church of St Peter, Finsthwaite	xxv
4 A page from the account book	xxxii

THE GENEALOGY OF CLEMENT TAYLOR

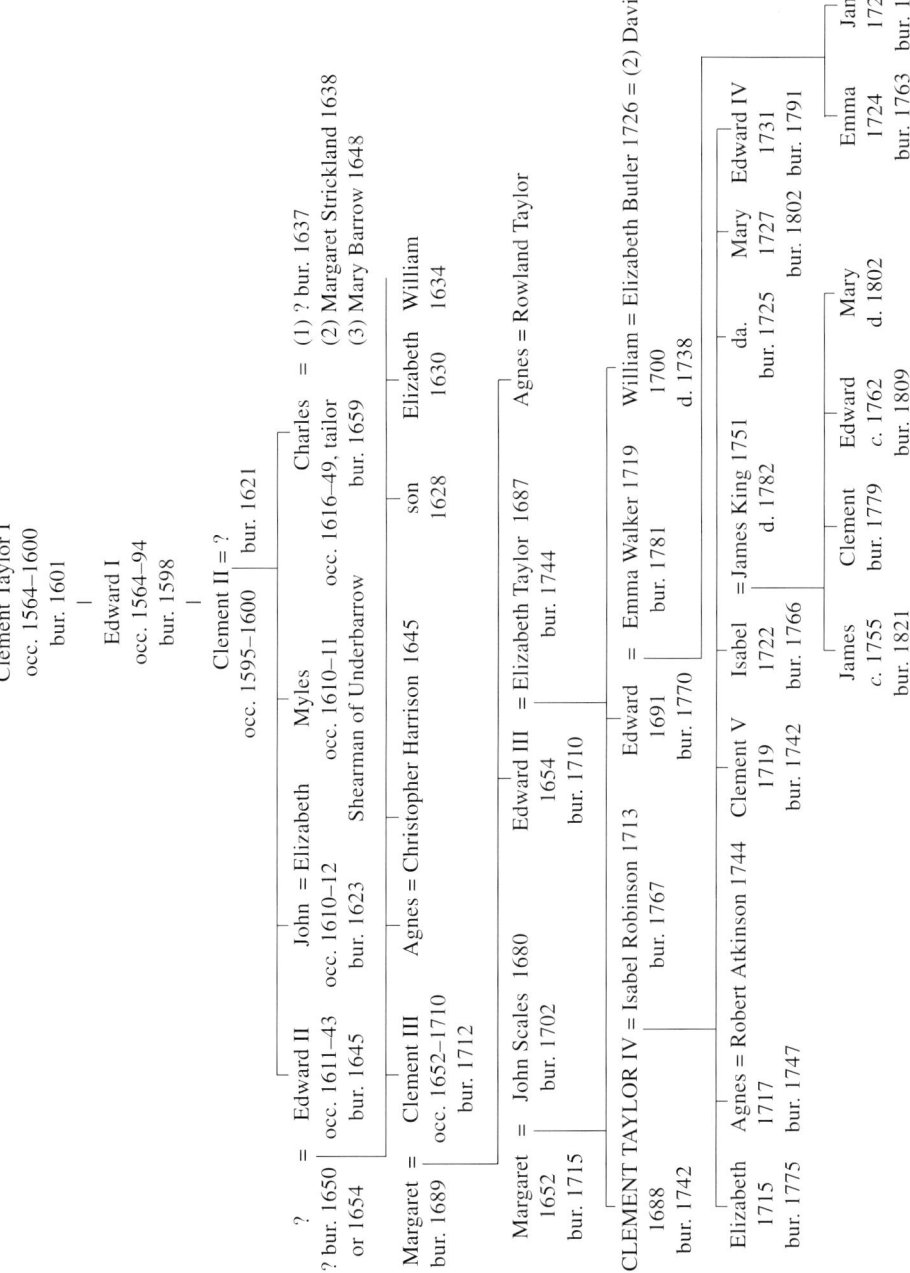

INTRODUCTION

Clement Taylor's account book[1] is one of the archives of Finsthwaite House, in which his successors still live today.[2] It contains notes of receipts and payments from 1712 to 1742, when he died, and it was then continued by his wife to 1753. The latest entry, an isolated one, was made in 1756. The book reflects the accretion of his estate as well as the building of the oldest parts of the present house, and a great variety of personal and local affairs.[3]

Finsthwaite is a settlement which stretches for more than a mile and a half along a valley just to the west of Lake Windermere at its southern end, from Town End in the south to the outlying hamlets of Low and High Stott Park in the north, and including the group of houses in what was known as Plum Green, close to the church. The parish also includes Lakeside, in Clement Taylor's day called Landing, where there was at least one house at the western end of one of two fords across the lake. The fords had largely fallen out of use when the fine stone bridge at Newby Bridge was built in the sixteenth century and attracted to itself an inn and a nearby blacksmith's business on the Finsthwaite side of the river Leven.[4]

In the middle ages the area was part of the extensive High Furness estates of Furness Abbey, whose tenants there were small farmers able to augment their livelihoods by exploiting the woodland which lay abundantly around their farms. In the sixteenth century they were making wooden bowls and platters, frames for pack-saddles, and baskets. Bark was trimmed for tanning and, most important of all, charcoal was made for smelting the iron ore mined in Low Furness and transported to places such as Finsthwaite to be smelted on primitive hearths.[5] When the abbey was dissolved in 1537 there were eleven tenants in Finsthwaite with four

---

1   LRO, DDPd 26/337.
2   The direct line of descent ended with the death of Clement Taylor's great-nephew, James King, in 1821. In his will, dated 16 January 1817, he left his Finsthwaite estate to his 'relation', Roger Taylor of High Stott Park. The precise nature of this supposed relationship cannot now be established. Roger Taylor was descended from the Ashburners who lived at Stott Park in the sixteenth century, and I can find nothing to connect his family directly with the Taylors of Finsthwaite House. Mary, daughter of Robert Ashburner (d. 1646), married Robert Taylor in 1637 at Hawkshead. Roger Taylor (1770–1849) was their 3 x great-grandson. On his death, his property was divided among his three sisters, and Finsthwaite House came to Elizabeth (1773–1857), widow of the Revd James Pedder (1767–1835), vicar of Garstang, from whom the present owner descends. James King's belief that Roger Taylor was a relation is an interesting survival of the clan ethos which must have been powerful among the sixteenth-century Taylors.
3   It was used by J. Fell in 'Some Illustrations of Home Life in Lonsdale North of the Sands, in the 17th and 18th centuries', *CW1*, xi, 1891, 368–98.
4   See below n. 15.
5   The early woodland industries are discussed e.g. by W.H. Pearsall and W. Pennington, *The Lake District: A Landscape History*, London, 1973, 264–7. See also A. Fell, *The Early Iron Industry of Furness and District*, Ulverston, 1908.

more at Stott Park.⁶ In the two parts of Finsthwaite, lower and outer (the distinctions related to their distance from the abbey), they all bore the surname of Taylor, and from one of them the owner of the account book presented here was descended.

Clement Taylor was baptised at Colton on 7 February 1688. His family is documented from 1564, when Clement Taylor I witnessed a deed of sale;⁷ he was buried at Hawkshead on 22 March 1601. He was the father of Edward I (buried 5 September 1598), who witnessed the same document, and he in turn was probably the father of Clement II whose wife was buried in the church at Hawkshead in 1621.⁸ Clement I was described only as a husbandman, but burial inside the church argues a rather superior social status. By 1561 'lower' Finsthwaite had become known as Finsyke, a name which is today only that of one house, but which was then applied to the whole southern end of the settlement.⁹ Clement I was 'of Finsyke' in 1570 and he bought half another 'farmhold' there in 1574.¹⁰

In 1612 another Edward Taylor (II), who was probably the son of Clement II, bought a property in Finsthwaite described as 'Clement Taylor tenement' from his brother John.¹¹ Whether this was another house owned by one of the first two Clements, or a virgin site, is uncertain, although 'tenement' might imply a dwelling, but it is clear that from then on Edward II and his descendants lived in a house on the site of the present Finsthwaite House. Edward II died in 1647 and was buried in Hawkshead church on 13 June. In his will, dated 8 June, he left all his property to his son Clement III, but made provision for a younger son William and an unmarried daughter Elizabeth, his other daughter Agnes having been provided for when she married in 1645. His inventory revealed a total personal estate of over £230, including £45 in cattle, a quantity of charcoal, over £60 in loans, and £77 in cash, so, for the time and the place, he was relatively well-to-do.

His son Clement III succeeded him and continued to prosper. He made some more additions to his property¹² and lived to a great age, being buried at

6   J. Brownhill (ed.), *The Coucher Book of Furness Abbey*, ii, vol. 3, Chetham Society, 78, 1919, 631. Fifteen people paid greenhew rent in both parts of Finsthwaite in January 1538: PRO, DL30/bundle 80/1083; in 1546 seventeen are named, and Landing is mentioned by name for the first time: LRO, DDSa 29/1. Each tenement must have supported more than one family.
7   LRO, DDPd 26/4; he also occurs 1570–1600; *ibid*. 26/6, 8–12, 17, 23, 28.
8   The early register of Hawkshead, where anyone of any consequence in Finsthwaite was buried, gives no place-names in this period. That of Colton begins only in 1623, is fragmentary in the 1640s and early '50s, and is completely lacking between 1651 and 1673, after which there are burials only to 1675 when it becomes compete. In suggesting the family's descent in its early stages I have made the assumption that there was an alternate series of Clements and Edwards, which is largely confirmed by surviving deeds and wills.
9   PRO, DL30/bundle 80/1086, Colton court roll, 2 July 1561. At this court eleven tenants in 'Finsyke' paid greenhew rent, and there were five in 'Plowmegrene', the old outer Finsthwaite, with five more at Stott Park.
10 LRO, DDPd 26/6, 9.
11 *ibid*. 26/45. Edward II was then living in Cartmel Fell, where he was perhaps in farm service as his father would have been in possession at Finsthwaite. In 1643 he bought a meadow near Rusland Pool: *ibid*. 26/99.
12 *ibid*. 26/106, 111, 118, 136–7, 149. In 1661 he paid £18 1s 6d to extinguish the tithes on his estate, more than was paid by anyone else in Finsthwaite except Richard Taylor of Waterside who paid £19: *ibid*. 26/122–3.

Hawkshead on 2 March 1712. By his wife Margaret he had two sons (one died in infancy), and two daughters, both of whom married yeomen farmers in the Rusland valley. His heir was his surviving son Edward III, baptised at Hawkshead on 5 June 1654. Clement's wife died in February 1689 and in the following December, for a payment of £100, he transferred half of his property in Finsthwaite to Edward, who was to have the rest when his father died.[13]

So the household from 1689 would have consisted of the widower Clement III, and Edward III and his family. Edward married Elizabeth, the daughter of John Scales of Thwaite Moss, at Colton on 4 May 1687. They had three sons, Clement IV, the writer of the account book (baptised on 7 February 1688), Edward (23 May 1691), and William (22 May 1700). In 1684 Edward III added another farm to the estate with the purchase of Cobby House from John Taylor, a tanner.[14] He died before his father and was buried at Hawkshead on 28 December 1710, when his eldest son, the heir to both Edward III and Clement III, was twenty-two years old. Edward's widow Elizabeth lived until 1744.

In 1713 Clement IV married a near neighbour, Isabel Robinson of Waterside. Her ancestors were also Taylors, descended from the Peter Taylor who had established a blacksmith's business there, close to the new bridge over the river Leven and on the road from Kendal to Ulverston, in the later years of the sixteenth century.[15] During the next century his family prospered and acquired more land, and his great-grandson Richard Taylor (d. 1706) was able to extend the house at Waterside on a generous scale. Richard had an only daughter Agnes, who married a Kendal joiner, Christopher Robinson,[16] at Witherslack in 1676. Her father added a rear wing to the house for them, with a moulded plaster overmantel bearing his own and their initials.

Both Agnes and Christopher died relatively young, he in 1690 and she in 1700, leaving a family of two daughters and two sons. Mary died in the same year as her mother. John (baptised in 1682) became a dissenter, probably a Quaker and perhaps through the influence of his wife, who, after he died at Bouth in 1712, married a

---

13 ibid. 26/164.
14 ibid. 26/152.
15 Peter Taylor first appears in 1572: *ibid.* 26/7. He was named as smith to Christopher Preston of Holker in 1582, and as smith of Waterside in 1594: *ibid.* 26/15, 23. His two sons, Richard (d. 1626) and Edward (d. 1610) were both smiths, and Richard's son Edward (d. 1637) may also have been one. If so, he seems to have been the last at Waterside. The later smithy was on the Cartmel side of Newby Bridge.
16 Christopher Robinson was a member of the company of joiners in Kendal, and was still 'of Kendal' in 1688: *ibid.* 41/1–2. In July 1663 he made a pew in Grasmere church for Sir Daniel Fleming of Rydal: M.L. Armitt, *The Church of Grasmere*, Kendal, 1912, 113. His origins are unknown, but he may well have come from Bouth and must have been related to the William Robinson of Bouth who was a party to the settlement made in 1680 by his wife's father, Richard Taylor of Waterside (LRO, DDPd 26/146–7), and his baptism is probably lost in the gap in the Colton register. He certainly had property at Bouth which he left to his son John, who also received a house in Kendal. Each of his daughters had legacies of £100. There is a copy of his will, 8 May 1690, at *ibid.* 26/165. His acquisition of Waterside after his marriage made him a farmer, as there were sheep and cattle in his probate inventory, as well as his 'joyner worke toolls' and timber valued at over £10. His wife's inventory is *ibid.* 26/171, and the administration bond for their daughter Mary is *ibid.* 26/172. Neither survives in LRO, WRW/F.

Introduction xv

known Quaker, John Caton of Hatlex, near Bolton-le-Sands.[17] Richard inherited Waterside from his grandfather and figures largely in the account book. And Isabel married his friend Clement Taylor IV.

Clement and Isabel had seven children of whom one, a daughter, died at birth in 1725. Their eldest child Elizabeth (baptised in March 1715) died unmarried in 1775. The next daughter Agnes (6 February 1717) married Robert Atkinson of Cark in 1744 but died three and a half years later and was brought back to Finsthwaite for burial. Clement V, the elder son, was baptised on 13 October 1719 and had begun to play some part in the affairs of the parish before his untimely death just after the Christmas of 1741,[18] although he is barely mentioned in the account book. Isabel (14 August 1722) married James King, a naval surgeon from Liverpool, at Cartmel in 1751. Their eldest son James became the eventual heir to the estate when his uncle Edward died in 1790. Mary (11 February 1727) was also unmarried, and lived latterly in Ulverston where she died in 1802.[19] The last child was another son, Edward, baptised on 18 December 1731, and so a child of about eleven when Clement Taylor died in November 1742.

Clement's brother Edward is a shadowy figure. In 1719, he married Emma Walker of Haverthwaite, mysteriously at Old Hutton, Westm., with which the family had no discernible connection.[20] They baptised two daughters, Emma (Emy) at Colton in 1724 and Jane at Finsthwaite in 1727; both predeceased their parents. Edward, who rented the house at Waterside from his nephew Edward from about 1750,[21] after it had come into the possession of Clement IV on the death of Richard Robinson in 1741, died in 1770, and his wife in 1781. Edward left an annuity of £60 to his wife for her lifetime, £100 to his sister Isabel's son Edward King, his godson, other monetary bequests of about £145, and the interest on £20 per annum for 'poor housekeepers' in Finsthwaite (his nephew Edward was the residuary legatee), so was not a poor man, but how he made his money is unknown.[22] His

17 One of the supervisors of John Robinson's will, dated 29 May 1711 and proved 22 February 1712, was John Pirt of Greenbank in Dunnerdale. The Pirts or Pritts were Baptists who appear before 1700 in the minute book of Tottlebank Baptist church now at Regent's Park College, Oxford: see *CW2*, 1991, 218, 229. But dissenters of whatever kind often had close connections, even in the nineteenth century: *ibid.*, 235 n. 55.
18 He signed the nomination papers for George Simpson's appointment to the living at Finsthwaite, 25 August 1741: LRO, DDCh 37/51, clergy bundle, Finsthwaite.
19 Mary was a wealthy woman with a considerable estate. Like her brother Edward and her sister Isabel's children, she was a partner in the Backbarrow/Penny Bridge Co. and at Cunsey Forge: CRO (Barrow), Z47–9. Her will is LRO, DDPd 37/5.
20 Edward may have had some connection with Blease Hall in Old Hutton. A seemingly stray document among the family papers is an abstract of title to the Blease Hall estate with the opinions of two layers as to a Mr Wilson's title to it, dated 1716: *ibid.* 26/203. Clement Taylor had a tup called 'Blease' who could well have come from there: see n. 256. The deeds for Blease Hall (CRO, WDRy 1/1/1) shed no light on the matter.
21 His rent is detailed in LRO, DDPd 26/338.
22 His will was witnessed by Clementina Douglas, who was buried in the churchyard at Finsthwaite on 16 May 1771 as Clementina Johannes Sobieski Douglas, spinster of Waterside. She was a lodger, with a male companion called James Douglas who also witnessed the will, at Waterside, and after her death their rooms were vacated and relet as 'the two Front Rooms which Captain Douglas had lately': *ibid.* The supposition that she was a daughter of the Young Pretender has been widely, and often wildly, canvassed.

father Edward III had specifically left him only 'the old bay mare', but he was the residuary legatee of both his father and his grandfather and undoubtedly benefited thereby.

William, Clement IV's youngest brother, was a boy of ten when his father died, leaving him decently provided for, with £400 'to go forward with him' until he came of age. Clement educated him at Browedge school, from where he entered The Queen's College, Oxford, in 1721, apparently with a bursary from his school, taking his BA in 1724. He was ordained deacon in 1726 and priest in 1728 in the diocese of Peterborough, and was successively curate of Farthingstone, Northants., and vicar of Long Buckby in the same county. He married Elizabeth Butler in 1726, and died of consumption in 1738.[23] There were no children of the marriage. Clement looked after his interests in the neighbourhood of Finsthwaite, where his money was invested, and dispatched boxes of potted char and preserved cockles to him. There is no evidence that they ever met again after William went to Oxford.

The charge of this youngest brother and his money may have been the occasion for Clement Taylor to begin his account book, as the first entries are concerned with William and his education. The writer evidently set out to be systematic, and continued with a list of 'Land Lett to farme', but although there is another section concerned with money that was lent out, some of which was inherited from his grandfather and some that belonged to William, most of the succeeding pages are in a rough chronological order. It looks as though the book was written up at the end of the day, whenever there was something to be noted. At the back there are sections devoted to bark sales, to the business of being parish constable, to the Hathornthwaite trusteeship,[24] to payments for the new house, to dealings with the butchers Edward Burns and William Coward, to overseer's affairs, to lists of bloomsmithy rents, and to sheep. After Clement Taylor died, the book was continued for some years by his widow and her man of business.

The account book is a volume measuring 308mm by 95mm, bound in tooled leather over paper boards, and now contains 268 pages, of which the first was originally left blank. The front endpaper has become detached, and the back endpaper is missing.[25] One or two pages have been torn at the foot, but generally the book is in excellent condition. It is transcribed here in full. Abbreviations have been extended, and the names of people referred to by initials are given in full where they can be identified with certainty, with the exception of the 'CT' or 'C. Taylor' by which the writer refers to himself. The pagination is mine, there being none in the original. All the dates in the original are Old Style. Unless otherwise indicated, the entries were written by Clement Taylor himself. Deletions in the text are indicated by < >.

Clement Taylor was twenty-two when his father died in 1710; two years later he inherited the rest of his grandfather's estate. It consisted of the family house and

---

23 His will is *ibid.* 36/9. His brother collected up some of his assets in Furness, loans to Richard Rigge of Force Mill and John Scales of Grizedale and paid them to his trustees in February 1739: *ibid.* 26/248. A mortgage on a house in Newby Bridge was called in in 1740: *ibid.* 36/10. See also n. 11, below.
24 See Appendix, 221 below.
25 Material from the endpapers appears at the end of the main text, as pp. i–iv; see 217–20 below.

farm, with the land belonging to it, and some other property nearby. Cobby House, which his father had bought in 1684, was available for letting, and was occupied by the Danson family throughout the whole period of the account book, in the persons of Edward Danson (d. 1730) and his son Thomas (d. 1754). At some point the farm at Town End which was leased to Thomas Johnson in April 1728 must also have been acquired, but its purchase cannot be identified among the surviving deeds. It may even have been bought in the sixteenth century. Clement Taylor himself bought Tom Cragg in 1713,[26] paying £320 to the previous owner, James Taylor. There is nothing in the account book about the purchase of the farm or who subsequently lived there, until it was leased to John Benson after Clement's death. It might have been James Danson, who was certainly a tenant, but there is no indication of where he lived; on the other hand, James Taylor was still working in Finsthwaite as late as 1727, and some arrangement may have been made for him to stay on at the farm in return for his labour.

In 1718 Clement acquired Charley Crag[27] from its aged owner, Jane (Jennet) Taylor, whose husband John, a collier, had left his little farm to his wife, with instructions that it should be sold. Clement bought it a few months later and subsequently managed Jennet's affairs for her. Her husband has specified that she should retain 'the new end' of the house, the tiny separate cottage on the north end, for her lifetime, and she lived there until she died in 1728. The main house was let to her son-in-law William Woodburn. Charley Crag was sold in 1729 to the John Taylor who was the father of Clement's right-hand man Peter, and Peter bought it from his father's trustees in 1734.[28]

In February 1741 Clement Taylor inherited the substantial house and farm at Waterside, and some other property, from his unmarried brother-in-law Richard Robinson. The following July he sold it for £500 to his son Clement V, evidently intending that the young man should set up on his own account, but the younger Clement fell ill and the transaction was reversed on 18–19 December 1742, by a lease which he signed in a pathetically weak hand and the next day by a release to which he could only put his mark.[29] He was buried two weeks later, and Waterside was leased to John Cragg. It eventually became the home of Clement Taylor's brother Edward.

Various pieces of land were also let, notably to Robert Sawrey who had his own house on the site of the present Green Cottage.[30] Clement Taylor was always ready to buy land whenever the opportunity offered. In 1715, for instance, he paid £3 for half of the close called Tarnhaw, near Boretree Tarn, and £24 15s in 1716 for two acres on Great Hagg.[31] His most extensive purchases were made when the estate of Henry Taylor of Landing came onto the market in 1735 and he paid £373 13s for 23 1/2 acres of land.[32]

26   LRO, DDPd 26/188.
27   *ibid.* 26/206.
28   *ibid.* 26/228, 236. It was eventually repurchased by Isabel Taylor in 1768: *ibid.* 26/301, 306.
29   *ibid.* 26/259–60. For the problems created by Richard Robinson's will, see below, xxix.
30   See n. 222, below.
31   LRO, DDPd 26/198, 200; see also *ibid.* 26/205, 210, 219.
32   See nn. 194, 196, below.

Only one of his minor land transactions is reported in the account book, perhaps because it was a joint venture with Myles Harrison of Stott Park. In 1726 they bought twelve acres of peat-moss on Rusland Heights from Abraham Rawlinson of Rusland Hall.[33] There may have been other purchases, for which no deeds survive, although the family was generally careful of its archives.

The tenants paid their rents in a variety of ways, partly in cash, partly in goods or services. In 1719–20 for instances, James Danson, paying £2 8s in cash, made up the rest of his rent by peeling bark, threshing, reaping, salving sheep, weaving, and 'helping to get Sheep in Severall times'. In 1726 Edward Danson at Cobby House not only wove twenty-eight yards of harden and seventeen yards of woollen cloth but also took bark to Penny Bridge.[34] In 1737 Thomas Danson paid £4 2s 1d in cash and made up the rest 'by Shoemaker Work'.

Clement Taylor, like most of his contemporaries in the area, continued the exploitation of his woodland. The manufacture of matting and pack-saddles, and of platters and bowls, had probably ceased by his time, and swill baskets were made by specialists, like Richard Newby from whom Clement bought his swills, but very considerable quantities of bark were produced on the estate and sold, notably to 'Merchant' Satterthwaite. It was prepared by both men and women in the village and measured out carefully in various barns and outbuildings.

Clement Taylor also sold charcoal or the wood for making it, and for that there was a ready local market at the furnace at Backbarrow which was established in 1711. In 1713[35] Clement sold all the wood growing in various parts of his land to the partners of the Backbarrow Company, reserving the 'lopping and topping' (the wood too small to be made into charcoal), as well as the ash, holly, and crabapple trees, which would have had other uses, and one oak. On this occasion the company was making the charcoal itself on Clement's land, and permission was given for making the pitsteads, for digging 'earth samell' to cover the wood while it was being coaled, and for making huts for the workmen. The company was to pay £180 in two instalments, but there is no trace in the account book of any money being received. It seems likely that payment was deferred until February 1717 when the company paid Clement £197 12s 10d 'in part of Two Bonds'.[36]

He continued to do profitable business with Backbarrow. In January 1723, for instance, he received a total of £100 for wood from two of the partners. In 1726 he delivered twelve loads and ten sacks of charcoal, and a further fourteen loads and nine sacks in January 1727. Relations with the company were not one-sided. Clement bought cider, a hogstead and six bottles, from William Rawlinson, one of the partners, in 1725. The company brought cider in large quantities, in ships returning from Bristol, as well as herrings.[37]

33 LRO, DDPd 35/4.
34 He also did carting work for the Backbarrow Co., as when he took four loads of iron to Cartmel and eleven loads to the Crane, the wharf on the river Leven at its highest navigable point, south of Lowwood Bridge; CRO, BDX 295/2.
35 LRO, DDPd 26/191.
36 CRO, BDX 295/2.
37 In 1718 the company paid for the carriage of '4 hogsheads of Cyder from Cark to Newby bridge . . . which Benjamin Ayrey Disposed of': *ibid*. For herrings, see n. 212.

Charcoal was also sold to the forge at Cunsey. In 1723 Richard Ford paid £22 14s 11d, and Anthony Wilson £67 1s 8d for forty seven loads. The Cunsey charcoal was taken up the lake by boat. The presence of the furnaces so close at hand meant that Clement Taylor was able to take full advantage of the opportunities for profitable trade and so extend his family's prosperity. His son Edward continued to sell charcoal to Backbarrow in considerable quantities[38] and invested money in the company (there is no evidence that Clement himself did), and his widow became a partner when Backbarrow was amalgamated with the Penny Bridge furnace in 1750.[39]

The Backbarrow Company would seem an obvious place in which to invest money, but there seems to have been no outside participation there until 1750. Otherwise there were few opportunities for a man to invest any spare cash which he might have accumulated. There was no bank in either Kendal or Ulverston until later in the eighteenth century. Shipping was one possibility, but the account book only records a single attempt in that direction, and that of doubtful success and towards the end of Clement's life.[40] Otherwise he seems to have contented himself with lending to friends and neighbours. When his father Edward III died, he had £419 lent out 'on specialty' and about £54 less formally, and, although some of this was William's money and was managed for him, and some seems to have been paid back when Edward Taylor died, Clement continued to record the payments of interest on the rest and to make other loans. It is difficult to calculate the interest he received, as some of the capital sums were probably paid back gradually and we have no idea of the terms upon which most of the loans were made. Interest seems to have been at about three to three and a half per cent in the early days, although when Clement himself borrowed £100 from Margaret Taylor in 1723 he paid her only two per cent. On at least two occasions, in 1728 and 1731, interest on loans was four per cent. It is clear that by the time he died he had, by careful management and a certain amount of good fortune, accumulated enough money to be able to make excellent provision for his wife and daughters and still leave an unencumbered estate to his son.[41]

Despite his commercial concerns, Clement Taylor would have considered himself primarily a farmer, and the business of farming figures largely in the account book. Records of cows being sent to the bull appear throughout, from 1725 to 1742. He appears not to have kept a bull himself and his cows were taken to neighbouring farms; the numbers vary from one in 1725 to as many as nine in 1732. The cows are described either by their appearance (blackhorn, great red, spinkt, and so on), or by the name of the man from whom they had been bought (e.g. Christopher Taylor cow), and some occur over a period of several years. The James Towers cow, bought in 1723, went to the bull four times between 1726 and 1731 and then disappears. The 'weggey why' had seven bullings between 1726 and 1734. If the first bulling was unsuccessful it was usually repeated, on one occasion

---

38   Detailed in his own account book, LRO, DDPd 26/338.
39   Fell, *op. cit.* 260–62; CRO (Barrow) Z22; LRO, DDPd 38/1.
40   See n. 207. Clement's widow had some interest in a ship called *The Jane*.
41   See below, xxx.

with two separate bulls, when the blackhorn cow was taken to Abraham Rawlinson's no fewer than six times between April and October 1739. The 'spinkt' cow occurs between 1733 and 1740 and in her later years was referred to as the 'old spinkt cow', to distinguish her from a younger one who appears in 1738–40. Some, like the 'fatt cow' of 1726, are only mentioned once. The fee for bulling was 1s or 6d.

Bulling took place at intervals throughout the year, in order to maintain a supply of fresh milk for the household. For the most part, the bulls were not those of particularly near neighbours, although John Robinson of Newby Bridge and Myles and Lawrence Harrison at Stott Park all supplied them. Abraham Rawlinson of Rusland Hall appears frequently in this context, and the cows were often taken to quite distant farms; the furthest was probably the Frith near Holker. Some heifer calves would no doubt have been kept as replacements, but it is clear that a number were sold either to butchers or killed to provide meat for the household like 'my wife why' in February 1727. Milking is never mentioned as having been done by anyone outside the household, and butter would also normally have been made at home, although it was bought on one or two occasions. In 1722 Clement Taylor bought a pair of oxen for ploughing and seems to have sold his old pair at the same time. Some cattle, which would mainly have been the bull calves, were sent away to fatten elsewhere, and he paid James Rownson for 'grassing' on several occasions.

There must always have been horses about the farm, but there is hardly any mention of them. In 1726 Clement accepted a horse instead of money due for the interest on a loan, paying the surplus himself. He would certainly have had at least one riding horse and when he was under-sheriff he bought a special saddle. His father had horses, valued with their 'fornatory' at £6, and he left the 'old bay mare' to his son Edward, while Clement inherited a grey gelding and a bay filly. In 1731 he paid for a pillion saddle so that his wife or one of his daughters could ride behind him. Pigs are never mentioned,[42] but hens would certainly have been kept.

The detailed records of sheep cover only the period 1715–24. Clement inherited 140 sheep from his father (sixty ewes, fifty wethers, and thirty hoggs), but only 125 were noted in 1715. There were then apparently no tups. By March 1720 the flock had increased to 216, and 230 were salved in October, including four tups. In 1724 there were 201. There the detailed records come to an end, but there is no doubt that sheep continued to be kept, as tenants were paid for shearing and wool was sold, as much as sixty-eight stone in 1730, although that possibly represented the clip of several years. Wool was provided for tenants' wives, who may also have done some spinning for the household. Only seventy sheep of various sorts were 'put to the fell' after shearing in 1744. Sheep were sold to William Coward the butcher and to neighbours. At his death, Clement left 170 sheep as 'heirlooms', to descend with the various properties as tied flocks.[43] Some sheep were let to tenants.

---

42 None was mentioned in his father's probate inventory.
43 For such heirlooms, see below n. 78.

James Danson had ten in 1713 and William Woodburn had nine. In 1742 John Cragg, leasing Waterside, had thirty.

The farm and its household were run throughout the period of the account book with the help of two servants, a man and a girl. Clement Taylor seems to have been a kindly employer. Jane Ormandy, who stayed with him for eight years from 1722 had 5s given to her in July 1730 'when her sister was not well', and Clement paid 2s for a 'painted Apron' for her in 1726. Margaret Birkett, hired in 1731, had an illegitimate child and in February 1732 Clement noted that he had received twenty-eight weeks' maintenance from the father, one William Braithwaite, which amounted to 18s 8d and which he was careful to pay over to her. It would have been very easy for him to have kept it. Generally the women servants earned about £2 a year at first, rising by small amounts in subsequent years, with an apron, an earnest payment of 1s, and with the premise of being provided with stockings or having their clothes mended. By the time Eleanor Newby was hired in 1735 the wages were £2 12s 6d, but after Clement died his widow paid her maid Isabel Fell only £2 a year.

The men earned more. William Taylor, who was Clement's servant from 1719 to 1724 had £3, rising to £3 12s 6d. Roger Jackson, hired between 1729 and 1734, earned £4 15s when he first came and £5 5s when he left. He seems to have been in Finsthwaite again in 1742 when he was paid for doing some work, and he married there in 1755. The servants sometimes received their wages in kind. Clement bought a Bible for Roger Jackson in 1730 at a cost of 6s and had a desk made for him by the joiner John Walker. Thomas Thompson, who came to be Isabel Taylor's manservant in 1742, was only paid four guineas.

Both male and female servants would have lived with the family. There were, however, other men who did a good deal of work but who lived locally with their families, not necessarily in houses belonging to Clement Taylor, and they probably worked for several employers. Jacob Park, a waller, was living at Jolliver Tree in 1729 but was at Landing when he died in 1735. Richard Fell lived at Town End, where he farmed in a small way, but he also made and transported charcoal for Clement; after he died in 1729 his widow Sarah worked in the garden and peeled bark. Peter Taylor, who appears constantly in the account book, was evidently of special importance on the estate. He made charcoal, peeled bark, carded wool, lent small sums of money, and even wrote deeds, and Clement evidently placed a great deal of trust in him. He lived in one of the houses at Finsyke and then at Charley Crag, which he bought in 1734, but after Clement died he went away to Trundlebrow in Browedge, where he died in 1749.

One of Clement Taylor's major preoccupations in the period of the account book was the building of his new house. We know nothing about the old house, which apparently occupied ground just to the south of the new one. It may or may not have been improved at the time of the general rebuilding which took place in the district after about 1650, when increasing prosperity and the decline and eventual disappearance of both plague and famine enabled many local families to improve their old houses, even though they might still be very small by modern standards. What is clear is that in the spring of 1724 Clement Taylor began to make very considerable purchases of timber and that they were not all intended for the new

xxii *Introduction*

Finsthwaite House from the south-east. The house built by Clement Taylor from 1725 ended just to the left of the small window in the centre of the ground floor. His wife extended it to the left after 1742.

church,[44] the payments for which are carefully separated, as in April 1724 when he bought wood from George Braithwaite, five trees for himself and one for the church. In March 1725 he paid 10d or 10^{1}/2d a foot for seventy-eight and a half feet of timber from eight trees in the Intack to Edward Kellett, the woodmonger who was felling there. Two larger trees provided a further fifty-two feet at 13d or 14d a foot, and he bought fifteen more trees in July, with other wood later in the year.

Millstone grit ridge-tiles and other pieces were bought from Richard Atkinson of Over Kellet a little later, and sent over the sands to Cart Lane from where they would have been brought to Finsthwaite by road. In May Clement laid in ten stone of hair for strengthening plaster. In June he accounted for a large purchase of nails from Lancaster: 4000 slate nails at 2s per thousand, 1000 of the second quality at 1s 10d, 5000 plaster nails at 18d, 500 'double spokes' at 2s 9d, 500 single ones at 1s 6d, and an unspecified number of flooring nails at 5s 6d a thousand.

There are few specific payments for gaining or transporting stone apart from that from Over Kellet. It must be assumed that all the stone for the walls of the house was quarried and carted by local labour from one or more of the small quarries on the estate. In October 1725, for instance, James Taylor was paid 1s 6d for 'getting stone' for three days, and there are other similar payments. A list of 'Money

---

44 See below, xxv.

Disbers'd to Walers' and covering the period from May to August 1725 names half a dozen men, including the John Walker who was possibly in overall charge of the work as well as being the principal joiner. In October Clement 'Rackned' with him for all work done until that date. Walker was paid a further £1 18s for fifty-seven days at 8d a day in February 1727, when John Holme received £3 12s 4d for 108 days and Solomon Armer £3 8s 10d for 118. Neither was a Finsthwaite man, and it looks as though these were the payments to professional masons for raising the walls of the house.

Slate for the roof arrived from the specialised quarries at Coniston in September 1725. John Sawrey and a man named George from Nibthwaite led 104 loads of slate from Coniston and were paid £2 8s, and the same 'George of Lords' brought a further six loads 'from Coniston Waterhead to my house'. James Taylor of Nibthwaite brought six more loads. The quantity of slate required was calculated by a Coniston slater, John Langram. On 19 September Robert Addison was paid 8s 6d for 'dressing and Lyeing Slate on The New House'. These payments were followed by those for the plastering which was done by the Crank family from Ulverston, who had also worked at the church, and a body of hired 'limers'. Numerous cartloads of limestone were bought at the cost of 2d a load, and there are payments for building and lining a kiln, and getting and washing sand.

The walls, roof, and internal plastering were probably completed by the middle of 1727 at the latest, but the fitting-out of the interior seems not to have been completed for another three years. Clement Taylor did buy a dozen new chairs and two stools, but there are no payments for fittings until 1730, although he paid £7 for glass and weights for the sash windows in February 1727. The windows themselves were made by the joiner, John Walker, with whom he made an exchange of seventy-eight feet of boards for '35 foot of Hamburge Boards', imported deals which would have been for flooring.

In April 1730 Walker and his man Jackey were building the stairs, and in June and July they spent four days making a bed. Six months later they were still working on the staircase and Jackey made some window-seats. Payments for laying the 'parler floor' were made in August 1731, and for the 'Cornish' in the parlour in October. They made more bedstocks and a little table in November. The attic doors had been hung and the floors laid in September.

Those are the last payments for work in the house which were recorded by Clement Taylor during his lifetime, except that for 109 yards of lead piping which were laid down by Anthony Strickland of Kendal in June 1734. One can only assume that the family was able to move into the new house soon afterwards. In 1742 the Backbarrow Company's ledger of sales of 'cast ware' noted payments of 5s 4½d 'To a Carv'd Back' (an ornamental fireback) and £9 8s 8½d 'To Balluster & Rails'.[45] As soon as her husband died his widow demolished at least part of the old house and did some building of her own. On 30 April 1742 she paid £2 6s to

---

45   LRO, DDMc 30/11. There is an iron fireback at Finsthwaite House which bears Clement and Isabel's initials, but it is dated 1723. It hardly seems a thing that anyone would buy before building a house in which to use it, so the payment in 1742 may well be for this one, the date being retrospective and not perfectly recalled.

'Reginald Grigg & Co for pulling down and rebuilding the late dwelling House at the South-End of Clement Taylor'.[46] Quite what was done is unclear, as Isabel's work has been overlaid by later additions, the precise chronology of which is doubtful. One strong possibility is that the old house was converted into a downhouse, or service room, perhaps only single-storeyed and backing on to the main chimney of the new part on the south side. Whatever was done, it was completed by August 1744 when the south wall was roughcast.

Further work seems to have been undertaken in 1748–50, as the account book contains a large number of payments to workmen in that period, though without specifying what was being done. It seems likely that the present library, the small room next to it, and the bedrooms above were added at that time. The style of the carved alcove in the small room fits well with a date of c. 1750. If so, the downhouse would have been substantially altered and provided with a second storey in order to connect Clement's work with these new rooms.

An exterior terrace seems also to have been made. In May 1743 Isabel Taylor purchased sixty-four iron 'ballisters' and four iron rails from the Backbarrow Company for £9 12s 2d. The following January she accounted for £7 2s paid to John Cornthwaite as the second instalment of £12 for 'Rigging, Chimney pieces, pillars, & copings for Pallisadoes & Troughs', that is for ridge-tiles and decorative pieces for the outside. The chimney-pieces were probably for the new library wing.[47]

In November 1725 Clement Taylor had set out the dimensions of 'our Fire House' in his account book. It measured twelve and a half yards by eight yards seven inches, and occupied an area of four square roods and thirty-five yards. Modern measurements approximate. The house, as it existed at the time of his death, was a tall rectangular building of three storeys, certainly comprising a large main room and a parlour (the best bedroom), with two other ground-floor rooms. One must have been a buttery; the other was probably a kitchen, as this was the period in which cooking was being moved out from the rooms in which people ate and sat. The staircase ran up through two floors to other bedrooms, and to the attics in which the servants would have slept. Three-storey houses were not common in this period, but his friend James Backhouse built a similar house at Jolliver Tree quite soon after Clement built his. There seems no doubt that the design of one influenced that of the other. Waterside was also extended in this same period by the provision of a third floor and a new roof. Clement also recorded the size of the 'little house', the outdoor privy, which was ten feet two inches long, and eleven feet ten inches broad over the roof.

The new house was not Clement Taylor's only involvement in building. Work

---

46   The house was always referred to as 'Clement Taylor'. Bark was measured in the old house in 1737: p. 203.
47   Clement's son Edward added a new front to the house, doubling its size. The date of that extension is not known, and there are no accounts for it, but it was certainly complete before he died in 1790. A payment for carting freestone in 1773 may indicate the date: LRO, DDPd 26/338. A valuation of the furniture which was to go to his sister Mary was made shortly after his death, and it is clear that the new rooms were in use by then: *ibid.* 26/340. The extension was built on made ground to the west of the old house, above a large cellar. The architect is unknown.

The old church of St Peter, Finsthwaite, 1724–5; demolished 1873.

was undertaken regularly on various barns and houses on the estate, and he was also deeply concerned with work at two churches. He had been a prime mover in extending the church at Colton in 1721,[48] and in 1723–5 he played a major part in establishing the school and church in Finsthwaite itself, the story of which I have considered elsewhere.[49] As one of the principal landowners he contributed £45 towards the building and future endowment of the church, and he and Richard Robinson went to Lancaster to visit 'Lawyer Gibson' who was dealing with the Commissioners of Queen Anne's Bounty in the matter of the endowment.[50] Some of the church accounts are set out in this book. He was presumably present on 24 July 1725 when the bishop of Chester came to dedicate the new church, and thereafter attended services there. Indeed he records lending two guineas to Henry Taylor of Landing in February 1728 'as we came from Chapel' and in 1740 he paid Peter Taylor 5s on his way to church. He was churchwarden for his own house in 1738 and for Cobby House in 1742, the year of his death. His relationship with John Harrison, the incumbent, was evidently cordial. Mr Harrison taught the Taylor children, both sons and daughters, apparently privately, and on one occasion came to help their father when a financial calculation got the better of him.[51]

The inhabitants of Finsthwaite also had obligations to their mother parish at

48 See n. 26, below.
49 J. Martin, 'The Building and Endowment of Finsthwaite Church and School', *CW2*, 1984, 125–139.
50 See n. 75, below.
51 See n. 192, below.

xxvi   *Introduction*

Colton. Clement served as one of the representative Finsthwaite churchwardens there in 1717 and again in 1742. Relations with Colton were soured for a time when the incumbent demanded dues from Finsthwaite[52] and the matter went to arbitration in 1730. Secular duties too made for close contact between the two places, as for civil purposes Finsthwaite was still part of Colton parish. Clement was overseer of the poor in 1713 and 1734, and constable in 1732, and the duties of both offices are reflected in the account book. In 1728, though not a constable, he was one of the assessors of the money raised for the expenses of that office.[53] He also made lists of the money owned for the bloomsmithy rents at three separate times, and we may presume that he assisted in their collection, as he also did for the land and window taxes, and for local parish levies. In addition, he was often responsible for the distribution of the various sum of money left as charities for the poor and for the school.[54]

His most important public office was that of under-sheriff to his neighbour Myles Sandys of Graythwaite in 1725. Under-sheriffs were sometimes professional men, acting as a county clerk, and were paid by their sheriffs, but Clement was not, and there is no indication that his was anything but a voluntary duty.[55] He would have had to attend the county court and the Quarter Sessions at Lancaster, and he wore some sort of uniform and had a special saddle for his horse, both of which he paid for himself. Such a connection would have brought him into contact with the wider world across Morecambe Bay. He visited Lancaster not infrequently, and also Kendal when business or the fair took him there. And he would have voted in Lancaster. Like his father, Clement Taylor was a Whig, supporting Walpole and the court party and unsympathetic to the Jacobites. In 1722 he was listed as voting for Sir Henry Houghton, the Whig candidate, together with Richard Robinson, Myles and Lawrence Harrison and George Braithwaite at Stott Park, Christopher Taylor of Plum Green, and Robert Sawrey.[56] The longest journey noted in the account book was to Askrigg in Wensleydale in 1725, when he went to look at a farm there as a possible purchase for the endowment of the church.[57]

But for the most part he stayed in the general area of home, where life was centred upon his family and farm. There were trips to the fairs at Hawkshead and Bouth, and on one occasion to the spa at Humphrey Head, after some time spent at Cartmel where his daughters had been learning to dance.[58] He evidently took great pride in his children, and his daughters, as well as his sons, were taught by John

---

52 See n. 154, below.
53 LRO, DDAr 331. There are lists of the churchwardens, constables, and overseers at Colton in CRO, BPR 17/C2/1, and of the Finsthwaite churchwardens in CRO, WPR 101/W1.
54 For the charities, see nn. 177, 182, 218, 231, below.
55 S. and B. Webb, *English Local Government . . . The Parish and the County*, London, 1906, 289–90, 304, 321.
56 LRO, DDSa 36/8; for his father, see *ibid.* 36/7. See also LRO, DDPd 26/251, a letter to Richard Robinson in 1740, seeking his vote at the next county election. On the election of 1722, see J.D. Alsop, 'Another Eighteenth-Century Election Poll: Lancashire 1722', *Northern History*, xvii, 1981, 256–8.
57 See n. 105, below.
58 See nn. 27, 106, and 64, below.

Harrison and his successor George Simpson. His younger son Edward went on to the grammar school at Browedge, where brother William had been and where Clement himself probably received his education. The account book shows him to have been literate and numerate, and to have some knowledge of Latin, if only of a limited kind. Browedge school was unsophisticated to a degree, having only stones and a plank for the boys to sit on before benches were installed about 1716, but the teaching was said to be good and some pupils went on to bigger schools like Cartmel, Hawkshead, or Sedbergh.[59] It was evidently held to be too far to go daily. Both Clement's brother and younger son boarded with people nearby, William with Benjamin Taylor at Hardcragg and Edward with a Captain Thomas Barrow, who probably also lived at Browedge. William was taught writing and accounts by William Birkett, the peripatetic writing master who also worked at Hawkshead,[60] and the copy of Ovid's *De Tristibus* bought in 1743 was probably for Edward. There are no references to the further education of Clement V, but he may well have gone to Browedge too.

The children chiefly figure in the account book because of the clothes that were brought for them, like Elizabeth's 'Calamaniah Coate' in 1723 and 'Clement Suite of Draget' in 1727. For the most part, everyday clothing would be made at home, either by Mrs Taylor and the maids or, in the case of men's garments, by a travelling tailor or one living locally, like James Leece who probably came from Booth. Isabel may well have made the shirts for brother William from the material brought at Hawkshead fair. Wool from the family's own sheep would be carded and spun in the house or by local women and was certainly woven by one or more of the tenants, principally by Edward and James Danson (who also wove hemp into harden), and then sent away to be fulled and dyed. Serge, being more specialised, was woven by a Thomas Holme, not in Finsthwaite. But cloth was also bought from at least one Scots packman,[61] and fancier materials were purchased elsewhere. On one occasion Clement bought a length of 'Persian' silk from a Manxman in Grange which it is tempting to think may have been smuggled. After Clement died his widow evidently made much of her surviving son, the eleven-year-old Edward, and elaborate clothes were made and bought for him before he went off to school in 1744.

Expenditure on food is an important feature of the account book. The staple cereal was oats for making the unleavened clapbread, which everyone ate, and for porridge. Some were grown on the farm, but oats were also bought. Wheaten bread was a luxury in this period, and was normally only bought for use at Communion,[62] but Clement mentions white loaves in 1729, bought from a William Walker who also provided bread for the funeral of John Taylor in 1732. There were also occasional purchases of wheat itself. The Taylors ate surprisingly large quantities of meat. The detailed accounts of Clement's dealings with the butcher, William

---

59   For Browedge School, see J. Addy, 'Dispute at Browedge school in Cartmel, 1727', *CW2*, 1972, 216–26. The Clement Taylor mentioned there on p. 223 is Clement of Hardcragg: see 239.
60   CRO, WD/TE box 20/4/1. This list of William Birkett's 'Schollars at Browedge' in May 1711, includes Henry (see 240) and William Taylor.
61   See n. 46, below.
62   When the church was dedicated 2s 6d was paid for '26 whit loves': *CW2*, 1984, 129.

xxviii *Introduction*

Coward, in the summer of 1727, indicate that the family ate a quarter of mutton each week, as well as veal, sheep's and calves' heads, and some offal. Mutton or lamb were most commonly eaten, but sides of beef and barrels of salt beef were also bought, and on one occasion, pork. Fish came from Morecambe Bay. Cheese was bought in large amounts, whole cheeses weighing sometimes 100lbs, mainly from Edmund Wilson in Hawkshead, who also provided salt, but on one occasion from further afield.[63] Sugar came from Thomas Hall in Cartmel or William Rownson in Bouth. Rownson also sold honey, but for that one assumes that the household generally relied upon the local beekeeper, William Danson.[64] The family grew some vegetables. Seed peas were bought in 1722 and other unspecified seeds for the garden in 1725. Potatoes are only mentioned once or twice, as when some were bought from John Machell in 1721, but later they were apparently grown as Margaret Braithwaite was paid for 'shearing off potates' in 1727. Apple, pear, and black cherry trees were planted in 1722 and 1723.

Beer for daily use would have been brewed at home. Clement bought his malt from Bouth and sometimes sent his own barley to be malted. But he also bought gin, brandy in considerable quantities, and occasionally wine. The lemons bought in Kendal in 1724 were probably for punch, which was certainly served after Clement's own funeral, when four gallons of brandy and rum were also paid for. There is no mention of either coffee or tea. Sometimes he noted expenditure on entertainment at the inn at Newby Bridge, usually in connection with meetings about parish or other affairs, and on one occasion struggled with either overwhelming sleep or the after-effects of too much to drink when setting down his notes after such an event.[65] Cockfighting is mentioned once, and on one occasion he lost money on a bet.

It is impossible to calculate the amount spent on food in any particular year, but the household was fed in much the same way as that of the much richer Humphrey Senhouse of Netherhall, Cumb., who spent £210 6s on provisions in 1727, except that he bought three 'fatt swine' and eighty pairs of rabbits.[66]

Very little emerges about either how the old or the new houses were furnished, but one must assume that the family ate at a long oak table and sat on benches or settles, with chairs for the head of the house and his wife. Beds would have been of oak, with mattresses made from harden stuffed with chaff, and clothes were kept in chests. New furniture was made or bought when the new house was built built. Clement notes the purchase of mirrors and chairs and stools, and the carpenter John Walker made a new bed[67] and a table. Lighting was by rush lights; sieves (rushes) for making them were bought, for instance, in 1735 and would have been dipped into melted tallow or mutton fat such as that supplied in 1734. But candles were also purchased, and on one occasion a lantern was mended, though that was probably for use outside. In the old house, the cooking would have been done on

63   See n. 209, below.
64   See 229.
65   See n. 277, below.
66   E. Hughes, *North Country Life in the Eighteenth Century, ii, Cumberland and Westmorland 1700–1830*, London, 1965, 67–8.
67   See n. 301, below.

the fireplace in the main living room, the firehouse, but in the new one there was probably a separate kitchen. In both houses the fires were fed with the peats bought in by various workpeople, sometimes by women.

Clement Taylor seems to have taken his responsibilities to his tenants and servants seriously. His kindnesses to his servants have already been mentioned. In 1725 he gave James Danson 1s 'when tore hand'. Like so many of his contemporaries he was in demand as an executor or a supervisor of wills, and in the case of 'Old Jennett' Taylor at Charley Cragg he seems to have managed her money for her. He was named as a trustee in the wills of neighbours at least seven times in the period 1712–42, helped to draw up at least five probate inventories, and was an executor or administrator at least three times.[68] These responsibilities would often have involved a considerable outlay of time.

It was usual in Clement Taylor's day for a man to make his will only when he felt that his death was imminent. He seems to have done so when the inheritance of Richard Robinson's property in 1741 made a very substantial, and complicated, addition to his estate. Robinson was buried on 10 February 1741, and his will proved on 12 March.[69] Waterside itself was freehold and presented few problems, although Clement took steps to obtain a final concord to assure his title, even before the will was proved,[70] and then sold it to his son. But Richard Robinson had also owned two customary tenements in Lindal, to the south of Ulverston, and Clement was subsequently admitted to this land at the manor court of Plain Furness.[71] There was some question as to whether the property could be devised by will and the opinion of counsel was sought in June 1742. The barrister, John Christian, said that Clement was indeed the rightful owner under Richard Robinson's will but that a fine should be obtained to confirm his title.[72]

---

68   There may have been more. I have looked only at the wills of people from Finsthwaite and others most particularly connected with Clement Taylor. He was also one of the trustees for the Jolliver Tree estate from 1729: LRO, DDTy 2/2/3–4.
69   LRO, DDPd 26/258 is a quitclaim from Leonard Stout (see 238), dated 1 April 1741 for the bequests of £200 to his wife Rebecca and £100 for the education of an unidentified 'cousin', Mary Orpin. For another bequest by Richard Robinson, see n. 240, below.
70   *ibid.* 26/257; the final concord, which is attached, is dated 21 March. There was some problem even about the title to Waterside; *ibid.* 26/255b is an undated statement, written by the vicar, John Harrison, about the position in which Clement found himself. In 1680 (*ibid.* 26/146–7) his wife's grandfather, Richard Taylor of Waterside, had settled his property on his only child Agnes Robinson by vesting it in trustees for her husband in his lifetime, with remainder to Agnes and her male heirs. If male heirs failed, it was to pass to her daughters. When Richard Robinson died, his sister Isabel Taylor was the only survivor of Agnes's children, and Richard left his property to her husband Clement. The questions posed in this paper, but not answered, were whether Richard had the right to devise settled premises by will, whether Isabel was the right heir in preference to her Uncle John's surviving daughter and granddaughter, and, if she were the right heir, how might she secure the property to her husband and his heirs? In the event, Clement and Isabel obtained Waterside, and it has remained in the estate ever since.
71   A copy of the court roll is attached to the probate copy of Richard Robinson's will, *ibid.* 26/254.
72   No fine survives, if it was ever obtained. John Christian's opinion is *ibid.* 26/265. Attached is a letter from John Law, the Ulverston solicitor, citing an instance of customary land in Plain Furness being devised by will. The Lindal land was advertised for sale in 1745, when Mr Law's bill was submitted: *ibid.* 26/273.

Perhaps with all this in mind, Clement Taylor drew up a first will on 21 July 1741.[73] In it he left £400 to his wife, and £500 each to his four daughters, with £1500 to his younger son Edward. The elder son, Clement, who was named as the executor, was to inherit all the property at Finsthwaite and Waterside, and the personal estate. The death of the younger Clement at the end of 1741 meant that another will had to be made. It survives only in a draft dated 9 February 1742.[74] In this, Isabel still had £400, with all household and other goods except those which were left as heirlooms in the various houses, but the legacies to the daughters were increased to £700, the interest on those to the two younger ones being available for their education. The real estate was left to trustees until Edward came of age, they being responsible for his education and the management of the valuable woodland.[75] Another updated draft[76] reduced Isabel's legacy to £200, and made provision for selling Richard Robinson's Lindal property, which Clement had already made over to his brother Edward and the solicitor, John Law of Ulverston. On the back of the draft wills are lists of moneys owed to Richard Robinson, which came to almost £3000, equal to the sum which he was proposing to leave in legacies, so his own estate would not have been weakened by having to sell property to pay them, assuming that the money could all be called in without trouble.[77]

Clement Taylor's final will, dated 23 October 1742, is a full version of the drafts. Isabel had £200 and his household goods, except the 'Bedstocks, Lockers, Cupboards, the long Tables and Ancient chests and arks in the several dwelling houses', and 170 sheep, all of which, he says, 'I desire may Stand as Heir Looms'.[78] The daughters had £700 each, Mary's to be paid when she came of age. Isabel, Clement's brother Edward, and John Law had Richard Robinson's customary lands at Lindal in trust to be sold, and all mortgages on other people's

---

73 *ibid.* 26/263. It was written by John Harrison, although John Law was consulted. He charged 7s 6d for visiting Finsthwaite, even when he was called out at night: *ibid.* 26/273.
74 *ibid.* 26/264.
75 It would have been important to see that the coppice woods were managed and regularly cut during Edward's minority.
76 *ibid.* 26/264.
77 Part of Richard Robinson's money was in a mortgage which he had taken out on 3 February 1724 on the property of one Matthew Noble, at Crag in Egton-cum-Newland, whose debts from 1727 to 1739 are listed in *ibid.* 26/251 and also appear on the dorse of *ibid.* 26/263–4. Noble, who was a ropemaker, had also taken on a poor apprentice, William Chapman, originally apprenticed to Richard Robinson, although the precise nature of the dispute over him is unclear. Noble refused to acknowledge his indebtedness to Robinson, and in June 1742 John Christian had said that he must produce receipts to prove that he had actually paid any of the interest or the principal on his mortgage: *ibid.* 26/265. The case was taken to the chancery court of the Duchy of Lancaster and in April 1743 witnesses were called to identify Richard Robinson's will and to testify that William Chapman's apprenticeship had been transferred: *ibid.* 26/268. Other depositions had been made in the autumn of 1742: *ibid.* 26/261. The outcome of the case is not known, but it lasted from the Easter term of 1742 to Trinity Term 1745, and John Law's bill came to more than £100: *ibid.* 26/273. For Matthew Noble, see 234.
78 Just as flocks of sheep were tied to a particular farm, so it was customary for specific pieces of furniture to descend with a property. Waterside still retains a table, now very fragile, which was part of its heirloom furniture.

property were transferred to them as well. The whole estate at Finsthwaite and Waterside was left to Edward to be inherited when he came of age.[79]

Less than a month later Clement Taylor died. He had made very few entries in his account book in the period after the younger Clement's death and one is tempted to think that he was perhaps overwhelmed with grief at the loss of his son. He was buried in Finsthwaite church on 14 November 1742, close to his own pew,[80] and the vicar, George Simpson, was paid a guinea for preaching at the funeral and for the fees. No fewer than 450 poor people attended to receive a dole of 3d each.[81] At the subsequent gathering beef, butter, and fruit were served, with mutton and veal and bread, and four gallons of brandy and rum were drunk, some at least in the form of a punch for which loaf sugar and lemons were bought. Isabel proved the will a week later, on 20 November 1742, paying a fee of one guinea. She appears not to have marked her husband's burial place with any kind of memorial stone.[82]

The impression gained from the account book is of a man poised between the old life of the seventeenth century and the new one of the later eighteenth. Clement's grandfather could not sign his own name, yet both he and his son had begun to amass the assets which made Clement's own son into a gentleman. He himself lived between the old life and the new. His dress and food and his occupations would not have seemed strange to his grandfather, but his new house and the small indications of gradual refinement which can be gleaned from the account book look forward, not backward. His speech was evidently local. He used local words and occasionally he wrote a word as pronounced, like 'dooer' for door. He also rarely used the genitive. Possession is indicated by such terms as 'Martha wage' or 'Edward cow', a usage common to northern dialects. But he read a newspaper and owned at least a few books. His legacy to his heirs was a well-founded estate, upon which his energetic widow and his son were able to built. Edward's business dealings were more extensive than his father's, and the new front which he added to the house transformed it from a farmhouse, albeit a large one, into a small country house. But the back stairs are still those made by John Walker in 1731, and Clement Taylor would be in not altogether unfamiliar surroundings were he to return to Finsthwaite today.

---

79   *ibid.* 26/277 is a quitclaim from Robert Atkinson of Cark for the legacy of £700 paid to his wife Agnes, 27 January 1747. The legacies to the other daughters were paid on 2 February 1750: *ibid.* 26/280. Isabel King's legacy was put in trust for her and her children in 1752: *ibid.* 26/282.
80   His place of burial is recorded in the churchwardens' accounts: CRO, WPR 101/W1. He was buried next to Richard Robinson but 'further into the Isle'. They shared a pew at the east end of the church.
81   See n. 232, below.
82   The wall monuments from the old church were re-erected in the new one built in 1874. There is none for Clement Taylor, but his burial place could have been marked by a stone on the floor which was not preserved. But burials inside the old church were continued until flags were laid in 1771, and occasionally afterwards, so floor monuments might not have been appropriate at a time when the earth was so often disturbed.

A page from the account book (p. 74).

THE ACCOUNT BOOK OF CLEMENT TAYLOR

[*p. 1*]

June the 10th 1712
Moneys Disborsed of William Taylor
Accompt[1]

	li	s	d
Imprimis for Bording at Schooll	01	10	00
Master Wage	00	05	00
Bording at Schoole	01	01	06
Master Wage	00	05	00
A hatt	00	02	06
A coote	00	06	00
Master Wage	00	05	0
paid Benjamin Taylor pro Bording	01	07	0
Master Wage	00	05	0
Pro Cote and Waist Cote	01	03	0
Master Wage	0	06	0
to Benjamin Taylor	2	1	2
William Lickbarrow	0	16	0
Mr Roskell	0	7	6
Mr Rowlandson	0	7	6

Chapel windows[2]
Top of Great Window	24
Low End Idem	48
7 windows 19 foot:2 apeice	136:2
two Steeple windows	017
foots	225:2

To The Reverend Mr Taylor
Curat of Farthingstone
to be left at the Post-House
in Daventry Northamptonshire

February 24th 1730 Isabel Dixon
paid Mr Burry[3] in part of his bill   14s
Test C Taylor

1 See xvi.
2 The next three entries on this page were added later. Finsthwaite church was built in 1724–5 [see xxv]; William Taylor went to Farthingstone in 1726 [see 242].
3 James Bury, apothecary, was buried at Ulverston on 26 March 1734, and it seems likely that he is the person referred to here. Nothing further is known of him, and his connection with the female servants and their wages is mysterious, unless he ran some sort of bank for them; see also p. 94.

2   *The Account Book of Clement Taylor*

[*p. 2 is blank*]

[*p. 3*]

March the 20th 1713
Accompt of Land Lett to farme

to Edward Danson	Imprimis Farr Hagg	1	00	00
	Little hagg	0	16	0
	Middow at pole[4]	0	11	0

to James Danson   House orchard garden parrick
Longmyre Cragg and Common
with 10 sheepe (to witt) five
hoggs three gimmer hoggs one tup
and one wedder hogge
Likewise two ews with lamm
one wedder [twinter *interlined*]
and two gimmers
twinters, price of the said sheep
is 3s hoggs & 3s.6 old ones
if his Stock happen to Dec[a]y
and Im to take it in my choice
whether I will have the price
afformentioned or Suchlike
Sheepe to the Judgment of
Edward Taylor & Edward Danson[5]
These Sheep was Livered the 11th
Day of March 1713

		l	s	
	James Danson Rent	2	15	00

to Robert Sawrey pinsher
Croft Dale pro 3 years
and to plow it two of
the said years so to Leave
it in Bigg Stubble suffi
ciently mannered price   0   15   00

?mand[6]

James Walker for Ileand & two		li	s	d
New Closes for 3 years with green		2	3	00
Side Up				

---

4   Rusland Pool, where the farms at the south end of Finsthwaite had their hay meadows.
5   *i.e.* if the stock of sheep on James Danson's farm decreased during his tenancy the landlord was to have money or similar sheep returned to him at the end of it; *cf* n. 76.
6   This is a later insertion, and of doubtful meaning.

February the 1th 1718 Land Lett
to William Woodburne pro House Orchard
Garden Beckingarth farrhagge
Jennethagge [& *interlined*] 1 acre & A halfe
in broad Middow pro 3 years pro 4ll 5s
yearly if he have Just reason to Complain
to have 2s 6d returned Gratis
And likewise he [*sic*] [the Same Houses &c *interlined*] is to be put in good
Order and Livered Up in Like Manner
at 3 years End

[*p. 4*]

[*miscellaneous calculations at side*]

May the 10th 1713			
Edward Danson Rent		2	14
topp of parrack		0	4	6
Robert Sawrey Longmiddow			
and the <Dry> ?Rms Shars[7]			
as the go about for			
3 years at 8s per year		0	8	0
		3	4	6
to Robert Sawrey pincher Croft Dale			
for 3 years to be manner'd			
the 2d year of his Ploughing			
According to Custome pro			15	0
idem halfe of Little Close			5s	0
and half of parick			5	0
			10	0
May 10th 1718			
Due to James Danson pro [Weaveing *interlined*] 16 yards			
of Hardn			2	6
more 5 days mowing			2	6
Idem pro Threshing			[*blank*]	
Idem a caf bedd			0	7
pro shering 3 days			1	0
pro mowing 1 day more			0	6
6 days Salveing			1	6
5 Lamms – 10s			10	0
pro 10 quarters Bark peeling		1	3	4

---

[7] The land referred to has not been identified; 'as the go about': as they go in rotation between one farm and another. The sum is *recte* £3 6s 6d.

4   *The Account Book of Clement Taylor*

August 1719	Debtor to James Danson pro peeling 5 quarter of Bark att 2s per quarter	10	s 0	
February 4 17[sic] paid J[ames] Danson			2	8

[*p. 5: torn at foot; no text lost*]

	li	s	d
July the 16th 1713 Accompt of money Disborsed Imprimis to Walers[8]	05	10	00

Aprill the 8 1719 Account of
Sheep Livered to William Woodburne
1th 3 Ews amd Lams <and>
3 hoggs 2 gimers and
one wedder Livered in the presence
of Richard Robinson Edward Taylor
and his brother in Law John Taylor

April 8 1719 Robert Sawrey rent	2	2	0

Then let to farme per C T to E[dward] D[anson]
for 3 years from the 2d February next
1719 Dureing the Said term, to pay
yearly and every year the Sum of [*blank*]
per annum Upon the 2d February

[*p. 6: torn at foot; no text lost*]

February 2d 1722 Debtor to James Danson
for peeling Bark in Knot 41.2

[*p. 7: torn at foot; some text perhaps lost*]

	li	s	d
February the 26th 1714 Land Rent Due to Clement Taylor			
paid Imprimis Edward Danson	2	10	00
paid idem more	2	08	6
idem more	0	14	0
James Danson	2	15	00

8   Wallers.

Robert Sawrey	<2>1	13	00
James Walker	2	3	00
William Lickbarrow	1	1	00
	12	<0>10	6[9]
J[ames] D[anson] paid february 2d 1714	1	0	0
January 26 1715 Rent Received	1	s	
Imprimis Edward Danson	2	10	
February 2d 1715 James Danson	1	13	00
March 29th 1716<5> J[ames] Danson	1	12<0>	00
February the 2d 1715 of Robert Sawrey	2	00	00
May 11th 1716 Edward Danson	1	1	6
february 6th Edward Danson	1	2	6
January 1716 Rent Received			
paid Edward Danson	2	10	0
paid more pro hagg	0	14<5>	0
paid James Danson	1	8	
paid Robert Sawrey	1	13	

[p. 8: torn at foot; some text perhaps lost]

May 10th 1718 Accompt with James Danson & he remains Debtor to me	3	14	5
James Danson rent Due May 1719	2	15	0
James Danson rent Due May 1720	2	15	0
	9	4	5
February 1719 James Danson paid in part of the Said rent	2	8	0
More 5 quarter Bark peeling at 2s per quarter which is	10	0	

	Sal[ving]		1	4
19 Salving Sheep 6 Dayes		0	1	6
20 Salving Sheep 6 Dayes		0	1	6
Threshing one Day		0	0	4
Shearing 2 dayes		0	0	8
Mowing 4 Dayes		0	2	0

9   recte £13 4s 6d.

one flannel Webb		[blank]	
one Linn Webb		[blank]	
helping to get Sheep in Severall times		[blank]	
James Danson rent due May 1721	2	15	0
James Danson a Harden webb		1	6
J[ames] Danson 1 day bearing Hay out of Iland		[blank]	
one Day Mowing in Myles Field &c		[blank]	
one Day in great field		[blank]	
one Day in Redding		[blank]	
James Danson rent pro 1722		[blank]	

[p. 9]

January the 18th 1720
William Taylor went to Oxford[10]
Received of Mr Hunter
Paid the Same to Nicholas
Marshall at Ulverston & Marshel
ordered it to be paid att Wittney
Near Oxford to Mr H with 20li more
pro William Taylor which was Answered there
by Nicholas friend

	li	s	
	30	0	0

	li		
	2	0	
	1	1	
	0	10	
	0	14	6
	0	<10> 7	
	4	12	6
	6	5	
		13	4
W[illiam] Woodburn			
	6	18	4
	4	12	6
	2	05	10
		4	

---

10   See xvi.

The Account Book of Clement Taylor 7

			2	0	
			1	1	
			0	10	
			0	14	6
			0	7	
		work	0	4	
			4	16	6
William Woodburn			1	s	d
Remains Debtor			2	2<1> 10 <.>	

William Woodburn remains debtor		s	d
For 20 april of old		14	0
1726 & for New Close & house			
for 1726	1	2	0
August 29th Received of Woodborn Wife		10	0
1727			
February 2 1728 of William Woodburn			
per Crossfield hand	0	1	8
February 2d 1728 Then Rackned with	li	s	d
Jaine Woodburn & She Remains Debtor	2	11	0
at may day next			

[*p. 10*]

May 15th 1729 Received of Jane Woodburn			
by the hand of James Danson Overseer	li	s	d
of The poor by my poor Sess	1	0	0
16th Sold Jane woodburn 3 hoops of		s	d
barley at 10s per bushel	0	1	10 1/2
June 11th To William Woodburn	5	0	0
25th To William Woodburn Wife			
in Little Close	5	0	0
July 16 in Cash	5	0	0
December 4 paid William Woodburn		4s	0
11th a peck of Barley			

[*p. 11*]

8   *The Account Book of Clement Taylor*

February the 26 1714			
Interest in Arear [11]	li	s	d
Imprimis Thomas Scotson	2	15	0
paid William Hirdson	0	16	0
paid James Capland	2	17	0
paid John Scales	1	10	0
idem per bill			
with Six years Interest	2	10	0
paid Frances [*sic*] Adinson	3	00	00
paid Richard Rigge	2	10	00
paid William Braithwait	3	00	00
paid Garnet Penington	{ 18	18	00
	{ 01	00	00
February the 2d 1715 Interest in A			
reare	li	s	d
paid Thomas Scotson	3	00	0
paid William Hirdson	0	16	0
paid Garnet Penington	1	00	0
paid James Capland	2	10	0
paid Richard Rigge	2	10	0
paid William Braithwait	3	00	0
paid Francis Adinson	3	00	0
paid John Scales	1	10	0
William Swanson	5	00	0
February 2d 1716	li	s	d
William Swanson paid 4li	5	0	0
paid William Braithwait	3	0	0
James Capland	2	10	0
paid Richard Rigge	2	10	0
James Adinson vidua	3	0	0
paid John Scales	1	10	0
paid Garn[et] Penington	1	0	0
paid William Hirdson	0	16	0

11 'Paid' at the side indicates that the arrears were subsequently discharged. The loans to Richard Rigge of Force Mill and John Scales of Grizedale were of £80 and £30 respectively, and the money belonged to William Taylor. They were still outstanding when William died. On 18 February 1739 Clement received a quitclaim from his brother's executors in Northamptonshire for £114 8s, representing the original loans and the interest due, which he had collected and paid over: LRO, DDPd 26/248. Just after William's death the executors had written to reproach Clement for not sending £100 which had been requested to provide for the widow, about whom they were concerned: *ibid.* 26/246. William had also had a mortgage on a house in Newby Bridge which was discharged in 1740: *ibid.* 36/10. There is a copy of his will at *ibid.* 36/9. At least seven of the other loans had been inherited by Clement from his father, Edward Taylor III, and are listed in his probate inventory: *ibid.* 26/184.

	li	s	d
Interest in areare 1717<8>			
Francis Chamney	1	0	0
paid Garnet Penington 2 years	2	0	0
James Capland paid in part	4	4	0
James Capland 2 years	5	0	0
Debtor to Francis Chamney pro Drowing[12] a Deed			
Francis Chamney Interest pro 1718	1	0	0

[p. 12]

	ll	s	
February the 2d 1718 Interest Due			
James Capland Interest pro 50ll 0			
Idem left Unpaid last year	00	16	
Frances [sic] Chamney Interest			
Due pro two years	2	0	
paid John Scales Interest in arear	4	0	
February 19th			
1719 John Scales left in arear	0	7	
John Scales Interest Due pro 30li	1	5	
	1	12	
2nd February John Scales Interest	1	5	
1720 James Capland in arear	2	1	8
Christopher Marr in arear	2	10	0
John Walker in arear	16	13	4

[p. 13]

November 19th A D 1720			
James Rowlandson Debtor for 10 Wedders att			
5s 9d apeice	2	17	6
Idem 16 Ews at 3s apeice	2	8	0
	5	5	0[13]
December 1th 1720 Rackoned with John Turner pro Swinbroach & backside wall and remains Due to me	0	13	0

---

12 Drawing up.
13 *recte* £5 5s 6d. The buyer was probably excused the 6d.

10   *The Account Book of Clement Taylor*

Swinbroach is 24 roods at 7d per rood
Backside 8 roods 5 quarters high Under Come[14] which
is 8 roods   H. M. was to have 10[d] per rood
paid H M in goods 7s & a horse to lead
Stones with

Received of Edward Danson pro [land *interlined*] rent	1	0	0
Robert Sawrey Rent is	2	2	0
J[ames] Danson Rent is	2	15	0
Edward Danson [ancient *interlined*] Rent is	2	10	0
Little House is	0	4	0
Half of top of parrack	0	4	6
Meddow at pool	0	4	0
Great & Little Hagg is	3	10	0
Edward Danson rent pro parchelj[15]	4	2	6
William Woodburnes is	4	2	6

[*pp. 14 and 15 are blank*]

[*p. 16*]

January 29 1720 Money Received

Imprimis John Stewardson Interest	5	0	0
Borrowed of Margaret Taylor	2	0	0
Borrowed of J[ohn] Dodson	10	0	0
Borrowed of Thomas Millerson	20	0	0
Borrowed of Thomas Rawlinson	10	0	0
Received of Edward Danson	4	10	0
More per John Turner	0	10	0
February of Francis Chamney	22	2	0
2d 1720 of William Woodburne	3	10	0
2 Borrowed Clement & William Taylor per bill	20	00	0
6 Received of William Braithwait Interest	2	10	0
6 Received of Richard Rigge Interest	2	1	0
6 of Executers of John Braithwait	2	5	0
6 of Robert Sawrey Land [rent *interlined*]	2	2	0
of Christopher Taylor pro a tree &c	0	2	10
2d Borrowed of John Taylor Dublin	10	0	00

14 Cam; the waller, H. M. has not been identified. On the rood, see B. Tyson, 'The root as a measurement of builder's work in Cumbria', *Vernacular Architecture*, x, 1979, 10.10–10.14; see also n. 107.
15 Parcels of land.

Edward Danson
17 Remains Debtor to me pro Last
year 1719   0   4   4
21 John Walker paid Interest   10   0   0
21 Christopher Marr Interest   2   10   0
John Scales Interest pro [anno *interlined*] 19   1   6   0

March
the 29   Received of William Wison's [*sic*] Wife
1721   for 7 stone of wool   2   12   0

Received of Edward Taylor in March 1721
1th the sume of   2   0   0
more in [March *interlined*] Idem E[dward] T[aylor]   1   10   0

March   Borrowed of Robert Rigge 10li at 10d
the 29 1721   per [*sic*] paid per annum   10   8   4

Aprill the 24 1721   li   s
Borrowed of William Danson   5   0   0

June   l   s
the 5th paid Agnes Carter   1   1
Idem more   0   10

[*miscellaneous calculations at foot*]

[*p. 17*]

Money Disborsed 1720   li   s   d
29 paid R[ichard] Robinson Borrowed in full   2   0   0
21 paid William Rownson Borrowed   3   0   0
29 paid Edward Kellet 10li per J[ames] D[anson] Order 10 00   0
31 paid George Taylor 20li per F.M. Order[16]   <1>20   0   0
28 paid Thomas Denny pro Smith Work &c   16   0
paid Thomas Rawlinson 2d February iron   10   8   4
paid William Taylor his Wage Due at
Whitsuntide last in full   3   0   0
12 February
paid William Rownson [Interest *interlined*] of his
<Interest> Brother Account   0   8   4
13 paid old Jennet[17]   8   2

---

16   F. M. is unidentified.
17   'Old Jennet' is Janet Taylor of Charley Crag; see 240.

12 *The Account Book of Clement Taylor*

more Idem which I received of William Braithwait		5	0
paid John Taylor pro Brother Edward 2lli which he left in my hand Last Candlemas	2	0	0
17 Rackned with Edward Danson pro all work Done by him or wife till this time and paid him for Idem which Is	0	8	2
18 James Taylor 3 dayes at Barn End	0	1	6
Samuell 3 dayes Idem	0	0	9
paid James Taylor 1 day Wholing flags	0	0	6
Debtor to James Taylor for Mosshead fogg	0	1	6
paid Robert Sawrey pro a Stubb Leah	0	1	8
paid Rowland Wainhouse in full for which I have his receipt	2	17	6
paid William Park 5 dayes Barn End	0	2	6
James Taylor Barn End 6 dayes		3	0
Samuel 6 Dayes B[arn] End		1	6
Edward Parke 6 Dayes [Sawing *interlined*] B bords[18]		3	0
John and Samuel Each 5 dayes		3	4
Edward Parke 2 dayes		1	0
Sam 1 day		0	4
John Parke 2		0	8
all paid			
March paid Thomas Benson in part 1th 1720 pro a pair of Oxon	8	14	6
remans [*sic*] Debtor to Thomas Benson	0	10	6
paid Richard Nuby 2 Swills	0	0	6
paid John Turner 29th March at Hagg Side in presence of Ralph & peper[19]	1	6	0
Aprill			
7 paid William Rownson pro Sugar &c		4	2
paid John Maychell pro Wheat & potetes[20]		9	3
Sent Mr. Chapman by R[ichard] Postlethwait man 3li 3s which I promised to answer him			

18 The 'B' is perhaps an error.
19 Ralph Leeming and Thomas Pepper; see 233, 235.
20 Potatoes were relatively new in Furness at this time. They were apparently first recorded at Swarthmoor in 1673: C.M.L. Bouch and G.P. Jones, *The Lake Counties 1500–1830*, Manchester, 1961, 101; see also W. Hutton, *The Beetham Repository*, ed. J.W. Ford, CWAAS Tract Series 7, 1906, 157.

[p. 18]

Money received 1721
<R> May the 1th John Dodson
per Clement Taylor of Jolivertree   2   12   6

John Dodson Debtor pro a pair
of Oxen & a heffer

John Taylor Debtor pro near 2
quarter of Barke   0   19   0

June 24
Received of John Dodson   6   6
of which I gave Brother Richard   3   3
which was Due to him pro Beas[21]
from J[ohn] Dodson

May
Borrowed of Margaret Taylor   1   1   0
of John Taylor pro Barke   0   19   0
July
27 of William Woodburne Wife   1   10
Borrowed of R[ichard] Robinson   2   2   0
22 November of Agnes Woodburne
1721   per her Father's Order   1   1   0
1 December   of Edward Danson
1721   which is in part of Rent   2   2   0

February the 2d 1721
Edward Danson paid per William Danson
being rent Due at Candlemas   3   2
February 2d   of William Woodburne Wife
1721   being in part of land rent pro 1721   2   3
9th of Christopher Marr Interest   2   10
5th of William Braithwait Interest   2   10
6th of John Walker   6   01
20th of Robert Sawrey   2   2
of John Stewartson   4   19

---

21 Beasts. Clement Taylor and Richard Robinson were perhaps joint owners of the oxen bought by John Dodson. For the use of oxen as plough animals, see S. Denyer, *Traditional Buildings and Life in the Lake District*, London, 1991, 101.

14 *The Account Book of Clement Taylor*

February 1721 Account with William Lickbarrow for 424 load of manner at one peny per load	1	15	4
More Due to him From C. Taylor for Dyeing	0	10	4
More from J[ohn] Taylor for Dyeing	0	8	
	2	13	8
William Lickbarrow Debtor pro bloomer ridding Land rent	6	0	0

[*p. 19*]

Disborsed March 29 1721 to Thomas Benson in full pro a pair of Oxen in presence R[obert] S[awrey]	1 0	s 10	d 0
March paid John Turner more pro coaling at Hag & New Close which was 75 roods at 1s per rood	2	9	0[22]
paid Agnes Carter 5s per J. T order		5	
paid John Taylor Master Wage		2	2
paid R[ichard] Postlethwait Land Sess &c	[*blank*]		
paid G[eorge] Banke poor Sess		5	0
paid R. Hirdson pro 1 botle of Jenne[23]		1	1
paid Margaret Taylor her 2s which I Borrowed		2	0
paid in June to Agnes Carter	1	1	0
more Afterward	0	10	0
paid William Benson pro 4 [bushell *interlined*] of oats		15	0
May paid Agnes Carter	0	10	0
paid Margaret Taylor 1.1 which I Borrowed	1	1	0
Lent R[ichard] Robinson	1	1	0
To Dr. Askew man pro [1 botell of *interlined*] wine & wheat bread[24]		2	6
Idem Idem [*sic*] by the above Said Orders		1	0
To Dr. Askew Servants		1	0

22 *recte* £3 15s but only part was paid.
23 Gin. R. Hirdson is perhaps Richard of New Close who baptised two daughters at Colton in 1717 and 1720.
24 Possibly for use at Communion, although Clement Taylor was not a churchwarden at Colton in 1721. Dr Askew is probably Adam Askew MD of Kendal, father of the physician and classical scholar Anthony Askew (1722–74): C. Nicholson, *Annals of Kendal*, Kendal, 1832, 248.

To Edward Bornes pro Lam [quarter *interlined*] &c		2	0
a quarter of Veall at Hawkshead		1	9
To Dr. Atkinson		5	0
<To Dr. Askew Man & maid>		<1>0	0
To John Corke pro a quarter of Lam	0	[*blank*]	
to potichary[25] September 30		6	0

August 53½ [foot *interlined*] of oke Board mesoured to			
25 Edward Kellet pro Coulton Church Door[26]			
gave Joseph Penny	0	4	6
for F[rancis] Chamney when he went			
to Lancaster Assizes versus Jo[hn] Corker			

Received Back of the 4s 6d		2	0
To Christopher Lang at H[awkshead] Fayer[27]		1	6
pro hart Lats 200		5	0
R[ichard] R[obinson] Land Sess	[*blank*]		
of William Woodburne wife 14s in full			
for rent & wooll for Anno 1720<1>			

[*miscellaneous calculations at foot*]

[*p. 20*]

to Edward Danson pro Shering in			
Harvest 1721 3 days		1s	0
of Edward Danson the 29th of			
May all rent Due being	1	6	6
1722 gave him 2s 6d gratis			
and [also *interlined*] 3 days plowing [in hag *interlined*] which			
is valued to		7s	6d

25   Apothecary.
26   Colton church was extended in 1721 by the addition of a new north transept. The licence to build it and to allot pews in it, including one for Clement Taylor, is LRO, DDPd 29/10, 20 February 1719. In 1720 other parishioners agreed to take part and to pay their share of the costs: *ibid.* 29/11. The work has been mooted as early as 1715. CRO, BPR 17/C9 is a bond in £50 from John Rownson of Bouth, Clement Taylor, and Francis Chamney of Stock to the churchwardens of Colton, to maintain that part of Colton church which they were to add to the north side. One parishioner took exception to the extension. LRO, DDPd 29/12 contains a series of depositions, dated 27 April 1721, including one from Clement Taylor himself, describing the activities of one John Robinson, who broke down the wall on 12 September 1720 with a 'Gavelock or Such like'. The schoolmaster, John Dodgson, witnessed his activities from the school in the churchyard, and Francis Chamney of Stock described how, when Robinson had pulled down most of the wall, 'he said that he was warm or hott and that he would goe to the Ale house and gett a Drink and lay by his Gavelock against another time'; see also R.H. Kirby *et al.*, (eds), *The Rural Deanery of Cartmel*, Ulverston, 1892, 83.
27   James I granted two fairs to Hawkshead, on St Matthew's Day [21 September] and the day following, and Ascension Day and the day following: H.S. Cowper, *Hawkshead*, London, 1899, 99. For their later history and development in the 19th century, see *ibid.*, 273. They were also hiring fairs.

16 *The Account Book of Clement Taylor*

[*p. 21*]

[*miscellaneous calculations at left*]

February 2d 1721 Disborsments			
Imprimis to Old Jennet	2	12	
to John Taylor Joliver	2	5	6
to James Taylor	2		
to Thomas Denny	1	1	0
to Margaret Taylor	1	6	0
Lent Thomas Denny	5	5	0
To John Taylor Land rent	2	4	10
to John Write Beddes[28]	0	2	10
to James Rownson pro grasing[29]		7	6
to Spent Idem		1	0
to my Wife at Haukshead		1	6
5th paid Edward Parke pro Church	1	5	6
Edward Barwick 2 days	0	2	0
to old Jennet	1	1	0
to the Same [for *interlined*] Interest	0	3	4
to the Same one Ewe	0	5	0
to Edmund Wilson pro Salt		5	0
to fish & Expences		1	5
8th to Mr. Chapman of			
Clement Taylor Joliver			
account	0	9	9
a hope of peies[30]	0	0	6
to Brother William at Oxford	11	5	0
to our Schole Master pro			
Cockpeny[31]	0	1	0
to Mr Dryden [of *interlined*] Church			
account	1	15	0
Lent William Danson	1	11	0
Lent Thomas Jonson	1	13	0
paid Margaret Taylor			
which I Borrowed of her	0	9	0
for 8 Bushell of oats	1	4	6

28 Presumably chaff beds.
29 Grassing.
30 A hoop of peas, probably for seed.
31 This was for the schoolmaster at Colton. A property at Cowridding was left by Adam Sandys of Bouth, by will dated 17 May 1662, the profits of which were to support a preaching schoolmaster 'that is sound in doctrine, life and conversation' to teach the scholars and officiate in the church. The school building was thought to date from 1745, but it is clear that there was a school in the churchyard by 1720: see n. 26. Mr Dryden in the line below is Henry Dryden, deputy registrar of the archdeaconry of Richmond.

to Edward Danson pro 2 trees		2	0	
to Gardiner for 2 apple trees & one pier tree[32]		2	0	
paid William Danson per his father in full	3	3	0	
to Jane Clifton	0	1	0	
to James fell	0	1	6	

[p. 22]

24th paid William Rowison In full of all Demands — 3 6

Aprill the 1th 1722 Then paid Old Jennet Taylor The 10li which I Received of George Braithwait which John Taylor Lent G[eorge] B[raithwait] <and> I Toke bill pro The Same which said sum I paid per Content of both Old Jennet and her Son John Taylor in the presence of Thomas Danson William Taylor Roland Taylor [& *interlined*] Susan Brockbank in William Danson Shoppe — 10 0

		lli	s	d	
March 1722	Received of Richard Rigg	2	1	6	
	Borrowed of Richard Robinson	5	5	0	
aprill	William Danson paid The Lent money	1	9	0	
	Thomas Denny paid The Lent money	4	16	6	
Aprill 28	to William Cowhird	0	5	6	
September 13th 1722	paid Robert Taylor Land Sess & Window Tax pro 1th half year	0	7	5	2
September 14	20 stone Wool Sold to Daniel Tyson att 6s per Stone[33]	lli 6	0		

14 paid William Cowherd ½ quarter <Mutten> Veall	0	11
23d paid William Walker pro ½ a Sheep	2	2

32 Pear tree.
33 Daniel Tyson is unidentified.

18 *The Account Book of Clement Taylor*

26th Borrowed of Brother Edward	10	11	10	
September 29th Received Interest of James Capland pro				
50li pro 1720	2	2	0	
October				
13 paid Richard Nuby pro 3 Swills		0	9	
13 paid Thomas Denny pro a peik[34] of Wheat	0	3	6	
26 paid Constable Sess to B[enjamin] T[aylor][35]	1	5	3	
October Then sold Edward Bland				
26 Six gimer twinters at 3s 6d a peice	1	1	0	0

[p. 23]

November				
7 paid Townson pro fish	0	2	6	
7 Received of John Dodson in part pro bease[36]	6	19	6	
paid Jonson pro 100 read balls[37]	0	0	6	
13 paid Jennet Taylor 10s in part of 26ll which I owe to her	0	10	0	
13 [*sic*] Then Bought of John Taylor 1722 of Joliver Tree half of a Cross-cutt Saw & a file belonging into itt price my part[38]	2	3		
6 Bout a Side of Bief at Ulverstone pro	1	19	6	
bout at Bouth a Side more pro	1	04	0	
6 paid William Walker pro quarter of Mutten in full	0	0	10	
17 paid Thomas Wayman pro butter	0	1	2	

34 Peck.
35 Benjamin Taylor of Nibthwaite was constable of Colton 1722–3: CRO, BPR 17/C2/1.
36 Beasts.
37 The sum paid for these red balls is very small, and continued to be. When Clement Taylor's son Edward bought 30 in 1751 he paid 1½d for them: LRO, DDPd 26/338. They were probably for marking sheep.
38 The saw was quite expensive, and was presumably a joint venture.

The Account Book of Clement Taylor 19

November 1721	Wheel Timber[39] Sawn per Edward parke &c		
November 1722	6 Axle Trees Hew'd per James Twisaday		
November	paid Edward Bornes pro 19lli of Sheep Suet at 2d^{1}/$_{2}$ a pound	4s	0
	paid Edward Walker pro Dressing 15 yards of Half Thick at 1d ^{1}/$_{2}$ per yard	1s	10^{1}/$_{2}$
	paid William Rownson pro Mend a lant Horn[40] &c in full	1	0
	Debtor to Our William pro a pair of wool cards	1	3
29 December 6	Lent Thomas Denny 2 Gunies & a ^{1}/$_{2}$ paid Myles Harrison the which I Borrowed In July Last	5 0	0

[*p. 24*]

December 22 Debtor to William Lickbarrow
<16 yards B> for Dyeing 16 yards of
Brown halfe Thick

[*p. 25*]

1710	s	d	qr
Land Sess	13	03	00
Bloomer Ridding		09	01
Smithy Rent	02	09	03
more for Bloomer Ridding		011	00
James Taylor estat[41]		02	1
payes att a poor Bill		09	00
more for Blomer Riding	00	00	02
Master Wage[42]	03	08	00

And pro James Taylor Estate
                    3s at 1li

Land Sess	<7> 08	04 <0>	00
A Single poor bill	0	11	3
Smithy Rent	3	5	0
more pro Bloomer Ridding	0	11	0
Bloomer Ridding	0	9	1

39 Carts at this time were the clog-wheeled variety, with solid wooden wheels fixed to the axle and moving with it; see Denyer *op. cit.*, 104–6.
40 Mending a lantern.
41 Tom Crag, the farm bought from James Taylor in 1713; see xvii.
42 For the school at Colton; see n. 31.

paid M[yles] Harrison Smithy Rent pro 1720

James Taylor		4	2
Old Jennet Taylor		1	2
Clement Taylor	2	9	3 <9>
Thomas & George Braithwait	0	0	2
Robert Sawrey	0	0	2
	3	4	3
Richard Postlethwait	0	1	2
Edward Nuby	0	1	1

which I Usually Used to Receive
of them [I *interlined*] paying my own with it to
the Collector but now the pay it
<the> them selves & soe much is
taken of me in the rentall
and set on their heads

[*p. 26 is blank*]

[*p. 27*]

Account of <Serving of>
Offices Servt by <me> Clement
Taylor

Imprimis Window Tax pro the year 1709
Over Seer of poor pro the year 1713

James Taylor Churchwarden 1700
Church Warden pro AD 1717[43]
The Land Tax & Window Tax pro 1721

John Coldin of Grainge Manksman
which I Bout I [*sic*] percionon[44] at 1li 06d
half peice being 5 yards & near ½

[*pp. 28 and 29 are blank*]

---

43 These are confirmed by the lists of parish officers in the Colton Church Book: CRO, BPR 17/C2/1; but James Addison of Newby Bridge was churchwarden in 1700, not James Taylor.
44 The second 'I' and the repeated 'on' after 'percion' are errors.

[*p. 30*]

December Then sent per Ulverston
Carrier to George Cocke att
Kendall 4s for 12lli of Candles
and also Left 1d for Carring
Box which Candles came in

		s	d	
Received of Brother Richard[45] towards Candles per C.T.		0	6	
15 Bout of John Jonson 5.½ of Comberland Cloth at 1s 9d per yard		9	0[46]	
3.¾ of Hollan at 2s 6d per yard		9 <2>	4½	
1 Silk hancorchive		2	8	
1 of Musslin		1	6	
	1	2	4	2
19 Thomas Denny paid in full		7	0	0

January the 26th 1722	li	s	d
to William Danson for Honney	0	1	0
to John Cowhird pro Work	5	0	0
to my Wif at Hawkshead pro Shert Cloth pro Brother William	0	5	11½
more to her Idem	0	5	2
to Edmund Wilson pro a Chese	0	4	0
Spent at Hawkshead Idem	0	0	10
to Randall	0	1	0
pro 15 apple Trees	0	7	6
to Newland Miller pro Drying 10 bushell of oats	0	0	10
to Idem pro Bun Meall	0	0	6
to Jonson in part for work	1	16	0
to Jonson More in full	2	0	0
to William Cowhird 5s toward Well Close	0	5	0
More to William Cowhird pro Work	0	5	0

45   His brother-in-law, Richard Robinson of Waterside: see 236, and intro. *passim*.
46   *recte* 9s 7½d; the total should be £1 3s 2d. John Johnson was probably an itinerant Scots packman. For later examples of such packmen, see T.W. Thompson, *Wordsworth's Hawkshead*, London, 1970, 234–46, W. Rollinson, *Life and Tradition in the English Lake District*, London, 1974, 55–6, and D.T. Jackson, *Roots and Records*, Heversham, 1989. William Johnston, 'a poor Scotch man', was buried at Cartmel on 16 July 1742. See also nn. 51 and 117.

to Thomas Wayman in full	0	4	6
to Christopher Taylor pro Bark leading	0	10	0

[*p. 31*]

	li	s	d
January 1722 for 16 Bushell of oats	2	18	8
to Roger Preston pro a grindstone	0	2	0
Spent at Ulverstone the same time	0	0	6
to James Rownson for Beas grass[47]	0	13	0
to Thomas Millerson pro a Letter	0	0	9
to John Cowhird toward his Work	0	5	0
to James Twisaday pro Work	1	4	6
to the same one stone of wool & a table	0	8	0
To William Rownson pro shop goods	0	1	6
To William <J> Cowhird toward Well Cloase	1	0	0
Spent at Bouth at a meeting about Church	0	0	6
paid pro Thomas Wife at Bouth	0	0	3
paid John Cowhird toward Work	0	11	0
paid James Dixon pro Bracken[48]	1	6	0
to William Rownson Sugar Lofe	0	4	0
to Richard Robinson which I had Borrowed of him	3	3	0
to William Danson pro shows[49]	1	13	6
to Idem which I had borrowed of him	2	2	0
to Idem for a Wash Leather skinn	0	3	0
to Jonson pro Cowhird pro a Bark Sack	0	3	0
to John Dodson for John Rownson and I Toke bill in from him	10	8	4
To Thomas Walker which I Borrowed	4	12	0
to Baine Bridge[50] pro Exchainge of a pann	0	1	8

47 Beasts' grassing.
48 On 12 January 1723 Clement Taylor bought permission to take a yearly 'daywork' of cutting bracken for thatch in the close called Far Hagg from James Dixon of Light-how, carpenter. The sum of £1 6s is that specified in the deed: LRO, DDPd 26/213. Clement's right to take the bracken was recognised in the deed of sale of Dixon's house and land on the same day: *ibid.* 26/212. It is surprising to find bracken being intended for thatch at so late a date; see Denyer, *op. cit.*, 158–9.
49 Shoes.
50 Possibly the John Bainbridge who appears as an iron-ore dealer at the Backbarrow furnace in 1712 and who may very well have also dealt in pans: A. Fell, *The Early Iron Industry of Furness and District*, Ulverston, 1908, 91.

for Corn 4 bushell	0	7	6
Spent at Ulverston	0	0	6
To Our William for his Wage for 1721	3	10	0
More to him which I Borrowed	0	16	0
to Edward park for work	0	12	0
To Scott[51] pro Cloth	1	2	6
to Old Jennet about Martin[52]	0	10	0
To Edward Rigg for old Jennet	20	0	0
More to Old Jennet	5	10	10
I remain Debtor to her	1	0	0

[p. 32]

January 1722 Disborsments	li	s	d
to Myles Harrison pro tarr[53] & Cows Bulling which I had unpaid him	0	2	0
paid William Danson which I Borrowed in full	2	2	0
paid William Park for 28 Dayes Work	0	14	0
paid James Taylor pro work	1	7	0
more pro 2 wedders	0	10	0
to Agnes Carter pro her Last year Wage	2	0	0
more to the Same of this year Wage 1722	1	0	0
to Richard Taylor Wife	0	3	0
To Clement Taylor of Jolivertree per our William for Interest	1	3	7
and more pro Mr Chapman	0	9	9
to Clement Taylor per Myles Harrison	20	0	0
paid Thomas Crosfield for 6li of fish had of Benjamin from Carr[54]	0	1	0
Spent at Nuby Bridge When I sold Little Close wood[55]	0	2	0
I had Nothing of Earnest of John & William Atkinson			
paid Robert Scales in part			

51 See n. 46.
52 Martinmas, 11 November.
53 The tar was probably for salving sheep, but it was also used, again mixed with butter, to grease cart-wheels.
54 Probably Cark, where there would be fishermen.
55 At the inn at Newby Bridge when he sold the wood from Little Close.

24   *The Account Book of Clement Taylor*

of the Church Account	2	2	0
More to him of the Sam [*sic*] Account	2	2	3 1/2
Advansed More of of [*sic*] Church Account Equall with partners[56]	0	8	8 1/2
Spent at Bowth 1s	0	1	0
paid William Rownson pro oyle of Torpintime[57]	0	0	9 1/2
to Elizabeth & Agnes Each 6d	0	1	0
paid Brother Edward for Black Cherry & plain trees	0	5	0
to Edmond Wilson for Chese 102li	1	1	10

[*p. 33*]

February 1722 Receipts	li	s	d
Received of John Taylor per James Rowson [*sic*]	20	0	0
Received of John Walker Interest in arear pro 1720	0	13	4
Interest pro 1721	16	13	4
Interest of the same pro 1722	16	13	4
Received of the princeple Money	40	00	0
Debtor to J[ohn] Walker upon bill[58]	21li		
of William Braithwait Interest	2	10	0
of John Stewrdson [*sic*] Interest Gave Idem 1722 1s	5	00	0
of Edward Danson Land rent	3	0	0
of John Taylor Interest	<3> 4	3	0
of John Scales Interest pro 1720 & 21	2	9	0
of James Capland per his Son Interest pro 1721	2	2	0
from Randall[59] per Mr ford Haukshead	0	10	0
of Mr Ford for Coles 17 load 2 Sacks	22	14	11
to Margaret Taylor pro Interest &c	1	12	6

56   For the extension of Colton church, see n. 26.
57   Turpentine.
58   This entry is a later insertion.
59   Randal Fallows; see 230.

February 6th 1722 Then Rackned with
Margaret Taylor & gave her a bill
for a hundred pounds which is [Due *interlined*] per
me [<to her *interlined*>] C. Taylor

February 8th of Robert Sawrey pro Land rent and for plowing in full	1	13	6
Received of Brother Edward 1li 18 6 in full of all accounts Exceping [*sic*] one hundred pounds	1	18	6
24 of James Danson for Land rent	3	0	0

[*p. 34*]

to Charles for 2 hatts for Elizabeth and Agnes	0	1	4
February 19th To Rowland Wainhouse for a Sute of Cloase & Stock-ins for Brother William	3	8	0
To The Same for a Sheloune petty Coat & other goods	0	6	0
Spent 2d at Cartmell	0	0	2
20th paid Robert Rigg pro Interest	0	16	8
2d Lent Brother Edward Taylor which I've Nothing to Show for	100	0	0
21 Bout fouer bushel of Oats at Ulverston	0	17	0
for ½ bushel of Beans	0	3	4
for ½ bushel of Cockels		1	8
Spent Idem	0	0	9
½ quarter of flanel	0	0	1 ½

21 gave Myles Harrison the
Receipt which Mr. Roskell
gave me for 40li at
Candlemas

24 Then paid James Danson for peeling 41 quarters & 2 bushels of Bark	4	9	4

26   *The Account Book of Clement Taylor*

Then paid him More for all Work which he had done for 4 years by past [a]c[coun]tts	1	19	0
24th [*sic*] 1722 James Danson remains Debtor which is not all Due till the 1th of May Next	3	13	5
25 to William Cowhird towards Coals	0	10	0

[*p. 35*]

February 11th 1722 Disborsments	li	s	d
to Rowland Wainhouse for Elizabeth a Calamaniah Coate	0	16	6
for 2 painted Napkins	0	2	6
of William Account 4d pro Buttons	0	0	4
for Agnes for Tape 2d	0	0	2
To John Barrow for 3 pecks of Wheat	0	11	0
Spent Idem	0	0	4

Six hopes of Cockles makes Six quarts of fishes Seasoning for the Same as Follows[60]			
one ounce & half of Mace		2	4
one ounce & a half of Cloves		1	1 1/2
one ounce & a half of white peper	0	6	0
one ounce & a half of White ranie Ginger	0	1	2
A good handfull of Salt			

March 25th		s	d
to Edward Walker pro Milling 28 yards of Blanketing at 1d per yard		2	4

30th 5 loads & 11 sacks of Cols Livered to Counsay per watter in 1722[61]

---

60   Cockles were preserved in the same way as char; see nn. 77 and 288.
61   The furnace at Cunsey was established in 1711 by Edward Hall & Co. on the site of a former bloomery: Fell, *op cit.*, 192–3, 209. Water transport was better for the charcoal which would arrive unbroken.

Aprill to John Cowhird towards Leading Coals		0	13	0
<To William Cowhird towards Cutting Wood			10	0 >
to John Cowhird			01	0
May 16 to Cowhird's Wife			10	0
To Richard Taylor			12	0
25th of Richard Rigg pro Interest		li	s	d
of 50li for 1722		2	1	6
25 to John Cowhird for leading Coals out of Knott in full		1	1	0
30th of James Towers pro a Cow		3	15	0
To School Master[62]		0	8	0
30 To Thomas Millerson pro Letter		0	0	9

[*p. 36*]

Spent at Ulverston		0	0	7
Lent R[ichard] R[obinson]		0	10	0
paid Agnes Carter at Candlemas in part of her wage pro 1722		1	0	0
More a Stone of yarn at Whitesuntide		0	12	0
In Earnest 6d		0	00	6
The Wole [*sic*] Duty of Man[63]		0	2	6
More in Money		0	13	0
	all paid	2	8	0
May 30th Then paid The Dansing Master				
1723 Shuttleworth pro Elizabeth 4 weeks		0	4	0
More to his son at Ball		0	1	0
Spent with him			2	6
June				
3d to Rowland Waynhouse pro Elizabeth 4 Weeks bord		0	9	0
to his Wife pro good [*sic*] for Elizabeth		0	5	0

---

62 Still at Colton; see n. 31. For the establishment of the school at Finsthwaite, see J. Martin, 'The Building and Endowment of Finsthwaite Church and School', *CW2*, 1984, 134–5.

63 *The Whole Duty of Man*, by Richard Allestree (1619–81), royalist divine and from 1665 Provost of Eton, published in 1658, with part 2 in 1683.

Spent when we went to Wells[64]	0	2	0
March Then Hired Jane 20th Ormandy pro 1722 & She is to have woll for Stockings & her Cloase mended and Made inth' house	2	5	0
	li	s	d
William Taylor Wage pro 1723 is	3	10	0
June 7 to Myles Harrison pro Master's table a quarter	0	17	6
More Idem pro Brandy		2	6
paid Robert Sawrey poor Sess		9	0
Received of R[obert] Sawrey pro plowing & 20 foot of Birch wood		7	0
7 to Richard Taylor Towards Coaling &c	0	5	0
12 William Danson paid the 2 Guneas which I Lent him			

[p. 37]

June 28 Then Sent to Brother William to Oxford	9	0	
to Carrier pro Carriage Idem	0	3	
8 pound of hungg bief Carriage	0	2	
besids to Ulverston Carrier pro Carriage to Kendall	[blank]		
June 28 Borrowed of Robert Rigg	16	0	0

---

64 The dancing classes were at Cartmel. Rowland Wainhouse, with whom Elizabeth boarded, was a mercer there: see 242. The dancing master, Mr Shuttleworth, makes no appearance in the Cartmel registers. The 'Ball' would be the occasion upon which his pupils displayed their skills; a practice still observed in the present century: see J.F. and T.M. Flett, *Traditional Step-Dancing in Lakeland*, English Folk Dance and Song Society, 1979, 8–9. The 'Wells' were at Humphrey Head, where a mineral spring had been known and visited for some time: see S. Taylor, *Cartmel, People and Priory*, Kendal, 1955, 107. Sir Daniel Fleming's children stayed at Flookburgh to take the waters in 1672 and broke a glass which cost their father 6d, but they went on subsequent occasions: *The Flemings in Oxford*, ed. J.R. Magrath, i, Oxford Historical Society, 1904, 462–3, 496, 503. Elizabeth ('Bett') went again to Cartmel in September: below, p. 37.

August
16th Borrowed of William Danson	1	10	0	
17th To Townson pro fish		0	3	6
17 To Miles Harrison Master Wage		2	2	
To Idem pro tarr	0	0	3	

1 September paid Old Jennet Taylor				
The 20s which she Left in my hand				
4 Borrowed of Our Margaret	0	5	0	
paid Richard penny for 13 dayes work	0	9	0	
paid Rowland Wainhouse for				
a fortnets Table pro Bett	0	4	8	
paid Thomas Millerson pro a letter	0	0	9	
paid to William Woodburne at Severall times				
towards Wood Cutting & Coaling in				
Knott 1th		5	0	0
more		5	0	0
more	1	10	0	
more	0	10	0	0
more	0	3	0	0
more	1	1	0	0
more	2	15	0	0
more	1	1	0	0
more Land rent due	<2>1	18	0	0
	8	08	1	0[65]

Due to William Woodburne pro bark peeling				
48 quarter at 2s 2d per quarter	5	4	0	0
Idem Bark Leading	0	5	7	2
Idem pro Cutting & Coling 8 load & 3 Sac [sic]	2	9	6	0
more 2 load & 7 Sacks	0	8	7	0
more 0 [load] 8 Sacks		2	2	2
	8	9	11	0

[p. 38]

November 1723
paid James Rigg 1s upon
John Turner Account which I Received
From Richard Harrison in the
presence of William Penington of
Bandridgehead at Coulton Church

65 recte £9 8s.

30   *The Account Book of Clement Taylor*

9 paid Richard Nuby pro swills		10d	0q
paid Birket Smith 4d Due upon the account of stone hammer[66]			
9 paid William Rownson pro hopps in full		10d	
paid William Hirdson pro li of Copperas		2d	
paid Robert Scales 6d for Ends[67] had <of William> of William Wilson Son			
paid Edmund Wilson pro 4 pecks of Salt		13	0
paid William Taylor pro Carriage of Books which he paid at Kendall		1s	0d
November 1723			
John Wilson debtor pro 12 stone of wool at 6s 2d per stone	3	14	0
Borrowed of Brother Edward 3 Gunnies[68] at Kendall Faier per C.T			
Mr. Chapman Debtor to me	1li	1s	
Debtor to William Danson 2li <G>			
William Rownson Debtor 1li 1s about Church			
<October John Wilson Debtor pro 12 Ston 1723 of Wool	3	14	0>
Debtor to Margaret Taylor	3	0	
Debtor to William Taylor	1	0	
Debtor to William Danson	1	0	
6li Candles	0	2	3
1 botle of Wine	0	2	0
To Jonson Wife at 2 Sundrey times	0	10	
William Cowhird towards Coaling in Knott	1	0	
paid Richard Fell pro Leading 2 load & 10 Sacks of Coals	0	7	1

66   William Birket, blacksmith, and his family gained a settlement in Colton parish in July 1729, but he could have lived there for some time before that: CRO, BPR 17/O1/12. Here he is being paid for a heavy hammer for breaking stone.
67   The meaning of 'Ends' is doubtful. It can mean lengths of cloth or the stems of a growing crop, but neither seems likely here. It can also mean lengths of thread, waxed at the ends, used in shoe-making.
68   Guineas. Formerly Kendal had two fairs, one about 28 October, the feast of SS Simon and Jude, and the other on 25 April [St Mark], but later there were four; for the fairs, see J.D. Marshall, *Kendal 1661–1801*, Kendal, 1975, 66.

[p. 39]

September 1723 Account of The 7 or 8 yards Long Whiell[69] timber Sawn on The back of Knott per J[ames] Twisaday Kendal Faire To young John Cowherd towards Leading Coals per his Father Order	0	5	0
January 18 To William Woodborne pro Cutting 1 load of Coles which istin Cold[70]	0	2	8
January 18 of William Woodborne towards Land rent pro 1722	1	17	
January 8 1723 William Woodburne left Unpaid of the rent pro 1722	0	13	6
February 1th 1722 [sic] of John Stewartson Interest	4	18	
of Edward Danson Toward Land Rent pro this year per Thomas Danson hand	2	4	0
<F>January of Mr Rawlinson pro Knot wood	57	0	0
of John Maychel	43	0	0
February 1th of Antoney Wilson pro 47 load of Coals	67	1	8
of Mr Ford pro 5 load 11 sacks of Coals & 10s of Randel Falloes Account	8	6	9
3d of John Taylor of Espford pro Interest of 50li	2	1	8
7th of Edward Danson Rent pro pincha Croft & tarnhaw	0	19	0

69   See n. 39.
70   *i.e.* isn't coaled, has not been made into charcoal.

32   *The Account Book of Clement Taylor*

7 of Edward Danson More Rent			
3 load ½ Coals leading out of Knot			
Edward Danson & set against 4			
dayes plowing pro Last year	2	16	0
7 gave Ditto again	0	1	0
17 to Thomas Jonson pro half of 10 load &			
11 Sacks at 2s 8d per load	0	14	8
To The Same pro 1 load 8 sacks at the			
Same price	0	04	6
To The Same pro putting a			
pitstead out	0	0	10
Idem Birch Tops 1s & riveing Coal Wo[od *torn*]			
a shilling			

[*p. 40*]

Knott Account			
17th James Danson part as on the other			
side of 10 load 11 sacks[71]	0	14	8
more one day rivein wood		0	10
More Idem Birch Tops		01	00
more Idem pro Scifting			
Coardwood 1 day	0	0	6
		17	0
17 paid Myles Taylor pro 2 bushel			
of oats	0	10	0
February To Myles Harrison per			
1723 Richard Robinson	10	0	0
5th of the said 10li I			
had Borrowed of Myles before			
February			
1723 To Robert Rigg which I was Debtor	16	10	0
To Thomas Danson which I was Debtor			
to William Danson himself	15	7	0
February to Margaret Taylor pro			
1723 Interest [2li in full *interlined*] & more 3li borrowed			
of her	5	0	0

---

71   This refers to the other half of the charcoal which Thomas Johnson made on p. 39. 'Rivein', on the next line, is riving.

The Account Book of Clement Taylor 33

February To Our William Taylor 1li which			
1723 I had borrowed of him &			
more pro his Wage pro 1723			
3.10 in all	4	10	0
To William Parke pro Waling at			
Back of Knot & other places	0	17	3
To Jacob Parke by his said Brother	0	14	3
To John Cowhird pro leading			
Coals out of Knot in full		15	0
To Peter Taylor pro Cutting			
Coal wood & Coaling the same			
in Knot 4 load & 8 Sacks at 2[72]	1	10	4
To Arthur Keen pro Coaling			
in Knot 24 load & 7 Sacks at			
4 & 3d per load paid at This time	3	1	6
pro 2 bushel of oats at Ulverston	0	9	7
To William Park of Edward park account	0	2	6
To James Taylor pro waling			
in full for this year	1	15	6
gave Idem pro Samuel	0	0	6
To Myles Harrison per Brother			
Edward <...> Lawrence Harrison Order	41	12	

[p. 41]

1723 To William Cowhird pro all Work			
done for me this year he rackined	1	s	d
pro plowing	0	2	6
February To Robert Scales pro Dansing			
1723 Master Enterance & pore Sess	0	15	6
To Dansing Master and Spent Idem		4	6
to James Twisaday pro a Stee &			
Work this year	0	6	6
Spent at Bouth with Mr Rawlinson	0	1	0

---

72 Something has been omitted here. The figure is undoubtedly '2', but it is neither 2s nor 2d. He may have meant something like 'at 2 separate times'.

To William Walker pro 2 <6d> 3d Swils pro School	0	0	6
To Robert Rigg Interest pro 6li pro half a year	0	2	6
of William Braithwait pro Interest of 50li pro 1723	2	10	0
To Thomas Danson of Brother Edward Account	10	0	0
February To Henry Taylor Test 1723 Thomas Denny	41	7	0
To Richard Robinson	14	15	0
Lent Idem before	00	10	0
Debtor to Richard Robinson pro a leter 8d & Sunment[73] or mace			
February To Thomas Hodsgsen pro Shoppgoods in full	0	3	0
To Edmund Wilson pro 100 Weight of Cheise	1	2	0
Debtor to Edmund Wilson pro 62li of Cheise	0	11	6
To Miles Taylor pro Oats	2	3	4
February Shertin[74] bought pro Brother William 1723 <1th 4 yards of Hollen> 1th 3 yards & 3 quarters of Hollen at 2s 6d per yard	0	9	<9> 4 $1/2$
7 yards & a half of Combrland [sic] Cloath at 1s 4d$1/2$ per yard	0	10	3 $1/2$

[p. 42]

February 25 1723 of John Walker pro Interest pro a bill 2li 10	li	s	d
More in Cash 5.10	8	0	0
22 of Thomas Denny 1li in part of Christopher Marr account pro Interest	1	0	0

73   Cinnamon.
74   Shirting.

March 1723
Money Disborsed of The School Account   s   d
1th To William Walker pro 2 swils   0   6
2d   to James Walker pro lime   1   0
A Lock pro The Dooer   2   0
to 29 foot of Oak bords
to two Ash planks
Ditto twenty & 5 foot of okewood   [blank]

Received of John <...> Walker
in part pro interest for 1723
when Chapel was builded   [blank]

Chappel Account[75]   li   s
1th to Lawyer Gibson   1   1
A Journey to Lancaster pro advice
About Chappel   0   3
To Lawyer Gibson   1   1
at the same time Expenses
to Lancaster when he Drew the Instrument
pro the Sidsmen & Minister to Signe
& also The writing which Brother Richard
and I am to Signe & Seal to the
Governor of the Bounty of Queen Ann
Spent with Mr Sympson   0   1   0
pro my Diner & other Expences
at the same time   11 1/2

May 8 Jorney to Lancaster with proposels
and request stayed all night Expenses   3   6
Spent at Ulverston & when we went to trout
beck & at Stotpark with B[enjamin] Brown   6d

[p. 43]

March 25th 1724[76]
Account of 60 Sheep belongin To t[he]
Farm at Plumgree [sic] Livered to
John Cowhird from Mr Henry

---

75 For the building of the church at Finsthwaite, see xxv. Robert Gibson (1767–1731), was recorder of Lancaster, and the Backbarrow Company's lawyer. William Stout, the Lancaster merchant, had a high opinion of him ('very moderat in his fees'): *The Autobiography of William Stout of Lancaster 1655–1752*, Chetham Society, 3rd ser., xiv, 208, 275, 277–8. Benjamin Browne (1664–1742), of Townend, Troutbeck, Westm., was High Constable of Kendal Ward 1711–32.

76 When a farm was let it was and, where a farm has a landlord's flock, still is the practice to have the sheep valued by independent assessors, usually two representing the landlord and two the incoming tenant. Here Clement Taylor is the only one. There is another example on p. 44.

Taylor & When The Said Henry
Taylor shall Come to Take
Liverance of they Said Number
of 60 Sheep The Detirmination
of any Diferance hapen to arise
is Left to Clement Taylor & price
of The Said Sheep is 5s apeice
& The Said H[enry] Taylor to have it
in his Choice whether to take
the Said Number of Sheep or 5s apece
for they same if C Taylor do not
Think them Worth the said 5s apeice
to the said H[enry] Taylor the said J[ohn] Cowhird
did of his own free will move the said
Motion   As Wittness My Hand
          Clement Taylor

John Walker
Joyner was present

Account of Sheep Taken of
the farm at plumgreen at
the abovesaid 25th day of March
1724
                17 Wedders two of them was [tups *interlined*]
                23 Ews
                29 hoggs
and at Michaelmas 20 more hoggs
                ──
                in all 89

Received of William Woodborn Wife
towards Land rent April
1724   2   0   0

	ounce	half
Sunement[77]	1	0
Cloves	1	2
Mace	0	1/2
Black peper a quarter		

    Charres

---

77 Cinnamon. This is a recipe for potting char; *cf* the one for the preservation of cockles on p. 35. Char, or Alpine trout, (*salvelinus alpinus*), are found in some northern lakes, notably Windermere. They were a prized delicacy in this period, and were preserved by being baked very slowly with spices in flat earthenware dishes, which were often decorated with fish. They would then keep for a considerable time and were frequently given as presents. Col. James Grahme had them sent up to London from Levens in the 1690s: *All Things is Well Here'*, ed. A. Bagot and J. Munby, CWAAS Record Series, 10, 1988, 21, 66, 68, 71–2. The Flemings of Rydal sent huge char pies at a rather earlier date, as well as potted char: *The Flemings in Oxford*, ed. Magrath, App. B. and *passim*, and M.L. Armitt, *Rydal*, Kendal, 1916, 281–301.

[*p. 44*]

March 28 1724
Account of Sheep Livered from
Mr Henry Taylor to His
Mother Mrs Margaret Taylor
in the presence of John Cowhird
& Christopher Taylor as
Follows

1th Ews	30	0
2 Wedders	10	
Tups	03	

valued per J[ohn] C[owhird] & C[hristopher] T[aylor] to
5s apeice wel worth

hoggs	17 at	

3s 6d apeice

[*miscellaneous calculations at foot*]

[*p. 45*]

March 30 1724[78]
Account of Wood Mesured
for Windows for Chapel
of Robert Taylor to J[ohn] Walker

		foot
1	1 tree	14
	2 tree	14
	3 tree	17
	4 tree	15
		60 foot

	s	d	q
May 1724			
Spent of the Chappel's account when we			
got Sidsmens hands	0	7	0
Item Six Side Swills	0	1	6
Spent at Stotpark when Mesured			
wood, J[ohn] W[alker] Robert Taylor			0
May to John Janson			
27 for Lyning lime Kill	0	2	6

---

78 The entries on this page and the next one are concerned with the building of the church; see xxv. The phrase 'when we got sidsmens hands' refers to the occasion upon which the sidesmen, assistants to the churchwardens, signed the petition for the new building.

To William Rownson pro a
pound & a half of Hopps   0   2

May Debtor to Edward Kellet pro principle
trees
      foot
1th tree   18 Intack
2d tree   22 1/2
3d tree   19 1/2

June 1th Lintren wood Measoured in
Green Slack per Myles Harrison

       foot
13 trees   61 1/2 at 4d per foot

10 Ribb wood Measured in Green
Slack per John Atkinson to R[ichard] Robinson
& C. Taylor 11 trees 77 foot
at 7d 1/2 per foot

<More> Sparr wood Measured at the
same time per said persons
4 trees 22 foot at
6d per foot
13th 2 trees pro Lintrens 12 foot
       foot
more 8 trees at 6d per foot 30 0
3 ribbs at 7d 1/2   21 1/2

[*p. 46*]

more of ribbs   foot
at 7d 2q per foot   55 0
One Sweeptree left in wood 5 1/2
one wholed [*sic*] tree pro a Lint
pro the great Window   5 0
[at 6d *in margin*]

June 18th one Sweeptree 14 1/2
one more   15 1/2
Measured per John Walker in Green
Slack

	foots				
<at 4d per foot	093<7>>				
at 6d per foot	126				
at 7d 2q per foot	235				
at 10d per foot	045½				
at 4d per foot	073				

		li	s	d	
foot					
73 [a]t 4d		1	4	4	
126 at 6d		3	3	0	
235 at 7d 2q		7	6	10 ½	
145½ at 10d		1	17	11	
		13	12	1	2

July to William Rownson pro [3li of *interlined*] White
Sugar 3li & 2d pips[79]   2   6
to James Guy pro 21li of
Cheise at 2d³/₄ a pound   0   4   9½
<pro 1li½ of Hopps   0   0 >
July 25 4 trees 6 foots 2 at 6d
per foot

[*p. 47*]

April 1724
Then Bought 6 trees of George
Braithwait at 7d per foot Nomber
of trees & foots as follows[80]

	foot	
1 tree	12	24 long
2	13	22
3	17	28
4	14	24
5	16½	276
6 pro Chappel	12½	& 10 foot Long

Myles Drinkel bout Slate at Trout
-Beck [park *interlined*] pro 18 pence per load at watter
& had Given over by the Seller at
3 C load 2 loads & two fine larg stons[81]

---

79 The hops and sugar would be for brewing beer for the workmen, who also had cheese and tobacco pipes; *cf* Fell, *op. cit.*, 297.
80 Clement Taylor is beginning to buy timber for his new house, which he distinguishes from that for the church. The measurements are in cubic feet and length.
81 *i.e.* 300 loads and 2 loads; for the Troutbeck Park quarries, see B. Tyson, 'The Troutbeck Park

40 The Account Book of Clement Taylor

Bords - Sawers Measour per Edward Kellet

	(Inchbroad/long)					foot	
1th Clogg	11	5	&	11	Bords	49	1/2
2 Clogg	10	5	&	11	Bords	44	0
3 Clogg	9	6 1/2	&	8	Bords	40	0
4 Clogg is						63	0
5 Clogg		6	&	9	Bords	45	0
6 Clogg	9	6	&	10	Bords	45	0
7 Clogg	11 1/2	6	&	11	Bords	60	1/2
8 Clogg	11 1/2	6	&	11	Bords	75	0

422 foot

	(Broad/long)						
1 Clogg	11	8.2	&	11	Bords	82	1/2
2 Clogg	10	7	&	9	Bords	49	1/2
3 Clogg	9	7	&	8	Bords	40	0
4 Clogg	11	7	&	10	Bords	65	0

237 foot

	bords			
1 Clog	12	is	96	0
2 Clog	9	is	47	0
3 Clog	10	is	50	0
4 Clog	11	is	66	0
5 Clog	9	is	54	0
6 Clog	8	f [sic]	40	0
7 Clog	11	is	44	0

397 foot

| 1 Clog | 12 | Bords | 90 | | |
| 2 Clog | 9 | Bords | 58 | 2 | 148.2 foots |

Slate Quarries, their Management and Markets, 1753–1760', *CW2*, 1984, 167–90. London slate, the best quality, was 1s 6d a load in 1753 so Clement Taylor was probably buying that here. The slate was brought to Ecclerigg Crag on the east shore of Windermere, where the slate company had a dock, and taken by boat down the lake. Although the destination of the slate is not specified, it was probably for the church as Clement's own new house was roofed with Coniston slate; see xxiii and below n. 299. A load of slate covered roughly one square yard. The measurements of wood below are in width in inches, length in feet, and number of boards, the final totals being in square feet. There is a slight margin of error in each case. Such errors were soon avoidable when woodmongers were able to use the tables devised by Edward Hoppus in his *Practical Measuring now made Easy* of 1736.

[p. 48]

		s	d
May 25 1724			
paid William Taylor in part of his wage		10	0
a pair of Cloggs		1	6
to my Wife pro a Napkin for him		1	6
June 14 to William Taylor per E[dward] Bland		1s	0
To [sic] of Chappel account	1	1	0
J[anuary] 31th To him more at Candle [sic][82]	0	10	0
To him more a Shirt	0	2	11

		s	d
May 1724			
To Jane Orondy [sic] in part of her wage		6	0
	li	s	
more to her [at severall times *interlined*] in full	1	19	0

Account of Boards Measured
in Knot from Edward Kellet
Hart Measured

	foot	
1 Clogg is	75	
2 Clogg is	35	2
3 Clogg	44	
4 Clogg	72	
5 Clogg	54	
6 Clogg	64	
1 part in all	344 1/2	

3 Cloggs	131	0
1 Clogg	71	0
2 part in all	202	

4 Clogs	80	
	69	
	140	
	34	
3 part	323 foot	
2 Cloggs	121 foot	
4 part in all	990 foot 1/2	

---

[82] Candlemas, 2 February.

[*p. 49*]

	li	s	d	
June Debtor to Edward Kellet pro 2 trees in The Intack	2	15	0	
4th paid Edward Taylor in full & also what remained behind of a Cow	0	16	0	

June 13th Clement Taylor Debtor to John
Atkinson To 12 yards of Linnen
at 1s 8d$^{1}/_{2}$ per yard   1 0 6
Ditto 5 Gallons 3 quarts   li   s   d
of Brandy at 5s 6d per Gallon   1 11 6
haveing the Cegg over at 1d
in all   2 12

15th Then Bout 6 trees at 10d per
foot in Green Slack of J[ohn] A[tkinson]
for C T 20 foot 12 11.2 11 14 10
one tree 2 foot one 16 foot   in all 78.2[83]

15 Received more of John Atkinson
in part of Little Close   1 1 0
20 of John Atkinson per my
wife   2 2 0

of Thomas Denny per his mother Margaret
Lent money toward paying Myles   li   s   d
Taylor pro 10 bushel of Oats   2 10 8
of The said Thomas Denny 5s at Cock
feight at Nubybridge[84]   0 5 0

July 9th Received of John Atkinson
The full Consideration pro Little Cloas
& Retorned 5 Gunies Gratis
August 13th 1724 Gray Cow buld
at A[braham] Rawlinson Unpaid

Edward Cow[85] Buld at M[yles] Harrisons
14th Day of March 1724 Broke

83 The 2ft and the 6ft trees are not included in the total of 78ft 2.
84 For cockfighting, see Rollinson, *op. cit.*, 141–7. This fight was at the inn at Newby Bridge, but at a rather late date Clement Taylor's son Edward held cockfights at Finsthwaite itself: T.E. Casson, 'The Diary of Edward Jackson, Vicar of Colton, for the year 1775', *CW2* , 1940, 6, 31.
85 The cow bought from his brother Edward. 'Broke' is short for 'broke bulling', a phrase which is now not used, but which indicates that the bulling was unsuccessful.

[p. 50]

	li	s	
July 1724 paid Arthur Keen pro Coaling 3 load of Coals in Becking Garth per W[illiam] Danson	0	12	
August 24 Interest of John Walker which was due 2d February last in part	4	0	0
24 of Jane Woodborn for land rent due 2d February last August	1 Matts[86]	1	0
October 1th of Richard <Harrison> Robinson	{0 {3	5 0	0 0
Borrowed of Myles Harrison	6	6	
October 19th of Richard Rigg Interest in part pro 80li at 10d per li	3	0	0
28 Borrowed of Myles Harrison	3	10	0
28 Boards 3/4 Inch 335 at 2d 1/4q per foot 11 Ditto 1/2 Inch 125 foot at 1d 3/4 per foot in all	4	1	0
Cartage to Ship Bord	0	0	4
pro Carrage from Liverpole to Grainge[87]		2s	6d

November 14 paid Myles Harrison
for all Tarr Had per me for 2 years
by past & for a Tarr Barrel
and for 2 stone of Salt & half
a Guney to Lawyer Chambers

paid Myles Harrison
in part of what I Borrowed of him   2   2
November more of John Walker
towards Interest pro 1723
a side of Bief 1li 4s or 5s
2s 6d pro Carrage of Bords from
Liverpool to Grainge

---

86 A later insertion and of doubtful meaning.
87 These are imported deal boards.

[p. 51]

	li	s	d	q
January the 29th 1724 Then paid George Braithwait for 5 trees at 7d per foot	2	2	3	2
30th Received of Edward Danson Towards the rent pro 1724	1	0	0	0
February of Edward Danson more per James 12 Twisaday for rent for 1724	2	19	0	0
Received of Edward Danson in all This Candlemas 5li 10s 0d for land rent Due				
30 Borrowed of Peter Taylor	9	0	0	0
More of The Same	1	0	0	0

	li	s	d
Received of Richard Robinson per[88] Brother William & Henry Bouton which said sum Henry paid on my account at Oxford to Brother William	8	8	0
More of Brother Richard in full	5	0	0
30 paid Adam Taylor pro 3 loks	0	2	0
paid Nicholas Crank of the Chapell account	3	11	10
30th of John Stewardson Wife Interest pro 120li	4	18	0
30 paid James Taylor for 23 dayes work	0	11	6
30 To Jacob Park pro waling	0	16	0
To The Same more paid for waling the Intack he being 55 dayes at 10d his man John 46 at 6d	3	8	10
More Jacob 6 dayes & his Man 6 dayes	0	4	0
31 To Sameuel Robinson in full for work & 6d Beverage	0	4	6
February 2d Received of John Walker in part for Interest	9	9	0
Received of John Atkinson per the hand of William Robinson in part for Green Slack wood	<.> 5	<.> 5	0

88 He means 'pro' [for] not 'per' [by or through]. Henry Bouton is unidentified.

More of J[ohn] Atkinson by the said William Robinson	14	15	0
April more per the hand of Richard 14 Robinson from J[ohn] Atkinson		5	0 [89]

[p. 52]

	li	s	d
February 2d 1724 paid James Rownson for Beast Grassing pro 1724	0	16	0
To Idem for Coals	1	0	0
To Idem for 6li of Sope	0	2	0
To Idem for Carriage Barley	0	2	0
To Idem About a wager	0	2	0
2 To Myles Taylor for 34 Bushel of Oats at 3s 10d per bushel	6	10	
2 paid To Thomas Holme for Makeing 26 yards of Serge at 1s 6d per yard	1	19	0
2 paid Thomas Hall in full for <Sope> Candles Glue & a book	0	6	8
2 paid Richard Taylor for furniter for Clement Coat &c	0	6	8
2 paid Bossmaker pro making 6 Bosses	0	1	6
2 paid James Brockbank pro 8 bushell & peck of Barley at 6s 4d per Bushell	2	12	3
paid John Scales for 4½ bushel of Big at 6s 2d	1	7	9
To the Same for makeing[90] of 9 Bushel at 2s 6d per Bushel	2	2	6
gave Idem pro buying 4 bushel & a half	0	0	6
2 paid Edmund Wilson in part towards 200li of Cheise & 3 pecks of Salt	2	2	0
2d Received of William Braithwait Satterhow Interest pro 60li 1724	li 2	s 10	0
<2d Received of John Walker Interest in part 360li nine Gunies	9	9 >	

89 Or perhaps £5; the sum is squeezed in at the foot of the page.
90 Malting; cf. n. 93.

46   *The Account Book of Clement Taylor*

of Antony Wilson pro 3 Duzen of Coals gave 6d to him	4	4	

[p. 53]

2d more of William Robinson per John Atkinson Order	5	5	
2d To John Wright pro a Sheet of Stampt paper[91]	0	1	8
Spent at Nubybridge with Maychel &c	0	2	6
7th paid John Cowhird for his part of two Walker brows	0	18	0
Received of Cozen Margaret Taylor the 2li 5s 6d which I lent her	2	5	6
8 paid Mr Ford for wood on the Chappel account & latts	5	0	0
8 To Mr Ford More of my own Account for wood Bought of Edward Kellet in the Intack in part	3	8	0
8 paid Edmund Wilson in full for Cheise & Salt & Candle Seavs & mustard in presence Margaret Braithwait at Haukshead	10	13	0
8 paid Charles Hatter pro Mograhs hatt 10d	0	0	10
8 paid Mr William Rawlinson pro a peck of wheat A Sider hoggshead & half Duzen of Sider in full	0	10	6
8 paid Mr Rawlinson more by Richard Postlethwait & John Maychel Order on account of Knott Bords	5	10	
Lent Mr Shiphird[92] 10li more per John Taylor 50	60	0	0

---

91   The Stamp Act, 5 & 6 William and Mary c. 21, prescribed that paper, vellum, or parchment used for legal or official documents must bear a government stamp.
92   Robert Shippard of Natland, Westm., gentleman, was buried on 5 January 1730 at Kendal. Six sons are mentioned in his will, proved in April of that year. See also *The Rake's Diary*, ed. A. Hilman, Curwen Archive Texts, 1994, 36, 75. The Shippards occur again on p. 54. No bond from them survives.

Received Interest of John Taylor pro 50li 28li.0 and the 50li also	2	0	0
8 of James Twisaday per Edward Danson Order in part for rent pro 1724	1	1	0
of Christopher Marr by the hands of Thomas Denny 2.10 being for Interest of 60li pro 1724	2	10	

[p. 54]

February 14 1724

	li	s	d
Bought a brass pot at Kendal weighed 44li at 6d per pound & 1s over	2	3	0
to potichary pro 2 ounce of the sperit of Hartshorn	0	1	0
Spent with Mr Robert Shippard when he & his 2 sons sealed bond	0	2	0
gave him for makeing bond & stamp	0	1	6
bout 2 lemons at Kendal	0	0	4
<February 2d of Edward Danson for rent for 1724 in part by the hands of James Twisaday	<0>2	00 <10>>	
21 More by Edward Danson for rent for 1724	1li	0	0
21 of Edward Danson for 3 dayes plowing for 1723/4		7s	6
gave Edward Danson against land rent		2s	6d

February 22d 1724 rackned with
Thomas Denny & paid him in full
for all Smith work & for a quarter
of swineflesh being 8s and
all other Accounts to this day
Excepting 3s which he is Debtor to me
Thomas Denny paid the above 3s

March paid John Leece for making 4 bushel malt peat Dryed	7	4

48   *The Account Book of Clement Taylor*

paid The Same for making 4 bushel more Sinder dryed Duty & all[93]		9	4
March 20 of William Woodborne wife towards Land rent		07	0
paid Thomas Denny of The Chappel Account	2	6	0
19 March Borrowed of Thomas Denny	2li	0	0
Borrowed of Our Margaret	1	1	0

[*p. 55*]

March 1724 Wood bout of Edward
Kellet in The Intack at 10d per foot

1th tree	at 10d$^{1}/_{2}$	10 foot
2	at 10d	9$^{1}/_{2}$
3	at 10d	10
4	at 10d	9$^{1}/_{2}$
5	at 10	10
6	at 10	7$^{1}/_{2}$
7	at 10	10
8	at 10$^{1}/_{2}$	12

More two principle trees
1th	26 foot	at 13d per foot			
2d	36	at 14 per foot			
July per J[ohn] W[alker] 15 trees at 7d		67$^{1}/_{2}$			
Borrowed of Thomas Denny			1	10	
one tree more of Edward Kellet Intack for Chappel at 10d per foot		16 foot			
Edward Bornes Debtor pro 4 lams				9	0
March left Underpaid by a former rackning				8	0
1724 a tup				5	0
Debtor to Edward Bornes pro Meat				17<16>	00

Bull alminick, dragens blood, burnt
alim of Each 3 drambs, mixt with
a little honey of roses

---

93   The duty on malt was imposed in 1697 under An Act for granting to His Majesty Certain Duties upon Malt, 8 & 9 William III. For the cinder-drying of malt, see *The Autobiography of William Stout of Lancaster*, 110, 258 n. 121.

A Calf
April   Edward Bornes a Calf 9s or 10s
10th   more a lamm he bout   2   9

12th Wood Bout of John Atkinson
in Green Slack   foot
1 tree   8 1/2   7d 1/2q
2 tree   15 1/2   per foot
New Wood in the said Close
1 tree   13 foot at 8d per foot
8 trees   45 foot
February   Edward Bornes Remains to
26   me [sic] When Rackned   3s   1d

[p. 56]

Account of Riggin & Wedder
bord Bout of Richard Atkinson
of Kellet to be Livered at
Cart Laine[94] at 1s 3d 1/2 per yard
Rigging   10 yards 1/2
Wedderbord   32 yards
2 Wa<ie>es   3li   0   0
Stayers   3   0   0
roof   2   10   0
flowers   0   0   4d
per yard

April 30th Received of Mr John Atkinson   li
in part for Green Slack wood   <1> 20
more Ditto per Thomas Denny   3   10
May paid William Dixon pro 10 stone of
6   plaster hare[95]   0   8   6
paid Ben Taylor Cunstable Sess
for 1724   0   2   0
paid Adam Taylor pro 2 letters   0   1   8
May paid Margaret Taylor Interest for 100li
4   in full for 1724   2   0   0

---

94 Cart Lane marks the Furness end of the route across the sands of Morecambe Bay from Hest Bank near Lancaster. Over Kellet quarry produced millstone grit, much used for millstones, but here for ridge titles: *John Lucas's History of Warton*, ed. J. Rawlinson Ford and J.A. Fuller-Maitland, Kendal, 1931, 145. 'Stayers' and 'Flowers' might appear to be timber for stairs and floors, but are more likely in the context to be stone for outside steps and for flooring. 'Wa<ie>es' is uncertain and the word is blotted.

95 Plaster was normally strengthened by the addition of hair, usually horse hair, but sometimes from cattle.

50   *The Account Book of Clement Taylor*

6 paid R[ichard] Robinson all I Borrowed of Him			
paid Jacob Parke on the Chapel Account		9	6
May paid James Rownson for The Old Whitefaced Cow	3	7	6
& he gave 1s for Luck			
May 16th Received Interest of Richard Rigg for 80li for Anno 1724	3	6	8
gave him again	0	1	0
16 paid Peter Taylor for Coleing 12 load & 4 Sacks		s 10	0
May 25th Great Why went To Freth[96] paid			

[*p. 57*]

1725 Money paid per C. T.
Upon The Chapel Account
1th To Thomas Denny pro ale
Ordered per H[enry] T[aylor] 1s M[yles] H[arrison] & C T

R[ichard] R[obinson] 6d in all[97]	0	1	6
Ditto pro mending bell Iron	0	1	0
To Richard Nuby for boddeming a hand riddle		0	3
To Wallers per the hand of Mr Harrison for waling Chapel Garth 28 dayes		14	0
To Rownson Taylor pro 7 dayes tableing him self 2s 4d			
To The Same for 7 dayes work		5	10
To Chapell One Stone of hare			11d
To The Chapell one stone of Hare			11

To The Chapel 6 pound of White lead
To the Chapel 1 pound of Spanish white
To the Chapel two Quarts of Lineseed
Oyle had of William Rownson
3 bords to Chapel Doors
being 17 foot

---

96   High and Low Frith are farms near the Leven sands, north-west of Holker, and some seven miles from Finsthwaite, a considerable distance to take a cow.
97   Henry Taylor [see 240, and below n. 194] either drank more than the rest or was more generous.

July to Brother Richard towards Concicr[ati]on fees for Chapel	4	4	0
To Chapel per Rownson half a Stone of Hare	0	<5> 0	5 2
Wood had of E[dward] Kellet in the Intack for Comunion Table			
September 20th To Rownson Taylor for washing Sand & Sarving Lymers at Chapel & Steepel 2 dayes [Table at *interlined*] at [*sic*] Richard Fells 1 day at His own house 12 at Jolivertree			
9 at William Cowhirds in all 24 dayes		12	6
To Elizabeth Jackson pro [26 *interlined*] whit Loves when Cap was Consicraited[98]	0	2	6

turn to the 4 Leave side

[*p. 58*]

June Received of Agnes Woodburne	li	s	d
9 upon her Father's Account pro Land rent in part	1	10	0
4th Edward <Cow Bult at William Barrows>			
June Broke bulling			
1725 Nailes Bought at Lancaster per William Danson for C Taylor			
1th 4000 of the best Slate nailes at 2s per Thousand		8s	0
1<000> thousan Second sort at 1s 10d per Thousand	[*blank*]		
5000 plaister Nailes at 18d per Thousand	[*blank*]		
half Thousand duble Spikes at 2s 9d	[*blank*]		
half Thousand Single Spikes 3s		1s	6d
floorings 5s 6d per Thousand			
June 1725 Received of Mr John Atkinson more in part for Greenslack wood		7	0
more 6 bottels of White Wine			

---

98 See xxv. Twenty-six loaves indicates the presence of a very large congregation at the service of consecration. The cross-reference is to p. 63 where there are further church accounts.

52   *The Account Book of Clement Taylor*

more per the hand of Thomas Denny
4 Gallons & a pint of Brandy
more a Barrel of Bief   1   12
July 16   more 8 trees   45 foot at 7d
more 4 trees   38 at 9d per foot
& a half

16   More in money   7li   13s

[*miscellaneous calculations at foot*]

[*p. 59*]

Edward Cow Bult at William Barrow 2d time
The 15th July 1725 Unpaid
July Debtor to Richard Crossfield & partners
for one Thousand sapp Latts
More Idem for A Thousand Hart
Latts
August 24th Then Rackned with [*sic*]
1725
paid James Danson for Knott, &
Becking garth & all other work
till This day above said
Knot Account   17s   0
Becking garth   16   0
A flannel webb 20 yards
at 2d per yard   3   4
More A harden webb
26 yards at 2d per yard   4   4
for his Maid Betty
& his own work pro 2 years   2li   0   0
Due to James Danson totall   4   0   8
more to James pro a Sall bill[99]   0   3   0

Remained Due Upon An Old
Account for Land rent   li   s   d
to Clement Taylor   3   13   0
More L[and] rent pro 1723   2   15   0
More pro 1724   2   10   0

Due to Clement Taylor   8   18   0

99   Sale bill.

The Account Book of Clement Taylor 53

James Danson <remains debtor> account				
Comes to in all		4	3	8
Clement Taylor account for				
Land rent Comes to		8	18	0
		4	14	4
April				
26 1725 Then rackned & [sic]				
and paid James Danson for all work				
Done till this abovesaid Day				
and James Danson remains				
Debtor to me		4	14 <5>	0
on other account		0	2	2

[p. 60]

September 6th 1725					
Received of Mr John Atkinson					
per The hand of William Robinson					
on the 2d February last the Summe		20li			
More of J[ohn] Atkinson per					
The hand of Thomas Denny		03	10		
2d May More of J[ohn] Atkinson per					
The Hand of Richard Robinson		05	0		
More of Mr John Atkinson		20	0		
More of Mr J[ohn] Atkinson		7	13		
More A Barrell of B[eef]		1	12		
More 4 Gallons of B[randy] at 5s		1	02		
6 Bottels of White [sic]		0	06		
More In wood For					
Chappel		13	12	1 1/2	
More In wood for My					
Selfe		14	0	6	
5 Gallon at 5s 6d					
which I've not Received		1	<5> 7	6	
		<88	3	1	2 >
More <in> Doubtfully		7	7	0	0
September					
6 More of J[ohn] Atkinson		4	10	0	0
	totall	100	0	0	
6th More of Mr John Atkinson					
The Sum of Twenty pounds					
10 More of Mr John Atkinson per					

54   *The Account Book of Clement Taylor*

the hand of Mr H[enry] Taylor			
twenty Gunies			
3 Looking Glasses	l	s	d
1 Charged		10	6
1 at		14	0
1 at	1	16	0
December per the hand of			
John Walker <about>	4li	1	8d
January 19 of Mr John Atkinson per the			
hand of Antony Wilson	li	s	
per William Atkinsons Order	38	12	
<To> of Mr J[ohn] Atkinson A Box			
which Looking [*sic*] came in	0	2	6
3½ foots of Lintren wood			
August of Mr Atkinson 15 stons of hare			
at 10d per ston & ½ ston over			
More of J Marshell 5½ paid			

[*p. 61*]

September about 28th Received of				
Mr John Atkinson in part		li	s	
for Green Slack wood		5	5	0
More of the Same a peice of				
Hollen Mesured, 20 yards				
at 1.8 per yard		1	13	4
More 20 yards of Linn at				
1s 2d per yard in all		1	3	4
October				
5th Received of Mr Atkinson		3	3	0
February 2d Received of Mr Atkinson per				
the hand of William Maychel		5	5	0
	total	104	6	7[100]
February 17th 1726 Then Ballanced				
accounts with Mr John Atkinson				
& he remains Debtor to me per				
a promisary Note		25 li	0s	0d

100   *recte* £104 3s 8d.

[*p. 62*]

September 1725
paid Myles Harrison pro 10 bushell

	l	s	d	
of Oats <per bushel> paid 4.6 per Bushell	1			
and 1s more for Peels care	2	6	0	
More Idem 11d pro a Sheep Skin	0	0	11	
21 paid William Collison pro Sheriffs Cloase[101]	4	8	0	
a quire of paper	0	0	11	
To Thomas Hodgshen for Sherifs Forniture for Saddle		18	0	
To The Same for a Silk [*sic*]		2	4	
21 To Adam Taylor for 2 Letter Louseing[102]	0	1	5	
21 To Edmund Wilson for 104li of Cheese at 1.3 pound & for Mustard & Candle Seaves in full	1	4	0	
September to Potichary in full	1	10	0	
25 to Hopps & other goods		3	0	
29th paid John Wilson Land Tax at 2s per li Finsthwaite being		8s	7d	1/2q
Blomer Ridding		0	4	1/2q

October Paid Isabel Beck for		li	s	d
3 Nursing My Wife[103] and other work		0	10	0
paid John Blendall pro Drying 30 bushel of Oats		0	2	6
To Myles Harrison for Sending the Sacks Over Sand[104] which the Oats Came in			6d	

101 Myles Sandys of Graythwaite was sheriff of Lancashire in 1725 and Clement Taylor was one of his under-sheriffs. He would have had some sort of official uniform and an ornamental saddle for his horse.
102 Loosing.
103 An unbaptised child was buried at Finsthwaite on 16 August 1725, so this is the payment for nursing Isobel Taylor in childbirth and afterwards. The cost of food at the funeral is entered at the foot of the page; see also n. 321.
104 Across Morecambe Bay.

		li	s	
September 21	paid William Colison for Sherifs Cloase & Stockings	4	8	
	To William Coward for meat this year		15	5d
	besids Childs Funerall		4s	6d

[*p. 63*]

October 10	to Crankes pro Ruffcasting at Chapel to Old Henry Crank 7 dayes to Young Henry Crank 11 dayes at 4d per day	[*blank*]		
18	paid Richard Fell in part towards Cranks table when ruffcast Chapel	0	6	0
21	Expences when I went Askrigg[105] to Look Roger Heighams Land	0	1	5
	Spent at Nuby Bridge with Mr Thompson &c about Crookland	0	0	6
	paid Edward Backhouse in part of his wage at Bouth Fair[106]	0	5	0
	more 2d February	0	10	0
	more paid William Satterthwait Tailer		0	4
	more a pair of Garters	0	0	2 ½
May 20	paid Edward Backhouse in full	2	9	6

9d per yard

James Taylor 2 Napkins		5s	0
William Parke one Napkin		0	10d
Jacob park one		0	10
James Danson one		0	10
peter Taylor a quarter of Cloth		0	6 ½
paid Jain Greenwood on James danson account	0	1	4
paid J[ames] Danson when tore hand	0	1	0

105 Askrigg, in Wensleydale, NR Yorks., so the expenses seem modest enough. The money given to the church by Queen Anne's Bounty in 1724 was being used to buy land, the rent of which would augment the vicar's stipend. The next entry probably refers to land under consideration at Crooklands, near Endmoor, Westm. A farm called Lindseys, in Garsdale, WR Yorks., was eventually bought: Martin, *op. cit.*, 134, and *cf* nn. 144, 166, 293.

106 There were still fairs at Bouth in the 19th century, but by 1848 they were barely viable. They were held on Whit Monday and the Saturday before or after 1 October: Cowper, *op. cit.*, 274.

October to buy Cloggs with	0	2	0
paid Thomas Hodgshon on J[ames] D[anson] account January 29 for a Ley	0	2	4
<when J[ames] Danson was not		about	
[illegible]	0	1	0>

[p. 64]

February 1th length of Little house	foot	half	
mesured by Thomas Scotson is	10	1/2	
Bredth over the riggin is	11	10 Inch	

Fire House is   4 roods   35 yards 3/4 quarters short
Little House is   0   13   3/4 over
The Mesure of Both
houses Comes to 5 roods   7 yards   1/4 quarter[107]

[p. 65]

October 28 1725 Then Rackned with John Walker for all work done by him till the Said Day & Remains Debtor to him Excepting Kendall Fair week	li 3	s 16	d 2
November Received of Edward Danson in part 14th for Land rent pro 1724	li 1	s 1	

Bark Mesoured to William Atkinson
for the Use of his son John
which was peeled in partingtree
per Peter Taylor 9 quarter & 5 Bushels

November Account of the Length
1725   & bredth of Our Fire House
Slate Mesoured per John Langram
Deepness of the House Side
is 8 yards & 7 Inches
Length of the House 12 yards & 1/2

December paid James Towers in part for a Cow by the hand of Robert Atkinson	2	11	0
30 paid James Rownson pro Beast Grass	0	18	0

---

107 The Westmorland rood of 6 1/2 yards is being used here. The 'Little House' was the privy.

January of Jane Woodburne in			
2 part for Land rent pro 1724	0	14	6
7 Account of Lime Stones Ledd			
at fair rigg 26 Carts			
at 2d per Cart	0	7	4[108]
paid Richard Harrison Upon the			
Account of Slate	3	10	
paid Francis Chamney for			
3 Heffers Grass	1	1	0
paid Clement Taylor which I had			
borrowed of him	2	2	0
paid Thomas Denny	2	16<0>	0
paid his wife in full about	0	2	0
paid Thomas Denny per C[hristopher] Marr	2	16	0

[p. 66]

	li	s	
paid James Towers in full for a Cow	1	2	
Bout Oats at Ulverston			
being 14 bushel	2	17	6
paid William Danson Borrowed Money	1	1	0
paid Miles Harrison Borrowed Money	12	10s	
paid James Taylor for ash boughs[109]	0	1	6
more for Mosshead fogg	0	1	6
more 3 days Getting Stons	0	1	6
paid him towards Greenslack			
wall	0	10	6
Due to peter for peeling 9 quarter			
& 5 bushel	1<.>	2<1>	6<0>
for 2 horses going Over			
Sands[110] for oats	0	1	6
for 2 days himself mend			
ing Little Nook	0	1	0
His Horses Leading peats		1	0
January 31			
of Robert Capland Interest for 50li			
for 1724 & 1725	4	4	
of John Stewartson Interest for 120li			
for 1725	5	0	

108   recte 4s 4d.
109   Ash was widely used as fodder in the district: see Denyer, op. cit., 81–3.
110   Over Morecambe Bay.

31 Gave again		2s	
paid Edmund Wilson for 3 pecks of Salt		9s	0
paid him More for Chese		11	6
paid Adam Taylor for A Letter & ale when we led flaggs		5	8
Received of Couzin Henry Taylor per the hand of Mr Ford	10	0	0
paid William Danson for work	1	14	8
Received of Him for plowing at The Same time		2s	

[p. 67]

Edward Danson rent 1725		
Antient	2	10
pullmiddows	0	12
Top of parrack	0	4
pincher Croft & Tarnhow	0	19
Haggs	3	0
Little House	0	4
	7	9

One Wooling Webb 20 Ell	2s	6
2 load of Coals Leading	2	6
2 Horses 2 dayes Leading peats paid for all work done	2	0

Rent for 1725	li	s	
of Edward Danson per William Danson	1	12	
more of Edward Danson in Cash	3	8	
gave him	0	2	6
paid 2 February 1725 to William Taylor per the hand of his Brother Clement being in full for his Wage for 1724	3	12	6
paid Myles Taylor for 20 bushell of Oats	4	3	6
paid to the Same pro 10 bushell of Barley	3	8	4
Jacob Park Debtor to me	5	0	0

60   *The Account Book of Clement Taylor*

2 February 1725 Received Interest of
Mr Shipphird per the hand of
John Taylor   2   13
January 21/22 My Wife Black why buld
at A[braham] Rawlinsons
26th My wife Brant Why Bult at
A[braham] Rawlinsons

February 3d paid Margaret Taylor Interest   li   s   d
in full for 1725   2   0   0

3 paid Mr Harrison for Agnes
& Clement Learning   0   8   0
7th paid Mr Ford per the hand
of Edward Kellet for wood
Had Out of Intack   1   14   6

[p. 68]

7th paid Mr Ford for wood
Had by me in the Intack per
the Hand of Mr Henry   li   s   d
Taylor   10   0   0
in full of all Accounts

July 2d Bought of William Soame
1725   a Comunian Cup weight 8 ounce 5 quarter 12 pennyweight
        at 6s per ounce & 11d[111]
with a box 4d   3   1s   0
Carriage & post Letters   0   1   0
                                                   ─────────────────
                                                   3   2   0
Received the Contents in full per
William Soame

February 10th paid Mr Harrison
Interest for 60li   2   8
at The Same time he alowed
me the 2li which he Owed me [in part *interlined*] for

---

111 The communion cup survives and is at present lodged in the cathedral treasury at Carlisle. Troy weight, by which silver was weighed, did not normally include quarters, but they occur here. Grains, of which twenty-four made one pennyweight, are evidently not meant. The cup was made in London and is signed G.S., the mark of Gabriel Sleath: C.J. Jackson, *English Goldsmiths and their Marks*, London, 1905, 164, 173.

Table & also Interest of 5li 5s which was in William Robinson hand paid him in Cash		3s	6d
	li	s	d
15th paid William Rownson pro Shopp Goods in full	1	2	6d
16 Received of William Braithwait interest pro 60li per A Horse	2	10	
paid the said Braithwait the remainder of the Horse price	1	10	

February William Boodburne [sic] Account for
21   work 1th Horse 2 dayes
1725   Wife Shering 3 days
The Same Working Hay 6 days

21 paid John Coward for Walker Brows	18	0	
paid William Park per the hand of James Taylor pro 7 days Work at ridding wall	0	3	6

[p. 69]

1725		s	d
Bought Kendall 2 brusshes		1	10
Bout Elizabeth a Bermods hatt		3	8
February Send Brother William per Oxford Carrier	36li	0	
25 pro Carriage of The Same	0	12	
paid Towers The Taylor for making Sherifs Close[112]	0	10	
Spent at Kendall	0	0	11
Bout a li of Black pick	0	0	3
Red Drying Ointment 1d$^{1/2}$ per ounce			
March paid Richard Taylor Linsty & Bedd 1 Lace	1	6	0
To the Same for a Great Coat	0	14	4
To the Same for a pound Hopps	0	2	8
To Thomas Hall for 1000 floorings		5	6
To The Same for plaister Nails	0	4	8
To Rowland Wainhouse for Elizabeth quilted Coat		3	0

112 See n. 101.

62   *The Account Book of Clement Taylor*

paid Bouth Potter for 40 bricks[113]		1	6
in presence of My Wife & James Leece Wife			
To thomas Hall pro Suger	0	0	8
1 March paid William Rawlinson for 46 Carts of Lime Stone at 2s per Cart	0	7	6
paid Richard Nuby pro 8 Side Swills & boddaming a riddle	0	2	3
4th Received of Edward Danson for 3 dayes Plowing for [Anno *interlined*] 1725	0	7	6
4th Chirrey[114] Why Bult at A[braham] Rawlinsons paid			
9 paid James Taylor for [6 days *interlined*] Working Ground work & 4 dayes at Cragg[115] before Low House doore in full pro Days Work	0	5	0
paid John Holme pro 60 foot of Bord for pew			
by Wheel wood		4	6
by 2 days table		0	8
by 2 bords		2	0
In money		2	6

[*p. 70*]

1725

March paid John Leece for Making	li	s	d
11 9 bushels of Malt at 10d per bushel	0	7	6
for Duty for the Same	1	1	0
11 paid Lewland [*sic*][116] Miller for Drying 14 bushels of Oats	0	1	2
Gave to the Same pro Bun Meal	0	0	4
11 Bout 10 bushels of oats at Ulverston which Cost	2	4	10
Bout at Ulverston two Skins	0	2	6
paid Jopson for a pound of Bacc'	1	0	
11 Spent 3 Garden Seeds 3½ [*sic*]		00	6½

113   Perhaps for a bread oven. Potters were often itinerant, selling their wares at local fairs, but this one may have lived at Bouth; *cf* n. 213.
114   Cherry.
115   At Tom Crag, where James Taylor perhaps stayed on after he sold the farm in 1713, although there is no note of any rent paid by him.
116   An error for Newland, near Ulverston.

Bought of William Rownson man			
Sope & Mohair	0	0	10
Left Silk unpaid for			6d
12 paid Leece & Satterthwaite			
Tailers in full	0	6	8
Gave 6d Beverage	0	0	6

April   Then Livered to Peter Taylor
1th   3 Wedders & had Livered to
1726   the said Peter Last year one Wedder
4 hoggs & 5 Ews from James
Danson from William Woodburn
Wife One Ewe & Lam & one Gimer
hogg in presence James Danson on 8th
April

June 20<4>th of Edward Danson in full			
for Land rent pro 1725	2	9	
paid him at the Same time			
for weaving a Harden web		3s	6d
20th Borrowed of James Taylor	7	15	

[*p. 71*]

April 1th 1726			
Then paid for a painted Apron for Jane			
Ormady [*sic*]	0	2s	0
paid to the same pro my mother a napkin		01	6
paid to the same pro Peter pro quarter of Cloth		00	6 ¹/₂
Gave to Workmen about Schoolhouse			
Chimney being my part Equall			
with Some Neighbours		01	3
paid Jonson Scotshman[117] pro Check	0	8	1 ¹/₂
5th paid John Wilson Land Tax & window	0	7	0
Received of Barbon pro a Ston of Hemp		3	6
he left behind 2d			
April			
29 Rownson pro 1 day filling Town End Barn	[*blank*]		

4th May James Towers Cow Bult at Hulliter[118] paid

---

117 *cf* n. 46.
118 The cow bought from James Towers. Hulleter is in the Rusland valley.

May
27 paid Jane Ormandy   1   5   0

July 11th Account of Bark Mesured <out>
at Town End   Quarter   Bushel
Thomas Braithwait   7   3
Thomas Taylor   2   0
Peter Taylor   39   2
James Walker   12   0

paid Thomas Wife pro peeling Bark
paid James Walker 10s 2s 2s 6s per J[ames] D[anson]
November paid James Walker 10[s] February 2d 3.6d
September 7th Weggey why Bult 2d time
at Hulliter <as below paid>
November Bark Taken Mesure of per E[dward] Danson
of our own peeling 3 quarter
August Weggey why Bult at Hulliter
29   paid
September 1th Then had Livered by Ralph
Leming out of Lending Knott
9 bunches of Sapp latts

September 7th Then had Livered per Richard
Fell 500 sapps in George Braithwait
wood Brought per J[ames] Danson
700 Sap Latts in top of parrack
<.>1003 of Sap 4 of hart went to Ulverston
Caried per Myles son & myself

[p. 72]

September 23 Great Black Cow
1726   paid Buld at Huliter
paid 28 fatt Cow buld at A[braham] Rawlinsons
October   Then paid Jane Ormady [sic]
5th   what remained of her wage pro 1725   0   18

5th Lent Jane Ormady [sic]   0   3   0
more paid for an apron for her   0   1   1
November Then Borrowed of M[yles] Harrison   5   5
remainder at whitsuntide   21   0
More at another time   6   0
January 10th Coals livered to
Backbarrow in all to this
day 12 load & 10 sacks   17   19   0
one sack more to the Hatter

January paid Thomas Hall in full		1	4	6
24 paid John Leece pro making & duty for 9 bushell of Malt		1	1	0
at the same time Gave him a Guley [sic] to buy barrley with		1	1	0
24th paid Dister pro dieing 21 yards of Brown & Coat Lining & Stockings & a pair of Blew Stockins in full		0	4	6
27th Received of Edward Danson pro Land rent for anno 1726				
In Cash		1	8	4
pro Weaving 28 yards of Harden		0	3	6
for Weaving 17 yards of Wolen		0	4	3
for Leading 13 quarter & 6 Bushel of Bark to penny Bridge		0	9	2
more paid to William Danson pro Shoes for 1726 & a duzen of Candles		1	14	9
Gave <him> Edward Danson 2s 4d				
	in all	5	0	0[119]
paid for leading 4 load of Coles		0	6	0
Received for 3 dayes plowing in 1726		0	6	0

February 15th retorned to Thomas Denny two Stainchers weyed 13li
Even Wey at 3d$^{1}/_{2}$ per pound

[p. 73]

January 31th 1726				
To William Park pro 47 days		1	3	6
To James Taylor pro 47 days		1	3	6
To Sam Wells 22 dayes		<0>	11	0
to the Same pro waling townend Barn at 4d 2q per yard		4	6	3
More to the Same at 2d per day advance pro Slating		0	3	4
to for [sic] Slate to James Taylor		0	4	6
to James Taylor pro working at Highwayes		0	1	0
To James Taylor [more *interlined*] towards Walker Brow wall		0	9	6

---

[119] *recte* £4.

66   *The Account Book of Clement Taylor*

February 1th paid William Cowhird on James danson Account	3	0	0
1th February paid Myles Taylor <which was T> on George Brathwait Account which was torned to John Cowhird & he ordered me to pay it in part of Walker Brow	0	11	3
More of John Cowhird for High wayes which was torned as payment in part of Walker brow rent	0	3	0
1th February paid Myles Taylor for 30 bushel of oats at 4s 8d per bushell & 21 bushell to Score	5	10[120]	
1th February paid William Rownson for Glass	3	0	0
& had paid him before for Glass & plumms for windows & other Goods	4	0	0
paid Margaret Taylor what I had Borrowed of her being	1	9	0
paid Brother Edward pro Bloomer Ridding	1	4	0
paid him at the same time A guney which I had Borrowed of him	1	1	0
Received of Brother Richard what I had Lent him being	1	11	6
February 1th Cherry why buled at Hulliter paid in full			

[*p. 74*]

February 1th 1726 John Walker Account	li	s	d
a dale board	0	1	0
Halfe a beife & 2 tounges	1	9	6
10 dales	0	10	0
one Gallon of Linseed oyl	0	4	0
for making 4 Sash Windows[121] & Cords 6d	1	4	6
a pewter dish	0	1	9

120 *recte* £7.
121 Sash windows first appeared in England about 1680, and might well have been novel features in Furness at this time.

John Walker 57 days at 8d per day	1	18	
John Holme 108 days	3	12	4
John Kellet 4 days	0	2	8
John Wilson 45 days	1	2	6
Solomon Armer 118 days	3	8	10
Received 2 February in Cash for the Kings arms Framed[122]	6 0	0 10	0 6
1th February paid Mr Harrison towards his Sallery	2	10	0
to the Same for Clement & Agnes Learning	0	8	0
1th Received More of John Walker for Interest pro a bill of Chappel Work		3	1
1th paid Jacob Park pro Work in part	1	10	
1th paid Mr Abraham Rawlinson for peat Moss on the height[123]	20	0	0
1th Received of Myles Harrison in part for Top of parreck wood	31	0	
paid Mabby Barrow pro being Middwife[124]	0	5	0
7 February My Wife why Buld at Hulliter			
11 February paid John Coward pro leading 7 quarter 1/2 of Bark at 8d	0	5	0
more in full [for *interlined*] Walker brow	0	3	9

[*p. 75*]

February 14th 1726 paid John Wilkinson pro a fender	0l	1s	6d
15 paid Mr Harrison more in part for Interest of his Sallery	11	10s	0
February 16th paid Peter Taylor for peeling 39 quarter 2 bushel at 2s 2d per Bushel[125]	li 4	s 5	0

122 For the church, and evidently on a painted panel; for royal arms in churches, *see* G.W.O. Addleshaw and F. Etchells, *The Architectural Setting of Anglican Worship*, London, 1948, 101–2.
123 On 25 November 1726 Abraham Rawlinson of Rusland Hall sold a turbary on Rusland Heights to Clement Taylor and Myles Harrison, twelve acres for £36: LRO, DDPd 35/4. The £20 was evidently Clement Taylor's share of the purchase price.
124 Mary, daughter of Clement Taylor, was baptised at Finsthwaite on 11 February 1727. On p. 76 Isobel Beck was paid for nursing Isobel, as she had done at the birth of the child who died in 1725; *cf* n. 103.
125 *recte* 2s 2d per quarter.

68   *The Account Book of Clement Taylor*

To The Same pro leading 4 load 2 sack of Coals – 1d ½ per Sack	0	6	3
To The Same pro leading 11 quarter 2 bushel at 8d per quarter	0	7	6
To the Same pro Coaling 12 load 11 sack at 4s per load	2	11	8
to The Same pro Cutting 10 load & 8 Sacks of Coalwood at 3s per load	1	12	0
To The Same pro Interest of 10li pro 1725 & 1726	0	16	0
More as appears before in This book in January 31 1725[126]	1	6	0
More to the Same for a wedder	0	3	6

	li	s	d
February 16 1726 Received of Peter Taylor in full for Land rent for 1725 & 1726 the Sume of	11	5	0
paid peter in full for his work	0	2	6
February 20th of William Woodburn per the hand of Richard Crossfield	0	8	0
More of William Woodburn pro leading 5 quarter & 5 bushels at 8d per quarter	<3>0	3	8
More of the Same for 3 days Shearing in 1726	0	1	0
More of Jenet Woodburne in Cash	0	14	6
paid James Walker for one day at Highwayes on J[ohn] Coward account	0	1	0
March paid John Wilson <Land> Window Tax of James Walker Account	0	2	0

[*p. 76*]

February 21th 1726 paid John Preston for half a bushell of wheat per the hand of Miles Harrison maid	0	7	6

March 2d Then Borrowed of Mary Gurnel 14 bushell & a half of Lime in Stones out of Kill

---

126 On p. 66, where £1 6s is noted as being 'Due to peter' for several items. The loan is on p. 51.

4 Gave My Mother at Edward Christening[127]	0	2	6
paid Isabel Beck for Nurshing my Wife for 4 Weeks of Mary	0	4	0
Myles Harrison Gave her	0	4	0
My Mother & Good Mother Sarah[128] gave her Each <2>1s	0	2	0

March the 8th Mesoured Abraham
Moss dike[129]
Next to Greenhows Side is   21 rood
More ajoining to the Same   3
Low End   10
More at Low End which Abraham
is to pay for   10
the price is 8d per Rood
11th paid John Walker for diking 34
Roods of the Above Said Dike at

8d per Rood	1	2	8
11 paid John Taylor for driveing plow 3 days at 4d per day	0	1	0
10th Borrowed of Brother Edward	5	5	0
16th paid Thomas Millerson pro all Letters Carraige	0	7	0
part of the above said on E[dward] T[aylor] account	0	1	8
April 10 paid John Leece pro making 5 bushels of Malt	0	4	2
& 1.1.6 behind for barley	1	1	6
& Duty 1.1.0 paid him before barley was 7s per Bushel			
2 Napkins	0	3	4
Aprill Received of Mr Shippird Interest pro 60li.0 per the hand of John Taylor for Anno 1726	21li	13	0

---

127 'Edward christening' is that of Clement's niece Jane, daughter of his brother Edward, baptised 4 March 1727.
128 Goodmother normally means mother-in-law or stepmother, but neither is applicable here. Sarah is probably Sarah Taylor, widow of Christopher Taylor of Jolliver Tree (d. 1712), and James Backhouse's mother-in-law; see 224, 242. She was perhaps Clement Taylor's godmother.
129 *cf* n. 123.

[p. 77]

April 1727
Received Interest of William Braithwait pro 60li
for Anno 1726   2 li   10 s   0   0

<Clement Taile Coat of Draget>
Clement Suite of Draget Cost   1   5   6
My Frock Cost   1   0   2
20 paid J[ames] Leece in full   <10>00   10   1
29th paid Thomas Jonson pro damaige
done to two Stone wombles &
a plugg Lost per C T in firing   0   1   0
paid Jonson toward Diking   11   8
29 paid Thomas Jonson towards diking
East side of Abraham Moss   0   10   0
July 30th to Jonson wife toward Diking   0   05   0

May 8 Great Black cow went to Frith
1727   on the said 8 day yeat at tarn was
        hung[130]
15th   paid Edward Walker for Woaking[131]
28 yards of Blanketing at 1d per yard   2   4
Then Exchainged with John Walker
78 foot [of *interlined*] Bords which I had of Edward parke
for 75 foot of Hamborge Bords [& I am *interlined*] to give
him a penny a foot in Exchainge & 3d over
Gratis which is in all   6s <0> 3d[132]
20 Mr Taylor Miller for drying
    20 bushels of oats at 1d per bushell   0   1   8
22 paid Agnes Ashburner pro a Trunk   0   1   0
Entrence 1s 1d to Mr Beirdwell
pro Agnes Going to dansing school
at Cartmel & 1s per weeke   0   1   6

130 In 1727 Clement Taylor was involved in a dispute about rights of way for cattle going to graze on Windhaws and Yewbarrow, through a pasture called the Brows which belonged to Richard Robinson and George Taylor of Elinghearth. In May the testimony of two elderly residents, Margaret Sawrey and Jane (Jennet) Taylor [see 237, 240] was sought, and both declared that within their memories cattle had always used the right of way, being driven up in the mornings and finding their own way back in the evenings. Richard Robinson had, about nine years before, 'made an Offer of Hanging a Gate at the Far-end of the said piece of Pasture, but the Gate being within a little Time pulled down, they gave no farther Disturbance': LRO, DDPd 26/225–6. In July an award was made by William Benson of Mansriggs and Thomas Rigge of Nibthwaite, whereby, in exchange for the route up the Brows, a new way was to be provided between the Sinderhill Beck and a new wall near Bortree Tarn. One of the landmarks in this wall was a 'gate called tarn haw yeat belonging to . . . Clement Taylor': *ibid* . 26/227.
131 Walking.
132 The Hamburg boards are imported deals; the sum is *recte* 6s 6d.

paid On Top of Parrack account				
To Christopher Dixon	0	2	6	
Spent at wood Trailing	0	1	0	
To Margaret Burnes per D[ixon] In Earnest		1	0	
pro housing & drissing[133] Bark				
and she is to have 1s pro housing				
7d per quarter pro drissing & Chopping		s	d	
October 1727 paid Margaret Bornes pro drissing				
5 quarter & 6 Bushel at 7d per quarter	<0> 0	<3> 2	10½	<2>
To The Same for Leading it	0	3s	2d	2q

[p. 78]

June 6th 1727 Received of Edward Danson				
More in part of Land rent for 1726				
per by Weaving 28th [sic] yards of Blanketing	li	s	d	
at 1d½ per yard	0	3	6	0
More of the Same by weaving				
17 yards of twill Sack<ing> web at				
2d per yard	0	2	10	0
More of the Same in Cash				
in full for Land rent for				
1726 – gave him 8d	1	16	8	0
		<Thomas Denny>		
6th Bout a Gallon & a half of B– –y [sic] at	li	s	d	
6s per Gallon of Thomas Denny	0	9	0	

paid Thomas Denny for the Abovesaid B[randy]
1th by 6s which remained behind
of Interest from Christopher Marr
due at Candlemas Last the remainder
being paid per Thomas Denny by smith work
per Marr's Order More 2s 6d pro Ale
Licence paid him 6d in full for the
said B– –y [sic] per C T

paid Edward Burnes for half quarter Veal			
Brough [sic] by George Cowhird	0	0	10

Black cow came from Frith
Wednesday 21th June

---

133 Dressing.

72 *The Account Book of Clement Taylor*

June [Wedensday *interlined*] 28 Cammey Why Bult with
Russland Hall Bull & Studd of her
self[134]

July 1th James Towers Cow bult
at Russland <...> Hall
paid July tuesday 18 Cammey Why
bult 2d time at Russland Hall paid

Fryday July 21th James Towers Cow
paid bult at Russland Hall paid 2d time

July Fryday 28 Bready Why bult
at Rusland Hall paid
Tuesday August 1th Great [Black *interlined*] Cow bult
at Rusland Hall Stud of her self

[*p. 79*]

November 24th 1732 Christopher Taylor
Cow Why Bult at Edward Riggs

[*p. 80*]

June 1727			
paid Edward Barwick in part towards			
peeling Bark in Brianway			
parrack & he was to have			
2s 6d per quarter	1	1	0
August 4th paid Edward Barwick more			
<at> towards buying meat at			
his Childs Christenig [*sic*][135]	0	5	0
paid Edward Barwick	1	1	
paid The Same	0	5	
paid the Same	0	12	
paid the Same per Margaret Taylor	0	10	
20th paid William Rawlinson pro 40 Carts			
of Lime Stone at 2d per Cart	0	6	8

134 'Stud [stood] of herself' [perhaps *recte* 'stood off'] is an expression which is now unfamiliar, but it evidently meant that the bulling was unsuccessful as the cow went to the bull again three weeks later.
135 Samuel, son of Edward and Margaret Barwick, was baptised on 5 August 1727.

20 paid Thomas Hall pro a daffey bottel
which James Danson brought
about 3 years before & When I paid
him for it Could not find it in
his book paid before his Wife   0   <2> 1s   2d
bout 2 more at the same time
which I paid for   2   4

20 paid paid [*sic*] Dansing Master 4 weeks
pro Agnes in full   0   4

20 Gave Mr Brockbank maidens
head maid 1s Under maid 6d
when Agnes & Elizabeth was there
a Munth
29 paid George Taylor pro peice of   li   s   d
Girthwood in full of all   0   2   0

[*p. 81*]

September 1727
paid To Thomas Wife pro peeling   2 quarter 2 bushel
William Cowhird   16   4
paid to Margaret Burnes   05   6
      2s 6d per quarter
paid Edward Barwick   17   6
                                 ─────────────────
                                  42   2

October Account of Coles livered out of
1727   parrack 10 load & 8 Sacks at 1li 10s

October Received Interest from
2d 1727 Richard Rigg per the hand
of Strickland Tanner
for 80li pro anno 1726   3   6   0
October 31th paid Edward Barwick
for Cutting 3 load & 8 Sacks at
2s 6d per load   0   9   6
November Received [of] Miles Harrison
more towards Top of parrack   li   s   d
wood   4   4   0
25th Measoured from James
Taylor The wall from the Cragg
below Gree [*sic*] Slack yeat to topp of

walker Brow being 45 roods
at 10d per rood for waling
& C Taylor Gott what Stones
wanted besides

January 23 Received of Anthony Wilson 1727 for 14 load & 9 Sacks of Coals Livered at Backbarrow out of Townend parrack & Thomas Hagg Coppey at 30s per load	22	2	6
Received of Edward Danson for 2 Days plowing in 1727	0	5	0

[p. 82]

	li	s	d
January 31 1727 paid James Taylor for 32 days Table He & partners waled Top of parrack wall	0	10	8
more of My own account to J[ames] Taylor for 5 days	0	2	6
paid James Taylor for Latter End of Walker Brow wall	0	17	6
paid Jacob Park which remained behind Last year	1	2	0
To the Same more this year he & his man Each 13 days at Tarnhaw[136]	0	10	10
Received towards rent for 1727 by William Danson for Shoues	1	9	8
4 load of Coals out of Town End parrack at 1d $\frac{1}{2}$ per Sack	0	6	0
more for weaving 8 yards of Harden for a Caff bed of Edward Danson alowed on James Danson account	0	0	10

136 *cf* n. 130. Clement Taylor was responsible for part of the cost of the new wall.

Towards Christopher Table	2	10	0
more of Edward Danson in Cash	0	18	6
January 31 Received the abovesaid Debtor to James Walker for Cutting 2 load & 3 Sack & 1 load 10 Sacks	5	5	0

February 1727

5 paid Edward Taylor for a Tup twinter		6s	6d
paid more pro bloomer Ridding for anno 1727	1	5	0
paid more for Interest of 5li 5s for 1727	0	4	0
paid more Borrowed money	0	10	6
paid more on account of Cheese	0	1	0
Received 1s for Letters paid for him	0	1	0
paid him in full Except 5.5s 0			

[p. 83]

February 10 1727

paid Mr Harrison Interest for 103li 13s at 4li per cent for 1727 on Chapel Account	li 4	s 3	d 0
More to the Same which I had Left behind in 25 or 26 on account of Interest	0	6	0
paid Mr Harrison <Int> for Clement Learning for 1727	0	4	0
paid the Same more for Isabel		2	0
16 paid John Leece for making 9 bushel	1	s	d
& Duty for the Same	1	1	0
paid Dansing Master for Enterance & Learning for Clement & Agnes	0	6	6
17th Bought at John Coward Sale 18 half Inch oke boards at 7d¹/₂	1	s	d
per board	0	11	3
February paid Thomas Holme pro making 27<6> yards of Serge at 1s 6d per yard he Abating 6d & Casting one yard in	1	18	6
19th Cherry Cow Bult at Russland Hall			

76   *The Account Book of Clement Taylor*

Borred [sic] of Robert Taylor 2d February	100li		
Borrowed of Thomas Danson 2d February 1727	030li		
February Then Lent Mr Henry Taylor			
paid as We Came from Chappel	2	2	0
March 5th Received of John Walker per the			
hands of Thomas Hall in part for			
Interest 10li	10l	0	0
8th Received of Mr H[enry] Taylor			
the 2li 2s which I Lent in February	2l	2s	
March paid Leece Taylor for work	0	9	6
Gave him more 6d Beveraige			

[*p. 84*]

March 20th 1727	li		
Borrowed of Thomas Strickland	30	0	
paid George Robinson on Chapel			
account per Miles Harrison Order	29	14	
about			
26 Borrowed more of Thomas Strickland	07	0	
January paid Thomas Strickland the abovesaid			
30 sumes & Interest towards			
1728 the same 17s – which is in all	37	17	
April 3 1728 Then Let to farm			
To Thomas Jonson 3 parchels[137]			
as below	l	s	d
1th Jennet Hagg	0	15	0
Iland, and Little Cloase	0	18	0
per annum for one year per C T			
April Then Let to farm The			
Law Half acer in Broad			
Middow at 6s per annum	0	6	0
& also The Top of parrack			
at 12s per annum for 2 years	0	12	
Then Let to farm the far hagg			
& Long Myre for one year	1	0	0

137   Parcels.

Then Let to farm The [Town End *interlined*] House
orchard & Garding & aples in
The Hagg & also in Becking Garth
Except Some in Becking Garth
& town End midow

In March 1727 I hired Jane
Ormady [*sic*] at Stoney Cragg
for 2li 5s & a Shilling In Earnest
& my Wife to Mend her a Shilling
and wool for Stockings

[*p. 85*]

	li	s	d
April 5th 1728 paid Thomas Denny for all Smith work Done in anno 1727 being	1	18	3d
at the Same time he paid me Interest for 60li for Anno 1727	2	10	0
and for Iron Stanchers returned wey'd 13li to Thomas Denny	0	3	0
at the Same time I paid him for 3 bottels of Brandy	0	4	6
June 5th Received of Edward Danson 1728 in full for Land rent for 1727	2	0	0

Tuesday July 23 Weggey why
Bult at Russland Hall & Studd of her
self unpaid

	li	s	d
January the 30th 1728 Then Receivd of Edward Danson towards Land rent for that year by his Son William	1	12	6
& more his Son James	2	00	0
of Edward Danson by peeling bark &c 14 quarter & 1 bushell at 2s 2d per quarter	1	10	5
more of Edward Danson by Cutting 3 load & 5 Sacks of Coal wood at 2s 6d per load	0	8	6 <2>0
of The Same more by Glassing of a window	0	1	8
	5	13	1

more by weaving a flanel
webb being 28 yards at 2d 2q
per yard [blank]
plowing paid in 1728 li s d
more of Edward Danson in Silver 0 7 0
which is in all 6li
& paid Edward Danson for all woork done
till the above said Day 1 s d
February 24th paid Edward Taylor for Bloomer R[idding]
                1 5 0
& more to him for Interest of 5li 5   4s

[*p. 86*]

February 26 1728 Then paid William Rownson
for 4 bottels of Daffey 6li of Candles
Thred Silk & metridate [& *interlined*] Treakle &c
about 9s 6d in full all accounts
at my own house

February 27th Then paid James Backhouse
for the 34 load of Coales money which I
Received at Backbarrow of H[enry] Taylors
account & his per for me [*sic*] Disborsments
on James Backhouse account
& at the same time & also ballonced
all other accounts & he remained Debtor
to me 11s 3d which he paid me at the time

paid Edward Walker for teising[138] 28 yards
of Flannel at 1d per yard   2s 4d
Then paid Richard Nuby for <6> 4 side
swills at 3d apeice   1s 0d

February 26 Then paid Peter Taylor
2s 9d of James Walker account
& of my own account   10li 8s
which is in full of all accounts
per me C T

March 14th Then paid James Goad
for 12 dale at 1s 2d apeice
& for 2 Gallons of Brandy at 3s

---

138 Teasing; this will be the twenty-eight yards of flannel woven by Edward Danson at p. 85.

per Gallon & 2 bottles of white wine at 1s per bottel	1li	2s	0d	
1728 paid William Taylor Land Tax at 3s per li		s	d	q
for my own Estate		12	11	1
Bloomer Ridding		0	6	3
Window Tax		6	0	0
	0	19	6	0

[*one page torn out*]

[*p. 87*]

March 31th 1729
Then Hired Roger Jackson the 2d   li   s   d
year for anno 1729 for   4   15   0
The Same Day Hired Jane
Ormady [*sic*] for anno 1729
for   2   6   0
and her Dame to Mend her 1s &
a pound of wool

April 8 Then paid Henry Fisher
for 12 Chaires at 2s apeice &
& 9dey [*sic*] Stool over [at them *interlined*] paid him more for
for 2 Stool 1s 6d in all   1l   5s   6d
April 20th 1729 My Wife Cow bult
at Robert Taylors

June & July paid Roger Jackson
In Cash towards his wage for 1728
In Money   1   11
A Shift Cloth   0   02   6
more in Cash   0   19   6
Rest in my hand paid   2   2   0

June 15th 1729 Received of Edward Danson
Last May Day rent   2li 5s
in full for Land to the [above *interlined*] said Day
8 paid Jane Ormady [*sic*] [what remained of *interlined*] her wage
which [*sic*] for 1728 in full   1   5   0

July 16th 1729 Received of John Scales
Interest <of Jo> for a bond of 30li
for anno 1727 1728 per me
Clement Taylor on my Brother
William Account being all Interest
till Candlemas Last

[p. 88]

1729

Thomas Wife Debtor to me for wool	0	1	3
more 1/2 a peck of Barley	0	1	3
In Money about 15th May to buy oats with	0	9	0
16 more Idem a hope of Barley	0	<7>0	7 1/2
July 24 To Thomas wife	0	2	0
August 4th paid Margaret Braithwait	12	00	0
11th paid Thomas Wife	01	0	0
October 10th To Margaret Braithwait		8	6
November 3d To Margaret Braithwait in full for peeling Bark		4	9
Thomas Braithwaite Bark is 12 quarter 5 Bushel paid the same at 2s 3d per Bushel[139]	1li	8s <3>	4 1/2

	s	d
May 27 Richard Fell Debtor for a peck of barley	2	6
Richard Fell more in Cash	2	6
Richard Fell more 10th June	2	6
24th Richard Fell more	4	0
July 8 more	1	0
Ditto half a peck of Barley	1	3
August 4th more Ditto	2	0

Margaret Braithwait Debtor 3d & 2d
November [Martinmas *interlined*] 1729 paid Margaret Braithwait

                                                                                  01   5s   0

	quarter	Bushel
Edward Danson peeled Barke in the Middlemost Hagg	15	0
J [*sic*] Little Close	11	4
	26	4
November 20th Measured Bark 1729 from Richard Fell Wife out of Little Close being	quarter 8	Bushel 5

139 *recte* per quarter.

[p. 89]

August 1th 1729 paid William Rownson for 2li of hopps & a quarter Tobacco in full of all Accounts per C.T.			2s	0

September 5th Weggey Bult at Robert Scales paid
November 20 James Towers Why paid bult at Robert Scales, Stud of herself

November 24 Mesured Bark from Jane Woodburn at Charley

	quarter	Bushel
Cragg being	16	4
More at Town End	5	1

December 30th Account of Coals Livered
1729   out of East Side of Little Cloase

	loads	Sacks
Imprimis William Woodburn	4	3
Richard Fell	3	8
Edward Danson	2	11
Thomas Braithwait	2	8
Edward Danson in th'Hagg	2	4
in all	15	10

	li	s	
January 27 paid To Mr Bury of Jane Ormadys [sic] account	0	7	0
June 2d J[ane] Ormady [sic] a Smock	0	2	3
More Siserser [sic]140	0	0	5
More 1.1s at Whitsuntide	1	1	0
paid Roger Jackson per William R[ownson] for a Bible	0	6	0
per J[ames] Dixon141	0	2	18 [sic]

More 1s about Christmas
2li 2s which I was Debtor to R[oger] all which J[ames] D[ixon] had from me C T being 5li on Roger Account

---

140 Scissors.
141 This account with Roger Jackson appears again on p. 96, where it is clear that the 2s 18d is *recte* £2 18s.

[p. 90]

	li	s	d
January 1th 1729 Then paid Sarah Fell for peeling 18 quarter & 5 Bushel at 2s 3d paid the Same more for Cutting 3 load & 8 Sacks at 2s 6d per load in all	3	2	2
paid of the abovesaid pro Land Ren [*sic*] for 2 years Last past	2li	0	0
More paid to her Late Husband[142]	0	15	9
More in full to her Self by the Hand of J[ames] Dixon	0	6	5 1/2
in part of the 6.5.		3s	6d

	li	s	d
Januery [*sic*] Then paid Jane 13th 1729 Woodburn for all Work Done per her & her Husband & upon ballonsing accounts She remains [Debtor at *interlined*] May Day Next	0	13	6

	li	s	d
Januery [*sic*] 31th 1729 Received of Edward Danson Land Rent for Anno 1729 by peeling 26 quarter of Bark & 4 Barrels at 2s 3d per quarter	2	19	6
pro leading Bark	0	2	6
pro Cutting 5 load & 3 Sacks of Coal wood at 2s 6d per load	0	13	0
pro Coals Leading	0	1	0
pro his son William Book for Shoes[143]	1	5	0
more of him per Cash	1	4	0
total	6	5	0

[p. 91]

		s	
January 31 Then paid Jacob Park for all work done in anno 1729 per Crook	0	5	
in Cash	0	14	
	0	19	0

142 Richard Fell [see 230] was buried on 21 October 1729.
143 i.e. his shop book, the amount Clement Taylor owed for shoes.

	li	s	d
February Then accounted with Miles			
1729 Harrison			
13 quarter Tarr	0	3	3
Wood in Lowther Busk	1	16	0
1000 Sap Latts	0	10	0
paid to Christopher Coulton	1	2	0
Borrowed of Miles of Bounty[144]	2	18	0
Carriage of Chest	0	3	3
An old Ballance of Account	0	2	9
60 Herrin	0	1	0
Due to Miles	6	16	3
Due to C.T.	7	5	0
Ballance Due to C.T.	0	8	9
Due to Miles for 60 Herrin	0	1	0
Due [for *interlined*] black wool to C T	0	3	0
Lent Miles Harrison	1	0	0

16   Received Interest of Mr Shippard
per the hand of John Taylor the
Sum of 3li 14s being [Due *interlined*] for a bond
of 60li for the year 1729
Then paid J[ames] Backhouse Rent for
Bloomer Riddings   1   4   0
at the same time he paid for top of
parrack 4[s] for my share for
anno 1729
2 February   Received Intrest of Christopher Marr
for 60li for 1728 & 29 per Elizabeth Denny

16th Received from Mr Fetcher [*sic*]			
pro 60 [half to Mr Machell Account *interlined*] Dale at 1.2 per peice			
	3	10	
pro 30 more Ditto	1	15	
pro 8 more Ditto	0	9	4
In Cash	11	6	7
pro Tarr for Mr Maychel	4	0	0
more Unjustly Charged on 60 dales		4	7 1/2

---

144   In 1730 Queen Anne's Bounty made a second grant of £200 to the church which was used to buy a farm called Dyke Hall, in Dent, WR Yorks.: Martin, *op cit.*, 134. The parish raised a similar sum. Myles Harrison was evidently looking after the money; *cf.* nn. 105, 166, 293.

84   *The Account Book of Clement Taylor*

[*p. 92*]

		li	s	
February 10 1729 Then paid peter Taylor for Coaling 15 load & 10 Sacks at 4s per load in Little Cloase		3	3	
February 1729 latter half year	paid Robert Taylor Minister of Coulton's Sallary in the presence of George Bank in Miles Harrisons House at his daughters funeral[145]	0li	2s	2d

Then acounted with Mr Harrison
& I paid him 11s Shillings [*sic*] in full of
all accounts Except 10li Given per
Margaret Taylor[146] which he is to have
the Intrest of yearly while he
Enioye finsthwait Chappel C T

28 Jacob park 2 days at Little Cloase	0	1	0
John 4 days George 4 days	0	3	0

paid Thomas Danson in part of 30li Ditto more which I Borrowed at Michaelmas 10li Remains 20li	10li	0	
March 2d	Received Intrest for a bond of 60li for the anno 1729 of of [*sic*] William Braithwait	li 2	s 10
paid Henry Croasdal for 3 Caggs[147] & Nothing Else due to him	2s	6	

11th March 1729
Then Received Intrest of Mr H[enry] Taylor
for a bond of 32li for anno
1727. 28. & 1729   4   0   0

---

145   Jennet, daughter of Myles Harrison, was buried on 18 February 1730. Finsthwaite continued to contribute to the salary of the vicar of Colton even after it had its own church; but *cf* n. 154.
146   In 1727 Margaret Taylor of Finsthwaite [see 241] left £10, the interest of which was to go to the schoolmaster there. There is a copy of her will in the churchwardens' account book: CRO, WPR 101/W1. In 1765 the £10 was put towards the sum of £200 needed to obtain a third grant from Queen Anne's Bounty: *ibid*.
147   Kegs.

March 12th 1729 Then paid William
Rownson for all Shop goods
had of him till this time   ss
being 17s   17

[p. 93]

Debtor to Miles Harrison for a quarter of Tarr
More ½ quarter Tarr Half Bushell of B[arley] 3s
more a quarter of Tarr

March 1730 Jacob 1 day & George 1 day at
Danson Barn more Jacob John & george Each a
Day a [sic] Lime kill
                                                                        s   d
Then paid William Holme   5   2
& Gave him 10d Beverige   0   10
being in full

April the 8 1730 Account of what
Money is Due for buring in
finsthwait Chappel Since the
Consicration after Deductions
for Chappel ses which Remainder is   1li   15s   4d
R[obert] Taylor being Chapellwarden
M[yles] Harrison George Taylor Mr
Harrison J[ames] Backhouse Richard
Robinson & Clement Taylor
being present at the Settlement
of the Above said Accounts & also
agreed that Every Fyre House
that keeps a Smook is to Serve
Chapel warden at their own
Cost Except bread & wine
which is to be take [sic] out of the
Offering money for that time[148]

May 15th 1730 My Wife Cow
Buld at T[homas] Barrow's Stud of her
Self paid 6d per R[oger] J[ackson]
1730

148 'Smook' is smoke, as pronounced, and keeping one seems to mean the presence of a substantial fireplace. The churchwardens were appointed from the principal houses in the parish in rotation, starting in 1726 with Landing [Henry Taylor's house at Lakeside], working north to Stott Park, and then south through Finsthwaite to the inn at Newby Bridge. The first sequence ended in 1753, a total of twenty houses, though at least one other was added as time went on. There is a list to 1851 in the churchwardens' account book: CRO, WPR 101/W1. The cost of bread and wine was met from the offerings given at the four yearly Communion services, at Easter, Whitsuntide, Michaelmas, and Christmas.

86   *The Account Book of Clement Taylor*

May 1730 Then Hired Roger Jackson for this year for	5li	0	
and also Jane Ormady's [sic] wage is for 1730 & 31	2	0	

1730
Minde

[*p. 94*]

May 1730 Received of Thomas Danson for plowing for anno 1729 for 3 days plowing		7	6
May 30th Jacob John & George Each one [day at *interlined*] Lime Kill it being wet <Kendall> 30th paid John Fell for 10 bushell of Coals at 10s 6d per quarter per Roger Jackson & in presence of L[awrence] Harrison		13s	0d
May 1730 <G> [Gave *interlined*] Thomas Danson bill for	22li	10s	
More 4th of June on the back of the said bill which I Borrowed of him that day	5li	5s	
5th Jacob & John Each one day at Lime Kill Lying [sic]¹⁴⁹ paid in full		7s	
paid Jane Ormady [sic] pro a Smock	2	3	
a pair of Sisers	0	0	5
paid Mr Bury	0	7	0
at Whitsuntide	1	1	0
a bottel of Daffey	0	1	2
Mid Summer day a bottl Daffey		1	2
Blooding – remember To Mr Bury in July when her sister was not well	0	2 5	2 0
half a yard of Camrick¹⁵⁰		1	8
	1	s	
<July paid Roger Jackson	0	10>	
October 24 A bottel Daffey	0	1	2
January 1 yard ½ yard of Half Thick	0	1	9

149 Lining.
150 Cambric.

Thred 1d		0	1
February 1th an apron Dying		0	2
March 2d paid Thomas Denny Wif		0	8
April 3d 2 yards & 1/2 of Edgin		2	2
at Easter		0	2
Blooding		0	3
May To Mr Burry pro wage part		5	0
June 6th pro Edging		0	6

[*at side*] to Mr Milner   4s   6d

[*p. 95*]

July the 7th 1730 my Wife Cow bult
at Thomas Barrows Stud of her Self paid
Second time Bulling
16th Brand Cow whye Bult at
Thomas Barrow's Stud of her Self paid 1s

Father's Advice to his Children
per William Lancaster Imprimatur
1694[151]

August the 5th Christopher Taylor Cow bult at
Robert Scales paid 6d

16th Borrowed of Mr Harrison	3	3	0
paid him for 2 ounces of aloes			4d
& more for 30 pills of Mr Dawney's	0	1s	0

19th Thomas Fisher 2 yards of Gold Twist
6d per Margaret Braithwait
21th Debtor to Christopher Harrison for
6 stone of plaster Hare   0   5s   0

Mr Maychel Bottle holds
1 Gallon 1 pint & about a Jack
August paid Mr Bury pro 10 dram of Bark   2   6
September 23d Borrowed more of Mr Harrison   2li   2ss
23 7 ounces of Oyl of Turpentine
the daffey bottel holds [*sic*]
from William Rownson per Christopher T[aylor]

---

151 I have been unable to trace this work. There is, however, an anonymous *A Father's Advice to his Son*, printed by the heirs of A. Anderson in Edinburgh in 1693.

September 25th 1730 Great Cow Why
bult at Thomas Barrow's [broak bulling *interlined*] Stud of herself
paid 1s

October 6 Borrowed of Brother Edward   4 li

[*miscellaneous calculations at foot*]

[*p. 96*]

1730
paid Roger Jackson towards
his wage for the year 1729
a bible to William Rownson   0   6   0
to James Dixon   2   18   0
More when he lent J T[152]   0   10   0
at Christmas 1s if not mistaken   1   0
a Sute of Close   1   16   0
paid Jane Ormady [*sic*] in the above said
year
1th to Mr Bury   0   7   0
a Smock Cloth for her   0   2   3
a pair of Sissers   0   0   5
at Whitsuntide   1   1   0
More to Mr Burry   0   2   2
a yard of Lin Cloth for
her Brother   0   1   0
3 bottels of Daffy   0   3   6
when her sister was
not well in October   0   5   0
mind this is put down before
in this book[153]

October plaister Nails Had   <0>
of John Coward   1360
November 2d of Thomas Hodson   3000

Great Cow why buld at Thomas B[arrow] 2d time
2d of November Stud of her self

November 1730
had plaister Nales of Thomas Hodson
7000d

152 *cf* n. 141; 'J T' is probably an error for J D[ixon].
153 On p. 94.

more of Thomas Hodson a pair of Card [sic]
& 1000 plaister Nailes

November 21th Great Cow Why
bult at Thomas Barrows the
3d time

[p. 97]

September 30 1729 Received of my Neighbours H.T. R.R. J.B. M.H. G.T. R.T. G.T.[154] Christopher Taylor & Clement T[aylor]	2	0	0
Disbursed of the Same as below Spent at Lancaster with Mr Taylor & 3 of my Neighbours	0	0	10
To Lawyer Gibson's Clark for Coping our Case	0	1	0
Spent at Nuby Bridge when we Consulted [about *interlined*] the Chapel Difference [at first *interlined*]	0	0	10
at Lancaster when drew The Cause R[ichard] R[obinson] M[yles] H[arrison] C.T. was There	0	0	5
To Lawyer Gibson	1	1	0
January 23 to Lawyer Gibson per the hands of J[ames] Backhouse	0	10	6
October 19th 1730 To Isabel Dixon	0	6	4
at The Same Time Spent at Ulverston when Com[missary] was There	0	1	3
November 1730 Spent at Nuby [bridge *interlined*] at the 1th meeting on the Acount of Refferance with Mr Batman [sic]	0	0	6
November 14 Spent at Bouth on a disign of Sealing arbitration bonds		1s	

154 Henry Taylor, Richard Robinson, James Backhouse, Myles Harrison, George Taylor, Robert Taylor, and George Taylor of Elinghearth. Robert Bateman, vicar of Colton, maintained that he was still entitled to receive fees from Finsthwaite, although it now had a church of its own. The more substantial inhabitants raised money to fight his claim and on 16 February 1730 Clement Taylor and James Backhouse were chosen to represent them: LRO, DDPd 29/15. The expenses in the case, and notes of further contributions are continued to the foot of p. 99. Henry Taylor, perhaps not surprisingly, seems never to have paid his share, a fact recorded on the back of the articles of agreement: 'Henry Taylor payed nothing'; see 240 and n. 194. The position of George Braithwaite of Stott Park and George Taylor of Elinghearth, who were dissenters, was uncertain and they did not sign the articles of agreement, although George Braithwaite did contribute [p. 99]. The principal protagonists are named again at the foot of p. 98.

Spent at Lancaster and Caton in in-quiring of Mr Taylor & others About the dues of Coulton with J[ames] Backhouse Spent 10d more at the time	0	5	9

Our Journeys Uncharged
as for goeing as above to Lancaster & Caton

February 8th J[ames] B[ackhouse] & C.T. a Journey to Lancaster with John Case Spent J[ames] B[ackhouse] paid more 1s 3d$^{1}/_{2}$ at same time	0	2	9

March the 7th J[ames] B[ackhouse] & C.T. a Journey to Leavens Millthrop[155] & to Lancaster when Mr Batman Libeled 1th against Mr Harrison & J[ames] B[ackhouse] To Lawyer Gibson for Drowing an answer to the same	0	10s	0
Expenses paid per me on that Journey being two Nights out J[ames] B[ackhouse] more	0	2	10

[p. 98]

more Charged in his bill on that Journey

	li	s	d
July to Biggins pro Carr[ying] Letter	0	0	1
November 12th paid pro Carr[ying] Letter to Giles Man	0	1	0

February 1731 Received of Brother Richard at Little Nookyet[156] <toward> towards Suit which I paid Mr Harrison the Same Day	1	0	0
he had advanced before which Lawyer Chamber had	0	10	6

3 paid Mr Harrison on Account of [suit *interlined*] & [towards making up of *interlined*] Mr Sandys Money	1	0	0
March 12 paid Giles pro 2 letters	0	0	2
18 To Giles pro a letter from york	0	0	4

155 Levens and Milnthorpe, Westm.
156 Little Nook gate.

26 Spent with Mr Lambert
on Sunday before laying
of the Costs & to forward the
same   0   0   6

Received per C T   7li   <5>0 s

April 26th at This time C T
1732   hath Advanc'd 2l 16s<6> 10d 2
towards Suite

	l	s	d
James Backhouse	2	17 <2>	3 <½>0
Richard Robinson	1	17	4
paid Miles Harrison	1	14	1
George Taylor	1	05	6
Robert Taylor	1	6	0
Christopher Taylor		2	0
Mr Harrison		16<2>	3<9>

Each part 4li 2s 6d
Mr [Harrison *interlined*] hath the accounts
settled in the presence
R R   M H   C T G T
Ro T   J B   C T

[*p. 99*]

April 27 Received of Miles Harrison	li	s	d
Towards Batman's [*sic*] Suit	2	8	5
more of Miles Harrison being			
on Case account returned Idem	0	8	6
28 of Christopher Taylor Wife	2	2	0
February of Christopher Taylor more	1	1	0
May 21th of Richard Robinson	2	5	2
	1	1	0

June 23 1733
of George Taylor on Winscar
in part towards Suite   3   3   0
23d of Robert Taylor
at our own dore   3   12   0
July 4th of George Braithwait
at our own Door   3   16   6

December 1732 A Further advansment per
the Neighbourhood of Finsthwait [of 5li apiece *interlined*] as
below toward the Suit with Mr
Batman [*sic*] Now Curate of Coulton

Robert Taylor	0	2	0
George Braithwait	0	17	6
George Taylor	0	14	6
Christopher Taylor	2	16	
Miles Harrison	0	17	5
Richard Robinson	1	11	8
James Backhouse	[blank]		
Clement Taylor	[blank]		

June to William Taylor a retainer
and postaige   0   5   6
October
25 My dismisson fee   0   6   4
To Usher or Clark of Hawkshead
& Cartmel for Copies of [they *interlined*] Regesters
December a letter from York & one
from Lancaster   0   0   6

Henry Taylor   4   15   0
Debtor toward the Finsthwait Charges
versus Coulton

[*p. 100*]

November 1730 Then paid John Coward wife
for all Shop Goods had of her
& her husband as apears Crosd
out in ther Book Nails being
last

	li	s	
January 26 Then paid Brother Edward	5	5	
More for a Cow & a Calf	4	5	
More Borrowed Money	4	0	0
More a Letter	0	0	10
more a Sheep Skin	0	0	10

January 30th 1730 Received of Thomas			
Danson for Land rent	li	s	
by Shoemaker Work	2	15	
by Interest 22li 10s	0	17	
by cash	3	8	
Gave him 2s 6d Gratis			

The Account Book of Clement Taylor

January 31 Spinkt why buld at
Mr Rawlinsons paid 6d Sud [*sic*] of her [self *interlined*]
of Graithwait

paid William Coward for half of Walkerbrow for 1730		5s	
February the 1th 1730 Then Received from John Schales for Interest of a bond of 30li for 1729 & 1730	2	9	6
February 3d 1730 Then Received of John Walker for Interest			
by Work	2	11	8
by a Web of Linn	1	6	6
by 6 pecks of Barley	0	10	0
in Cash	20	0	0
February 3d Remains Due to C Taylor for Interest	l	s	d
in arear	12	11	1

2 days over Charged per J[ohn] W[alker]
& Interest of 15li for one yeare

[*p. 101*]

Januery [*sic*] 30th 1730 Thomas Danson rent	li	s
antient	2	14
Two Haggs	2	15
pool Meddows	0	12
Pincher Croft	0	15
Tarnhaw	0	4
Farrhagg & Long Myre	1	0
Little Close		5
	8	5<0>

February 4th paid William Dixon pro 10li of hare[157]		5	6
7th Received Interest of Richard Rigg for 1729 & 1730 per Peter Nuby or James Walker	6	12	
Received Interest of William Braithwait at Kendal for 60li for 1730	2	10	

---

157 Hair; *cf* n. 95.

94   *The Account Book of Clement Taylor*

Received Interest of Brother Edward for a bill of 100li pro 1730	4	0	0
paid Christopher Taylor pro a pilion Seat 3s.5d pro a tup 6s	0	9	0
on William Garner's Account & J[ohn] Coward		8	0
13th Then Received of Lawrance Harrison Wife for Town End Meddow for one year	0	6	0
paid Holme Taylor[158] on John Coward account	0	4s	8d

16th February Weggey bult at Mr. Rawlinsons paid 6d
Then Sold Mr John Wilkinson 68 Stone of wool at 4s 6d Certain & 3d per stone Further if he Can Afford it 2s per pack being allowed To Mr Wilkinson pro profit

[*p. 102*]

		s	d
March the 2d 1730 Then paid William Holme		10	9
& gave him Beverige			9
in full till this time			
26th paid William Holme in full		0	8

April the 7th James [Towers *interlined*] Cow Whye bult at Mr Rawlinsons of Graithwait paid 6d

26th April James Towers Cow buled Second time at Mr Rawlinsons

	li	s	
May 10th 1731 Received of Thomas Danson in full for Last year Land rent	1	5	
More for 3 days plowing for Last year		7	6

---

158   Presumably Thomas Holme, who appears on pp. 52 and 83.

		s	d
May 10 paid William Holme		4	2 1/2
in full			
Beverige		0	<6>7 1/2

		s	d
15th paid William Danson for 5 stone of		s	d
hare		14	6

June the 4th 1731 Then hired Margaret			
Burket pro	2	10	
Roger Jackson Wage is	5	5	

Margaret Burket wage	2	10
& a 1s I Gave her Earnest		

		s	d
Mr Harrison Debtor for 8 yards 3 quarter		s	d
of Cloth at 1s 6d per yard		13	1 1/2
Received 10s in part		10	0
		3	1 1/2
Firr trees remained		2	5
	Due	5	6 1/2
	Received	5	6 1/2

[p. 103]

	li	s		
June the 18th 1731 Then paid Roger Jackson	4	4		
in part towards Last year wage	0	1		
more I had of him before				
Remains <15s> 20s				
paid him more pro a pair of				
Skins	0	2	8	
more when he went to Kendal	0	2	0	
per John Walker Desk	0	10	6	
2li Candles	0	0	2	
at Hawkshead Fair	0	9	0	
paid more May 27 1732 in full	0	2	10	2[159]

June 23d Account of Bark Measured	quarter	Bushel
Imprimis John Taylor	33	1
Thomas Braithwait	4	7
George Braithwait	2	0
September George Braithwait More	16	6
in all	56	6

[159] The total paid to Roger Jackson was £5 11s 2 1/2d, so he earned more than his five guineas. For Hawkshead fair, see n. 27.

96   *The Account Book of Clement Taylor*

9th August Margaret Birket Received [to *interlined*] [*sic*]
for her Daughter of R Atkinson
August 12 1731 My Wife Why
buled at Robert Scales

23d August Spinkt Cow bult at
George Robinson's
August Then had out of Park 500
Latts of Richard Crossfield

September 12th Then Received of William Walker
for half a Cord of Swillwood
had out of New Close   0   10 <.>
being in full of all accounts

September the 20th had more Sapp
Latts out of Park from
Richard Crossfield per the hands
of Henry Crosdale 300
paid Richard Crossfield for all
Latts per Jane Woodburn

[*p. 104*]

June 25th 1731 Then paid John Coward
in full for work & his wif for
Shop goods
Emetick powder, a vomit pro J[ames] B[ackhouse]

October 10th   My Wife Cow bult
1731   at Robert Scales paid 6d

October 16th Then paid [Nicholas *interlined*] Cranks [*sic*] Junior
in full for 5 weeks at
8d per day per the hand of   8s
William Crank Junior   12s[160]
October 28 Borrowed of Mr
Harrison   13   0   0
November Butt peice of
John Barrow Wife wood is 4 foot 2
Borrowed of Thomas D[anson]   5   5   paid

160 If Nicholas Crank worked for six days a week at 8d a day for five weeks, he would have earned
     £1, the sum of the 8s and 12s noted here.

January the 19th Spinkt Why Bult at
Robert Scales

20th Coppey Why Bult at
Robert Scales

February paid Richard Crossfield per the hand
of Jane Woodborne in full for
Latt   0   10 s   0

[p. 105]

Januery [sic] 29th [1731 interlined] Received of John Walker
per Dayes Work This year   2   19   4
per 2 Carre potts[161] & [illegible]   <1>0   <5>1   <0>5
pro Roger Desk   0   10   6
                                                                    _____
                                                                         3   11   3
Received more of John Walker
per the hand of Miles Harrison
in full for Interest of anno 1730
as will apear before in this Book [162]   9   0   0

February 1th 1731 Received of Thomas Danson
for Land rent of the said year   li   s
Imprimis by Shoemaker work   2   5   1
In Cash   4   15
                                                                   _____
                                                                        7   0   0
at the same time paid Thomas Danson
Interest for 22li 10s   17s   & also
Interest pro a bill of <5> 5li   5s   4d
for the above said year

February 1th 1731 Received of Miles Harrison   li   s
in part of Bark money   10   10
the whole being 35li 14s

On the above said Day paid
Jacob Parke for all work
Done Last year   15s

---

161 Char pots; see n. 77. As John Walker was a joiner it seems likely that the payment was for the boxes to pack them in. The desk was for the servant, Roger Jackson [cf p. 103]. It was probably of the type known as a Bible box, an oak box with a sloping lid for writing on.
162 On p. 100.

		l	s	d
To John Taylor pro peeling 56 quarter & 6 Bushel at 2s 2d per quarter		6	2	10
More to the same for Cutting 30 load & 3 sack at 3s per load		4	10	9
More for Coling 30 load 3 sack at 4s per load		6	1	0
pro leading 7 load out of Stot -Beck at 12d per load		0	7	0
6 load & 7 sack out of New Close Coppy at 1s 3d per load[163]		0	8	9
		17	10	4

[p. 106]

	l	s	d
February 3d 1731 Then Received Interest of Christopher Marr per the hand of Elizabeth Denny for 60li pro Anno 1731	2	10	0
paid John Taylor towards peeling Bark Cutting wood Coaling & leading coals	9	8	8
More Idem	5	1	0
the abovesaid semes to have a mistake in it C T hath paid more than is Charg'd February 28 1731 Received Interest of Paul Penington pro a bill of 20li for the said year	0	16	6

	li	s	d
February 1731 Lent Margaret Braithwait when her Father died[164]	0	5	0
14th Received of Margaret which I am to pay March of her account as follows	0	10	0
To John Coward pro Coffin	0	5	6
To Henry Croasdale for his dues at Chapel	[blank]		
To John Coward W[ife] pro W[inding] Sheet	0	3	2
April 8th Then paid George Braithwait of Kendal Dier for Dieing 71 yards of Scotch Stuff at 2d per yard & also for printing the same 1d per yard <in the> Witness Mr. E. Blackstock			

163 He paid for seven full loads.
164 Thomas Braithwaite was buried on 27 February 1732. Clement Taylor is dealing with the funeral expenses for his daughter Margaret; see p. 226.

		s	d
May 25th paid Luke Bradley 1732 for one stone of Drist Hemp		5	6
the same paid Betty of Dickies[165] for Bearing peats 2 days	0	0	6

[p. 107]

February the 3d 1731 Then paid Mr Harrison my part of Bounty Money being	22	0	
paid Borred [sic] Money	13	0	0
Ditto Interest for the Same for one year & 4 months[166]	01	3	5
Ditto paid Him Interest for 10li	00	8	0
Ditto paid him for Clement & Isabel Learning	0	8	0
at The Same time paid him for J[ames] Danson	1	1	0
at the same time paid 4li 4s being part of Mr Sansys [sic] Money[167]	4	4	0
4th paid Margaret Sawrey Intrest for 20li for anno 1731	0	16	8
8 I am to pay William Coward on Grace[168] account for Stot Beck		5s	

February 9th 1731 Then Let to farm
To Thomas Jonson town End house
Orchard Garding & Apples
in Becking Garth & hagg I

---

165 Elizabeth, daughter of Richard Taylor; see 239, and cf nn. 185, 302.
166 Clement Taylor's part of the parish's contribution to the second payment from Queen Anne's Bounty; see n. 144. The 'Borred' money had been a loan from the vicar in October 1731 [p. 104], so he was paying interest for a year more than was needed.
167 The meaning of this is unclear. The Sandyses of Graythwaite were not parishioners.
168 Grace Braithwaite; see 226.

haveing Liberty to get some my self for & <Jonson to have> one day work of peats	li 1	s 4	
Iland	0	14	
half acre In Broad Middow	0	4	
parack & hill	0	18	
	3	0	

Johnson And Clement Ta[ylor]
February 17731 [*sic*]

[*p. 108*]

Cammey Cow buld <7>8th February 1731
at Mr Rawlinson's paid

February 16th paid John Leece for making 9 Bushel of Malt & Duty	li 1	s 1	d 0
21th Received Interest of William Braithwait for a Bond of 60li pro 1731	2	10	0

March 23d 1731 had 6 Bushels
of Barley in part of the Interest of
the said year at 6s per Bushel
all the rest is unpaid besids for that
year more 4 Bushel 1/2 at 5s 6d per Bushel

April the 3d 1732 Then Let to farm to Candlemas next Old Jenet Hagg & Cinderhill Brow for· To Edward Barwick per C. Taylor & Edward upon Leive to have some sheep goeing in the Brow [a little *interlined*] afterwards	li 1	s 2	d 0
Richard Kurby pro diking 28 rood of Dike at 8d per Rood on South E[ast] Side May 7th I paid 9s & Miles 9s yeat unpaid Each 6d	0	s 18	d 8
paid Jonson [for Diking *interlined*] of the East Sid of Abraham Moss as will apear before in this Book[169] for 40 rood at 8d per rood	1	6	8

---

169 On p. 77; *cf* nn. 123, 129.

May 2d paid Margaret Sawrey the Interest of the 20li which is in Paul Penington hand (in her house)	0	16	6
May 2d paid John Leece pro William Coward & & [sic] my selfe in full for Duty & making of Malt	1 1	s 2	
on the 1th Day of May at Mill-Thropp[170] I paid James Barrow for half a Bushel of rye	1 0	s 4	d 4

[p. 109]

May 6th on that Day we had 1th penny Lofe[171] of William Walker all been paid before that Day			
9th paid Isabel & Mary Each one shilling in full of Borrowed Money			
27 Received of Thomas Danson May Day rent being what was Left at Candlemas unpaid for the Last year 1731	1	0	0
at the same time he paid pro 3 dayes ploughing	0	7	6
he did not pay pro Stirring Barley Land			
27 paid Roger Jackson per the hand of John Taylor Executors	4	0	
To him self being in full	1	5	
paid Margaret Birket Wage	2	10	
27 Roger Debtor to me pro hatt	0	1	11
December 24th to Roger	0	1	6
April 1th when he went to Cartmellfell	0	5	0

Margaret Singleton[172] Wage is 2li 5s
1732 & Either an apron or 1s which I Gave her
1732 Roger Jackson's is 5li 10s
if he stays a year, if he goes
away at Martinmas but 5l 5s

---

170 Milnthorpe, Westm.
171 Bought bread would have been a rare treat; cf Denyer, *op cit.*, 26. William Walker appears again in this context on p. 231 and p. iii, but is otherwise unidentified.
172 She was Mary, not Margaret, Singleton, and is correctly named further down the page.

102   *The Account Book of Clement Taylor*

paid Mary Singleton pro a Gown & Taylor wage	0	6	6
more in money	0	5	0
January A Musslin apren about about 24		4s	
February 6 Toward paying pro Coggs[173]		0	6
10th pro Camrick		3	1	2
March 20th a Camrick Napkin	<1>3	<6>1	<2>0
April Frenge[174]		1	4

[*p. 110*]

June the 12th 1732 paid John Holme in full pro worke till this time		3s	

June 26 rackned with Miles Harison
& I remain Debtor 8s 5d how Ever
& it apear that Miles have paid
J[ohn] Torner 2s & that I have paid none
in Liue of it but 10s 8d to Jonson
I shall be more in his debt
Quere about that paid Myles Harrison
The above said Ballance in full for
tarr an [*sic*] all other Accounts
and also John Case Money[175] 8.6
which [he *interlined*] is to pay To Clarks of Hawkshead
& Cartmel
July the 8 My Wife Cow Came from
Freth

July the 19th then Lent William Taylor per the hand of Thomas Strickland Received January 10th	10li	0	0

29 July Weggey Bul'd at
Robert Scales – Broke bulling

August 1th Benjamin Airey pro a Suck wood[176] in full	0	2	0

---

173 He means clogs.
174 *cf* p. 94, where the servant Jane Ormandy had 'edging' bought for her, which would be, like this fringe, for trimming a dress or apron.
175 John Case of Walney was married in Finsthwaite in 1728, although why he should have busied himself in the dispute with Robert Bateman [see n. 154] is mysterious, as he went away at once to live on Walney [see 227], but he paid part of the lawyer's bill in the case: see the loose paper inserted at p. 234.
176 'Suck' is what is written; he may mean sack, although it is unlikely that he would be buying a sack of wood.

2d paid William Rownson in full for
Shop goods
28th <August> July Bready Bul'd at
Myles Taylor's & came home
the 5th of August from Grass
August <12> 14th Weggey why Bult at
Robert Scales
27th Black Cow bult at
Robert Scales all paid
September 24th My Wife Cow Bult
at Robert Scales
December 10th my Wife Cow Bult
2d time at Robert Scales

[*p. 111*]

Christopher Taylor Whie bult at Edward Riggs
about 4 weeks before Christmas paid
December   My Wife Whie bult
15th   at Edward Riggs paid

December 23d The Interest of Thomas Strickland
1732   Legacy[177] to the poor Labourers in Coulton
                    parish of which was Distributed in
                    Finsthwait as Follows 1732

To Jane Woodborne	0	9
To George Braithwait	1	<6>0
To Dorathy Braithwait	0	6
To Agnes Daughter of Sarah Prudey		9
1732 Disborsed of Mr Penny poor Money to Some of the Same as above		
To Jane Woodborne	0	6
To Dorothy Braithwait	0	6
To George Braithwait & Wife	1	0
total	5	0

---

[177] Thomas Strickland of Iconthwaite left £60 for the poor of Colton parish by will dated 12 March 1728, 'one half to the Poor that Goes about to ask alms; and the other half to the Poor Labering People of the parrish'. The Colton register noted that he was buried at Kendal on 8 April 1729. 'Mr Penny poor Money' below is the bequest of £20 left by William Penny of Penny Bridge, by will dated 28 December 1676, for the poor of Colton, Egton, and Newland: *The Registers of Ulverston Parish Church*, ed. C.W. Bardsley and L.R. Ayre, Ulverston, 1881, lxxxvii.

January Edward Barwick 6 [Days *interlined*] work
at 3 Sunrey [*sic*] times
January 28th Then Let to Farm for two
years To Edward Barwick Old Jennet
Hagg pro in all 15s per annum   15s   0

February 6th Spinkt Cow Bul'd at Edward
1732   Kilners of Ayside paid 1s

A bill of Sale[178] Such goods & Cattels
as was Sold by J.C. of P in publick
Sale the 00 Day of 00 anno Domini
1732 The Order of which Sale is
all at or Under 10s <ready> present money
& all Above time for payment is
allowed Untill the 00 Day of 00
next Ensuing Upon giving good
Security for the same when
demanded

[*p. 112*]

January 24 1732
Then Received for Land rent
for Several parsels at Town End
of Thomas Jonson for the same
Imprimis by two & half Days
Mowing   s   d
at 8d per Day   1   8
Ditto for his Wife
Working Hay
8 days [at *interlined*] 4d per Day   2   8d
Ditto his Horse to Ulverston   6
Received In Cash   2   2   0

                                                                        2   6   10
February 6th more
in full for Last year   0   13   6

Gave Jonson 1s   3   0   4

---

178 A draft of the announcement of a public sale, perhaps for John Coward of Plum Green [see 227]. Cash had to be paid at once for purchases under 10s., but buyers had more time to pay larger sums. That appears to have been the usual practice: see H.S. Cowper, 'A Grasmere Farmer's Sale Schedule in 1710' *CW1*, xiii, 1894, 253. For Clement Taylor's own purchases at John Coward's sale on 17 February 1728, see p. 83.

Received of Christopher Taylor for the Iland Hay at the same time paid him for Bark Leading	0	12	0
6 paid Margaret Sawrey Interest of 20li pro anno 1732 February 19 Weggy Buled at Robert Scales 2d time paid paid before	0	16	0
24th Received Interest of James Backhouse pro 60li pro 1732 at the same time allowd him in the same 1li 5s pro Bloomer Ridding	1 2	s 10	

[*p. 113*]

January 27 1732 Thomas Danson Land
rent pro Severall parchels is 8li

		li	s	
Received per Shoemaker work towards the same		2	1	
by John Barrow Wife's Wood		0	1	9
by Interest of 22li 10s		0	17	0
by Interest of a bill of 5li 5s		0	4	0
In Cash		3	16	3
Gave T[homas] Danson 2s 3d	toto	7	0	0
27 Received of Antoney Wilson for 4 load & 7 sacks at 28s per load Gave him 4d towards Shott Gave Benjamin 6d Stocktaker		6	8	4
February 1th 1732 paid Jacob Park for all worke done Last year		1	15	6
February 12th paid Thomas Peper pro all smith work done Last year 1732		1 0	s 19	d 9
Margaret Braithwait Debtor pro one stone of wool at 6s per stone		0	6	0
March 26th Then hired Mary Singleton 1733 the 2d year for & an appron one shilling I paid her at Hiring of the same		2	11	

April 2d Elizabeth Taylor Debtor pro 1 stone ½ & 1li
of wool at 6s per stone

6th Then paid Richard Kitchin for Dying
Linnen & Woolin yarne & Stockings
being in all   0   6   6
his Wife being present

paid William Rownson in full the Same Day

[*p. 114*]

16 of April 1733 received Interest
of John Scales Widow pro 30li for   li   s   d
Anno 1731 & 32   2   9   6
18 paid William Holme in full
& for Satherthwait Man   0   2   8
on Mary Account   0   6

April paid William Satterthwait in
full for his & William Holme
man <when my> Coat was made   0   2   0

April paid Margaret Sawrey Paul Pennington Interest   16s
John Prudey Debtor pro wool at 6s per Stone
Elizabeth Taylor Debtor pro 1 stone & 1 li of wool at 6s per stone
George Taylor 20 stone of hay at 2d½ per stone
Edward Barwick <5> 40 stone of hay at the same
price

                    of Thomas Danson   li   s
May 10th 1733   Received in full for (land *interlined*) rent
                                                1   0
More per 3 days ploughing
in Last plough time   0   7   6

May 11   paid Roger Jackson in full for   li   s
Last Year Wages being 1732   5   10

paid Mary Singleton her wage
in full for Last year also

June 16th 1733   paid Mr Harrison
Interest pro 10li 8s & also for Clement
& Isabel Learning 8s Maley Free[179]

---

179 Mary ('Mally'), his youngest daughter, who would have been six years old.

July 12th   Bhy [*sic*] Built at
Robert Scales
The other bult 3 weeks before
St James[180]
12 October   Black Cow bult at R[obert] S[cales]
21th Great Cow built at R[obert] S[cales]
December 25th 1733   My Wife Cow
built at Robert Scales
all paid per Constable Sess

[*p. 115*]

February 17th 1733   Spinked Cow Buled
at Robert Scales   not paid

March the 9th   Then paid Margaret Sawrey
1733   16s in full of all Accounts
in the presence of Margaret Braithwait
of Town End (alias Dolies)[181]
& Agnes Dixon

March 11th James Backhouse Received				
of Benjamin Airey all ash wood				
Silver pro Bloomer Ridding	li	s	s	
being	1	1	8 1/2	
April 12th 1734 Then gave Edward				
Taylor's of Little Dicks Charety Money[182]		s	d	
Imprimis Jennet Woodburne		2	6	0
George Braithwait		5	0	
Dorothy Braithwait		2	6	
Agnes Fell		1	6	
Elizabeth Soabby		2	0	
Elizabeth Taylor		2	6	
		16	0	
April 29th 1734 paid J[ohn] Prudey				
for Cutting Coalwood in				
Bloomer redding being 11 load 3 sack	li	s	d	q
at 3s 8d per load	2	1	2	2

180 St James's day, 25 July.
181 Margaret, daughter of Dorothy, widow of Thomas Braithwaite; see 226, and n. 302.
182 Edward Taylor of Craikside [see 239] left £20 for the poor of Finsthwaite and Plum Green in his will dated 7 November 1727; there is a copy of the will in the churchwardens' account book: CRO, WPR 101/W1.

108 *The Account Book of Clement Taylor*

		s	d	
also Bark 5 quarter & 6 bushel at 2s 4d per quarter		13	5	0
which is in all	21	14s	7d½	

May 6th 1734 Then paid Henry Taylor
for himself & Thomas Massicks for
removing a pitt   s d
                         1 6

[*p. 116*]

			s	
Borrowed of Thomas Danson		0	10	0
Clement Stockens		0	1	6
A Hive		0		5
December A quart of Mustard		0	0	4
1733 More in Money		3	3	0
of Mr Harrison		6	6	0
of Roger Jackson		1	0	0

December 1733   Account of poor[183]

Nibthwait	16 poor persons
East Side	17 poor
West Side	11 poor
Russland	10 poor
Haverthwait	5 poor
Finsthwait	6 poor

December 1734 Finsthwait H[averthwaite] & Rusland
Devided to the poor this year
to Isabel Walker
to Margaret Walker
Josey Wife
George Braithwait Finsthwait
Ester Rownson
Margaret Burnes Widow

Devided to poor labrours
John Jackson
John Wilson Smith
George Braithwait Finsthwait
James Kurby
Isaac Jackson finsthwait

---

183 Clement Taylor was overseer of the poor for Colton parish in 1734. The next entries refer to his duties in that office.

[*p. 117*]

Decenber 21th 1733
The Devidend of Thomas Strickland
Gift[184]

		s	d	q
	The East & West Side	20	0	
	Haverthwait Finsthwait & Rusland	17	6	
16	Nibthwait	12	6	

East & West had 1s 3d more than their S[hare]
17. 6 being Devided among F[insthwaite] H[averthwaite] &
Rusland acording to poor bill

	s	d	q
Finsthwait Share	5	11	1
Rusland	7	2	2
Haverthwait	4	4	1
	17	6	

Disbursed to Finsthwait

		s	d	q
To Dorathy Braithwait		1	0	0
To George Braithwait		1	6	0
To Isaac Jackson		1	6	0
To Jane Woodburn		0	6	0
<J Har> Agnes Fell		0	6	0
Elizabeth Taylor alias Dickes[185]			6	0
Elizabeth Soalby		0	6	0
	in all	6	0	0

December   Received of Thomas Strickland
1734   Money being 2li 6d Interest
for Finsthwait Haverthwait

		s	d	q
& Rusland	0	16	1 ½	
of which Rusland had	0	6	1	2
Haverthwait	0	4	0	
Finsthwaite	0	5	6	0
East Sid of Coulton B[eck]		10	2	1
West Sid Ditto		8	2	2
Nibthwait	0	10	2	2

paid for out of Interest

A bond pro next year	2	0	0	

the money being in Frances
Chamney's hand Thomas Rigg being
bondsman for the Same

---

184   See n. 177.
185   See nn. 165, 302.

110   *The Account Book of Clement Taylor*

			s	
Disbursed to the poor of Finsthwait				
to Dorathy Braithwait			1	0
to Elizabeth Solby			0	9
to Elizabeth Taylor			0	9
to George Braithwait			0	6

[*p. 118*]

		li	s	d
to Jane Woodburn		0	0	6
to Isaac Jackson		0	2	0
	in all	<5>0	5	6

April 1735 then Disbursed Interest
of Edward Taylor money[186]

to Elizabeth Taylor	0	5	0
Jane Woodburne	0	3	0
Dorothy Braithwait	0	3	6
George Wife	0	2	0
Elizabeth Soalby	0	2	6
		16	0

by James Backhouse
Miles Harrison
C Taylor

February 4th 1735 Then Received
Land rent of Thomas Danson

	li	s	
by Shoemaker Work	3	7	0
in Cash	3	13	0
	7	0	0

about the above said time
I Received of Thomas Jonson   3   0   0
in part for rent for Ano
1735 more of Jonson for the Hagg   0   15   0

April 23d 1736 Then Disbursed Interest
of Edward Taylor Legacy to poor of
Finsthwait according to his Will

	s	d
Elizabeth Taylor	5	0
Dorothy Braithwait	3	0
George Braithwait	3	6
Elizabeth Soalby	1	6
Jane Woodburne	3	0
	16	0

---
186   See n. 182; the account for 1736 is below.

May 24th 1736 Then received of Thomas Danson
the latter [part *interlined*] of Last year rent   1   5   0
& also 7s 6d for ploughing   0   7   6

[*p. 119*]

January 18th 1734 My Wife Spinkt
Why buled 2d time at J[ohn] Robinson's paid

Coals   piggs
Sacks   li   s   d
27   6   10   0
30   6   17   6
24   6   02   6
34   7   7   6
20   5   12   6
Coals to advance ls When piggs
advances 2s 6d [tunn *interlined*] & fall after
the Same Manner or rate[187]

July the 27 1737 Brandt Why bult
at Miles Harrisons

[*p. 120*]

Alice Taylor Died 11th February 1734[188]

24th September 1734 begun
Ended with 35 weeks

[*p. 121*]

December 29th 1733
paid Jacob Parke for all work
done Except Blackredding   l   s
coall by his man John   1   4

March 1734 paid Mr John Couperthwait
pro an article between me &
George Rigg about partintree   2   6

[187] That is to say, that the suppliers of charcoal, probably to the Backbarrow Co., would get more for their charcoal if the price of pig iron rose.
[188] This refers across to the payment to Alice Taylor on p. 121. She was buried on 12 February 1735; see 241. The entry below refers to that for George Braithwaite on p. 121.

112 *The Account Book of Clement Taylor*

May 19th 1734 Account of what
pensioners There are within Colton[189]

Jonathan Wilson Mother			9d	per W[eek]
Alice Taylor		1s	0	per W[eek]
Smith Wife		1	0	per W[eek]
Elizabeth Burnes		0	6	per W[eek]
Chapman Wife		0	6	
<Christopher Dixon>	0	0	0	0
<George Braithwait		8	6	per Annum>
<Isabel> Isabel Walker	<2>	4	0	per Annum
Dick Nuby House rent		15		rent
Isack Jackson		10	0	per annum
Widdow Torner		8	0	per Annum
Rebecca <Coward> Rigg Dead				
<Elizabeth Taylor Nibthwaite>		1s	10	per Week
To a man Over Kellet never Claims 2li if he be Living per Annum				
Jane Keen		5s		per Annum
Elizabeth Readhead		2	6	per Annum
Margaret Readhead		2	6	per Annum
George Braithwait alowance began 24th September 1734				
William dodson	2li			per Annum
Charles Russel		0	1s	per W[eek]

[*p. 122*]

May 24th 1734
Then Measured Wood in
Green Slack to Richard Crossfield
30 foot at 9d per foot to [*sic*]
Livered at pool Bridge
per C Taylor

[<. . . . . .> *at side*]

June 9th Weggy Why Buled
at Mr Robinsons paid

---

189 Another piece of overseer's business. Rebecca Rigg, noted here as dead, was buried at Colton on 12 March 1736.

July 16th Great [read *interlined*] Why paid
Bult at Mr Robinson's
19th Weggey Why Bult
at Mr Robinson's 2d time paid
21th Brand Backt why
bult at Mr Robinson's
29th Bettey Denney why
July Bult at Mr Robinson's
Second time all paid per C.T.
in presence of Ann Robinson
August the 3d Great Cow Why
Buled at Mr John Robinson's
2d time all paid

10th My Wife Why Buled
at Mr John Robinson's paid

September 17th Great Red Cow
bult at J[ohn] Robinson's paid ls
January 26th <my> Spinkt Cow
Bult at J[ohn] Robinson's
18 My Wife Spink Why Bult
forgot putting down before paid

[*p. 123*]

February 4th 1734 Then Received
of George Muckelt 65li in part
of consideration Money due pro
partingtree by me C. Taylor
this is all I've Received on that account
Except some wood not Given in part

[*at side*] Less George Muckel 5s 6d
G[eorge] Muckelt April [more *interlined*] of Idem 10li 10s

March Edward Taylor Waited for Abrahams
14   with a designe to devide H[athornthwaite] money[190]

Direct to me by Davantry
bagg[191]

---

190 For this, see Appendix.
191 Part of his brother William's address.

114 *The Account Book of Clement Taylor*

March
24th   Borrowed of Edward Taylor
          paid Edward Taylor 2li 2s in <part> all   5li   5s

24th of Mrs Ann Robinson
or Mr John Robinsonson [*sic*]
the Sume of   5   5
paid Mr John Robinson 7th June 1735

paid Thomas Casson per his Dr Rigg
in presence of J Fox   2li   10s
in part of 8 Bushel ½ of Barley
at 6s & 4d per Bushel

George Muckelt hath paid
at Several times in part
of Purchas money as
below for Parting tree
1th   65   0
2   10   10
3   26   0
Table & <Wood> [Bark *interlined*] deduct   3   8
                                                        186   3
                                                        032 <.>   3   0 <3>
                                                          8   0
                                              ─────────────────
                                   in all   296   8
                                                        003
                                                        150
                                                         10 [192]

[*miscellaneous calculations pinned on at foot*]

[*p. 124*]

may[193] February 21th My wife spinkt
Why Buld at Mr John Robinson
3d time paid before

---

192 The accounts for the sale of the timber from Partingtree wood seem to have caused some problems, and eventually the vicar, John Harrison, was called in to sort them out on pp. 138–9.
193 Clement Taylor began to write 'may' for the entry at the top of p. 122 before he realised that the page was torn and that he had written it on p. 124.

[*p. 125*]

```
         8li  5s
February 2d 1733  Then Received of
Thomas Danson Land rent                    li      s        d
by shoemaker Work                           3    <.>2      00
in Cash                                     3     14       11
by Interest of 22li 10s                     0     17        0
by Interest of 5.5                          0      4        0
                                                 ─────────────
                        totall              7    17<6>   11<9>
```

April 1734
Then Hired Margaret Bornes
pro next year pro
paid her 6d in Ernest in part
of the same Rowland Taylor being present

```
                                           li      s
                                            2     13        0
```

Roger Jackson Wage 5li 10s
pro next year
October 7th 1734 Received of Thomas
Danson the latter End of Last   li   s   d
year Rent   0   7   0
3 days ploughing   0   7   6
Gave him sherring Further   [blank]

Account of Mr Henry Taylor Land
Sold at plumgreen November 27
1734[194]   li
    Cowper Redding   120
    Water meadow   <9>93   3
    Brookbank   201   1

[194] Henry Taylor [see 240] went bankrupt and his land in Finsthwaite had to be sold, after being put into the hands of trustees who endeavoured to sort out his affairs. He was the owner of his father's old farm at Plum Green with the house which had been created from its downhouse, the house and land at Landing, and one of the houses at Sinderhill. A list of his debts, amounting to £1370 11s 5d, with £85 16s 8d in unpaid interest and other costs, survives in CRO, BPR 17/M2/1–2, but in a late copy. That does not take into account the £161 which he raised by mortgaging land to James Barrow of Upper Newton in February 1732, nor the £100 for a mortgage of Wintering Park to the same man in February 1734: LRO, DDPd 26/231, 237. Drinking may have been one of his problems. He owed £70 to Elizabeth Denny, the innkeeper at Newby Bridge; she must have been remarkably forbearing. The trustees, Walter Chambre of Kendal, John Fletcher of Holker, and William Lambert of Kirkland, Kendal, took over the estate on 26 February 1734 [CRO, BPR 17/M2/1–2], and Clement Taylor is here recording the prices paid at the sale for the various pieces of land. The running total at the foot of p. 125 is *recte* £2250 6s, and the total amount raised was therefore £2497 9s. The sale must have caused something of a sensation, as a very considerable part of the parish of Finsthwaite was changing hands.

116   *The Account Book of Clement Taylor*

Wintering Parke	160	
Parrack fould	092	
Great Intack parrack		
of Height [& *interlined*] Hogghouse		
parack	346	2s
Low Intack	043	
Great field	350	
Walker parack	040	
Born knott	542	
Knott	103	
Low Redding	160	
	225	6 [*sic*]

[*p. 126*]

	li	s	
House & parrack & Common	192	10	
Height	42	5	
Brows &c	12	5	

1734
Debtor to John Walker [for *interlined*] Work [<for> *interlined*] done
& Barley livered

Barley 6 Bushell	1	16	
Barley 4½	1	4	9
Barley 9	2	14	
35 days Work	1	3	4
Jackey	0	1	0
Locks & Drops	0	2	9
John Waker [*sic*] paid	7	1	10
Received in Silver	0	18	0
& [more *interlined*] for Interest			
of upwards of 40li			
being for arrears			
of Interest	1	10	0

February the 1th 1736 Spinkt
Cow & White Backt Why
Bult at John Robinson's paid

February the 1th 1736 John
Walker Debtor for Interest   li   d
till this time   26   7
the above Said Received in part
of the above Said Sum   13   7
    by me C T

a mistak Due to C T from John Walker in the reckning	2	0	

[*p. 127*]

January 20 1734 Then Received of Thomas Jonson for land rent pro 1734	3li		
all Work [done by him *interlined*] being allowed in the Same for hag fogg paid		4s	0
Received towards beif		11s	0
Beif paid in full G[ave] ls again			

February 2d 1734 Then rackned with John Walker & [he *interlined*] Remains Debtor to me 400li principle
More [Debtor *interlined*] Interest of the Same 12li which is a Just Account between him & me at the same time paid or alowd with him for 19 Bushel ¹/₂ of B[arley] and all work done by him & <Thence> he remains Debtor to me as above & 12li [<....> *interlined*] which is all Interest Due till this time 1734

	li	s	d
November 1735 Then received of John Walker in Mrs Simson's	4	0	0
more by 10 Bushels of Barley at 6s & 8d per Bushel	3	6	8
More 2d February 1735 at Cartmel being in full for 1734	6	0	0

& 1li 6s 8d toward the Interest of 1735

	li	s	d
February the 2d [1736 *interlined*] Received more of John Walker by the Hands of Richard Robinson towards Interest of 1735	12	0	0
April 25th 1737 Received more of John Walker towards 35 & 36	8	0	

February 2d Received of John Walker towards 1736	11	0	
January 28 2 bushels of Barley	0	13	

[*p. 128*]

June 1734 Then Antony
Strickland of Kendall
Laid Lead pipe being
109 yeard & 2 foot at 2s 4d
by the yeard he Abating
20s at the whole & also
promises to repair what Lecks[195]
is in the said pipe at his
Own Expense Clement Taylor

February the 2d 1735 Then Borrowed of
Emmey Taylor   10li   0s

1736
<Margaret> Roger Jackson   20
Mr Harrison   20

May 16th 1738 Received of John
Walker toward Intrest
of 37   5   7
More 2 Bushel of Bar[ley]   13

[*p. 129*]

February 4th 1734 Received of George Muggelt
in part for Partingtree   65li
February 6th 1734 Then Gave
bill to James Barrow pro   186li   3s
payable without Iterest [*sic*] next year

Mr Henry Tayor whole
purchase of Winteringpark   160
Brookbank   201   1s
Brows   12   12
Height my part   14   1   8
                                                                        ─────────────────
                                                                         387   14   8

To Mr Lambert pro Lease &
Release <& Sessment>   1   0   0
Deed of Height my part
being a 3d   0   4   0

195 Leaks.

Spent that time being at Sealing[196]	0	4	0

February Then Gave bill
for 10li to Margaret Braithwait
payable with Interest at 10s
per pound Due 2d February Next

		s	d
April 9th Debtor to Roger Harrison for 5 yards ¼ of Lan'er Lin[197]		5	3
3 peces of Velvert		7	6

	li	s	d
Then Hired Elinor Nuby 1735 for Next year for	2	12	6

paid sixpence at Hiring in part of the same
July the 9th 1735 Then & before
paid John Walker & William Satterthwait
for all Taylor work pro C T

	li	s	d
<July> August the 2d then paid Elinor Nuby in part of her Wage	0	10	0
December paid for Elinor to pick stones	0	1	6
anapkine [sic]		<2>1	6
an apron		3	0
	0	16	0
paid her in full more	1	16	

[p. 130]

May 26th 1735 Then Received of Thomas
Danson Land rent in full for Last
year & at the same time paid him Interest
in full & all other Demands
plowing not paid for by him

---

196 On 3 February 1735 Henry Taylor and his trustees, with the mortgagee James Barrow, confirmed that they were to sell to Clement Taylor the woods and fields called Brooksbank, half of Wintering Park, and Walker Brow, and, to James Backhouse, Walker Parrock; LRO, DDPd 26/239. The next day, for a nominal sum of 5s, other pieces of land were sold to Clement Taylor and James Backhouse: the pasture called Plum Green Height and Yewbarrow Top, and 100 acres of furze and heath at Sinderhill: *ibid*. 26/241. Finally, on 4–5 February, by lease and release, Clement Taylor paid £373 13s for half of Wintering Park (nine acres), two closes, formerly one, at Brooksbank (nine acres), Slate Quarry or Sinderhill Brow (three acres), half of Walker Brow (one and a half acres), and an acre of pasture at Low Height: *ibid*. 26/242. A final concord was issued on 22 March: *ibid*. 26/243. The purchase price in the lease and release is therefore slightly less than that given here; *cf* n. 194.

197 ? Lancaster linen.

120   *The Account Book of Clement Taylor*

27th June Then lent Jacob Park   2li   2s
August the 13th 1735 Great Cow Bult
at John Robinson's Broak
21th Great Read Cow bult 2d
time at John Robinson's paid

December the 3d 1735 White
Backed Why Bulled at John
Robinsons paid all paid <1s more>
paid for one before to Thomas Robinson
at the same time

January the 18th 1735 Spinkt Cow
Bult at John Robinson's
April the 1th 1736 Black Spink why
Bult at John Robinsons

April the 20th 1736 Great Cow Why
Bult at John Robinsons
June the 12th 1736 paid [Roger *interlined*] Then &
before 20s & remains Debtor to
Him 10li paid in full
June the 22d 1736 Then [took *interlined*] measured [*sic*]
                                    quarter   Bushel
of Bark from Elizabeth Kurby   33   3
and from Prudence   12   2
by John Satterthwait & George Muckelt
C Taylor being present
August 20th from John Prudence quarter   Bushel
in my Barne   39   1
by George Muckelt & Marchent
Daughter Livered in to me
C Taylor
September 30th Grace[198]   quarter   Bushel
at Thomas Dansons   8   2

[*p. 131*]

December 1735 Then Thomas Strickland
Money Disbursed at followeth[199]
12s 6d for Finsthwait & Rusland   s   d   q
To   Finsthwait   5   7   3
     Rusland   6   10   1
     Haverthwait   4   1   ½
                                                  _____
                                                  16   7   2

198 Grace Braithwaite; see 226.
199 See n. 177.

			s	d	q
to	Dorothy Braithwait		1	2	0
to	George Wife		0	8	0
to	Elizabeth Taylor		0	8	0
to	Jane Woodburn		0	6	0
to	Elizabeth Soalby		0	8	0
to	Isaac Jackson		2	0	0
			5	8	0

			s	d
1736	to Isaac Jackson		1	6
to	George Wife		1	2
to	Jane Woodburn		1	0
to	Dorothy Braithwait		1	0
to	Betty Taylor		1	0
			5	8

[*p. 132*]

1738
February the 3d Then Received
of Thomas Danson for Land

	li	s
rent	3	2
in Cash	3	18
of Thomas Jonson	1	10

[*Edward Taylor*]

Antient Rent for
Cobby House Back meadow

		li	s
Wheat Garth & Butt Hills		2	14
Two Haggs		3	00
Pool Meadows		0	04
Pincher Croft Share		0	15
Tarnhaw		0	02
		4	01
		2	14
	In all	6	15

122   *The Account Book of Clement Taylor*

[*Clement Taylor*]

January 31th 1736 Thomas Danson
		li	s
Land rent as followeth			
Antient		2	14
Two Haggs		2	15
Pool Meadows		0	04 <12>
Pincher Croft		0	15
Tarn Haw &			
Little Close		0	5
		6	13
Far Hag & Long			
Myre		1	0
		8	1
Long Myre		0	10 [200]

[*p. 133*]

October the 12th 1736 Bark Livered
from Richard Robinson for Marchant
Satterthwait	quarter	Bushell
	18	2
13th from Margaret Woodb		
urn young wood Bark	2	0
More from the Same Old		
Wood Bark	2	0
More Young wood Bark	3	4
More old wood Bark	30	3

William Coward Led from J[ames] D[anson]
	39	1
from Grace	8	2
from Woodburne Wife	31	5
from John Prudence out		
of Old Stable Measured		
by Satterthwait Son	7	6
Peter Taylor	13	3
Margaret Woodborne in old [Stable *interlined*]		
	4	

[200]   This calculation is roughly written and does not add up.

The Account Book of Clement Taylor 123

January the 25 1736 Then Received of Thomas Jonson towards Land rent for this year	3	0	0
January 31th 1736 Then received of Thomas Danson for Land rent	li	s	
by Shoemaker Work	3	13	
In Cash	3	7	
May 10th More in full	1	1	
also ploughing paid	0	7	6

<January> February the 1th 1736 Spinkt
Cow and White Backt why
Bult at John Robinson's paid
September the 16 Bought Cow bult
at Myles Harrison's
November 10th Bought Cow bult
2d time at M[yles] Harrisons
January 1th Black horn Why
Bult at John Robinson's

[*p. 134*]

June the 18th 1737 Robert Dodshen[201] Came to be borded with me		
September 1737 To Mr Turner	1	6
a parsing Book	0	11
February 1737 Cock penny	2	6
April a quire of paper	0	6

Debtor to Peter Taylor 4
pows 6 [*sic*] at 8d per foot
for pool Bridge

[*p. 135*]

Good fryday April the 8th 1737
Edward's [*sic*] Taylor Charity money[202]
Disposed of as followeth for
the year 1736

Elizabeth Soalby	0	1	0
George Braithwait Wife		5	0

---

201 Robert Dodgson is unidentified, but he evidently came to be taught in Finsthwaite.
202 See n. 182.

Jane Woodburne		4	0
Dorothy Braithwaite		2	0
Elizabeth Taylor		4	0
		16	0

Good friday March the Last
Disposed of Edward Taylor money
for the year 1738<7>

to Elizabeth Soalby		1	0
To Thomas Wife		5	0
To George Wife		5	0
To Jane Woodburn		5	0
		16	

[p. 136 is blank]

[p. 137]

Money Received from George Muckelt
& by his order towards parting
tree as followeth

of himself		65	
Mar[chant]		10	10
J[ames] B[ackhouse]		186	3
Mar[chan]t		50	
		<28	8>
Lent him & in }			
table Woodburn } 28.8<3>		311	13
& Kurby }	Lent	28	8
		294<3>	5[203]
Wood		2	5
Self		8	0
Mar[chant]		10	0
Self		10	0
H[enry] Bar[wick]		150	0
	[illegible] paid	474	10
		<433>	
	Rem[ains]	164	10
	Received more of <G> Marchant	10	

[203] *recte* £283 5s. The calculation appears correctly on p. 139.

September 22d Bark Measured
out Cowhouse from Miles field
Busk   quarter   Bushell
                          19   6
Machent [sic] Saterthwait wife being
present

Debtor to George Muckelt
for Latts   0   1   6
Odments   0   1   0
Well Pipe   0   2   6
Tree in Law Wood

[*p. 138*]

[*John Harrison*]²⁰⁴

638   0   0   Purchase money
620   17   10 ¼   Received
─────────────
 17   2   1 ¾   Remains

[*p. 139*]

[*Clement Taylor*]

Received from George Muckelt
& by his order in part towards
purchas money for Parting
tree as followeth   li   s   d
of George Muckelt   65   0   0
of Merchant   10   10   0
of George M[uckelt] By J[ames] B[ackhouse] 186   3
of Merchant   50   0
                                       ─────────────
                                       311   13
Lent G[eorge] & in table
Woodburn W[ife] & Kurby
Wife   28   8
                                       ─────────────
                                       283   5
more by Wood   02   5
of George   8   0
of Marchant   10   0

204 See n. 192. The sums of money involved in this wood sale are surprisingly large.

126   *The Account Book of Clement Taylor*

of George	10	0	
of Merchant	10	0	
of George by H[enry] B[arwick]	150	0	
	473	10	
of George 10 B[ushel] of B[arley]	003		

[*John Harrison*]

A Copy of the Above was given
to George Muggett October 18th 1737

[*Clement Taylor*]

more of George 1th February	40l	0	
More of George M[uckelt] by			
Henry Barwick bill	70l		
		s	d
<A> 2 Quarts of &c [*sic*]		3	0

[*John Harrison*]

Shoe Upper Leathers		3	0
A Seal Skin		4	0
10 Joysts		3	4
Wood 11 Foot		9	7
	587	12	11
A Quarter of the Globe[205]	33	4	11¼
	620	17	10¼
Purchase Money	638	0	0
Remains due	17	2	1¾

February 2d 1737   paid in full

Allowed by Clement Taylor [*signed*]
George Muggelt [*signed*]

Witnesses
[*signed*] John Cragge
[*signed*] John Harrison

205   This at first mysterious entry refers to the ship in which Clement Taylor had a share; see n. 207. The sealskin above was presumably imported by George Muckelt as part of his coastal trading activities. In 1723 John Fell of Daltongate in Ulverston left to his brother-in-law, William Chapman of Bouth [see 227], 'one saddle-housin of seale skin': J. Fell, 'Some Illustrations of Home Life in Lonsdale North of the Sands, in the 17th and 18th centuries', *CW1*, xi, 1891, 371.

[*p. 140 is blank*]

[*p. 141*]

[*Clement Taylor*]

1737
Spinkt Cow Bult at Myles Harrisons
25th December bought Cow a week
before

White Backt <why> Cow Bult
at Mr Rawlinsons paid
16th March 1737
April 24th White Backt Cow
bulled Second time paid before
at Mr Rawlinson's
June 22d Lesser [Spinkt *interlined*] White Backt
bult at Mr Rawlinson's paid
28th White Backt
Why bult at Mr R[awlinson's] paid 1s
25th of August Great Read
Bult at Mr Rawlinson's paid 1s
31th of August Blackhornt
bult at Mr Rawlinsons paid

[*p. 142*]

	s	d
Delvered [*sic*] to C T	5	6

December 23 1737 disburs'd
Thomas Strickland Charety Moner [*sic*][206]

	s	d
To Jane Woodburne	0	6
To Grace	1	0
To Dorothy Braithwait	1	0
To Elizabeth Taylor	1	6
To Isaac Jackson Wife	1	6

---

206   See n. 177.

128 *The Account Book of Clement Taylor*

	li	s	d
January 25th 1737 Then received Land rent of Thomas Danson			
by Shoemaker Work	2	17	11
In Cash	4	2	1
May 23d Received of Thomas Danson in full for rent	1	1	
plowing paid for	0	5	
1737 Elkenah Taylor[207] Charge of Boat is	132li	19s	9d

Cubby Hagg[208]

	li
B 400	120
T 217	325
C 50	45
	—-
	490

[*p. 143*]

	li	s	d
March the 14th 1737			
To Peter Taylor Wife	2	0	0
15th To Peter Taylor	1	0	0
May to L[eonard] Stout Chese	0	7	0
to Peter when he Went to Ulverston	0	5	0
June 26 to Peter when he Went to Bishp [*sic*][209]	0	10	0
for Chese	0	5	3

207 LRO, DDPd 26/253 is an application for the opinion of counsel in the matter of the ship. Elkanah Taylor and George Muckelt [see 240, 234] built a sloop at their joint cost and sailed it with Elkanah as master, and one other seaman, Samuel Scales. Clement Taylor was persuaded to buy Muckelt's share, for which he paid £66 9s 10½d, half the sum named here. He sold half of his share to Peter Taylor [see 241] and gave the other half to his son Clement. After two years he fell into dispute with Elkanah over the management and accounting of the venture, and applied to counsel to know whether his son and Peter Taylor could replace Samuel Scales (who had by now bought a quarter of the ship), with 'another capable seaman' who would have equal status with Elkanah, or whether they had power to replace Elkanah altogether. The lawyer, John Christian, replied on 28 February 1741 that they could not replace Elkanah, who had the same rights as they did, but that they could seek to call him to account as master, through a Bill in Chancery. Nothing further is known of the matter, and it is not clear why the purchase price of a quarter of the ship, which appears on p. 139, is being treated in February 1738 as money which was being paid to Clement Taylor and not by him. The ship would have been engaged in coastal trading.
208 The position of 'Cubby Hagg' is not known and the calculation is unintelligible. The ground was possibly named for the Cuthbert Taylor who was living in Finsthwaite in 1600: LRO, DDPd 26/25. It appears on modern maps as Covey or Copy Hagg.
209 Possibly Bispham, Lancs., although it seems a long way to go for cheese.

paid Peter in Wood towards Bark peeled	1	0	0	
paid Margaret Braithwait for peeling &c 4 quarter & 5 Bushell	0	9	3	
August to Peter when he went to Ulverston	0	10		
September to Peter T[aylor] Brandy	[blank]			
A Hatt for Jaccey	0	0	8	
A hundred [sic] pro <.> <6> 9[li *interlined*] paid at 18s 9d per Hundred	[blank]			
Emey[210] 36 pound Idem	[blank]]			
Peter 2 Geese	0	1	6 1/2	
Old Ann[211] at Christing	1	1	0	
Peter 7ber one G[oose]	[blank]			
		s	d	
an ax	0	1	2	
a Coller	0	0	9	
18 poor bills	0	0	4 1/2	
when he paid William Coward	3	0	0	0
To William Masicks	10	9	0	
Brandy november Herren[212]	[blank]			
March 1738 to Peter Wife in our Loft	0	s 5		

[*p. 144*]

February 12th 1738 Then received [of Thomas Danson *interlined*] towards Land rent and also 4s & 6d Left unpaid Last year	li 3	s 0	
		s	d	q
Richard Robinson Land Tax		2	4	1
Windows		3	0	0
		5	4	1

---

210 Probably Emmy Morris, who had more cheese on p. 148.
211 Perhaps a term of affection for Peter Taylor's wife. Their daughter Elizabeth was baptised on 22 October 1738.
212 Herrings. The Backbarrow Company brought back Welsh herrings in ships returning from Bristol: Fell, *op cit.*, 306. In 1713 Nathan Kilner, the first agent at the Backbarrow Co., recorded a payment for sixteen barrels 'from Redwarfe to Beaumores att 10d per barrel bought of Owen Williams': CRO, BDX 295/2.

130   *The Account Book of Clement Taylor*

Constable Sess & poor	1	0	0
P[oor] Bills	8	0	0
Bigg 5 pecks	5	4	2

James Backhouse Debtor to C T	s	d	q
2 poor bills	1	1	1
<100 Bricks>213			
Newspaper	1	5	0
Well	[blank]		

February the 19th
Water Side Black
Hornt Cow bult at
Lawrence Harrison's paid 1s

[*paper in another hand, perhaps that of Mary Backhouse, pinned in here*]

1738 Cousin Clement Debtor			
July for two letters from		s	d
Mrs Taylor one 5d the other 9d		1	2
newcastle newspapers214			4 1/2
1739 September 4th paid wine at Kend[al]		10	0
for halfe bloomer reding ses		0	4
	li		
halfe Joseph Nusam thick cheese	1	17	2 1/2
halfe Carriage		1	5
John Gibson Cheese all	1	13	6 1/2
to Carriage		1	6
December to pay for Ann		13	0
	4 li	18	6 1/2
1739 September 25th Received			
	4	4	00
		14	6 1/2
2 poor bills		1	1	1
new's Paper		1	5	
		2	6	1
well paid John Cragge				
one shilling		12	0	

213 *cf* n. 113.
214 Probably the *North Country Journal: or the Impartial Intelligencer*: see G.A. Cranfield, *A Handlist of English Provincial Newspapers and Periodicals 1700–1760*, London, 1961, 72. There had been some early, but short-lived, newspapers in Kendal in the 1730s: *ibid.*, 10, and Marshall, *op. cit.*, 57–9.

[*p. 145*]

[*Clement Taylor*]

June 1738 Bark Livered from
Peter Taylor by C T Order
	quarter	
1 time	41	0
2d time to Margaret Wife	71	3

December 29 1738
Old Spinked Cow Buld
at Mr Rawlinson's paid 1s

December 23d 1739 Disburs'd
Thomas Strickland Gift to the Poor
of Finsthwait as followeth[215]

To Isaac Jackson	1	6
Dorothy Braithwait	1	2
Elizabeth Soalby	1	0
Jane Woodburne	1	2
James Danson	1	6
	6	4

December 22d 1738
Received Finsthwait Share
of the Interest of Thomas Strickland
Money being
Delt as below

	s	d
	6	1
To James Danson	1	7
To Dorothy Braithwait	1	6
To Jane Woodburne	1	6
& to Isaac Jackson	1	6

Good fryday April 20 1739
Edward Taylor Gift Disbursd

	s	
To James Danson	07	0
To Jane Woodburne	05	0
To Dorothy Braithwait	2	6
To Elizabeth Soalby	1	6

215 See n. 177. For Edward Taylor's charity below, see n. 182.

[p. 146]

February the 2d 1738
Then received of Henry Barwick
in part   li   s
the Sum of 6li 6s for Interest   6   6
February 1738 Received from John Satterthwait
by the Hand of James Backhouse   li
the Sume of   10   0
more of John Satterthwait
in April 1739   10   0

April 30th Blaikhorn Cow bult
at Mr Rawlinsons paid

June 7th 1739 Then received from   li
John Walker by his son   4   0
in part of 15li Due at Candlemas
Last
July the 3d Then received from
Mr Henry Barwick more in part   li
for Interest for last year   4   4
Remains Due 2li of
Last year
July 22 1739 Blackhornt
Cow bult at Mr Rawlinson's
2d time paid before

August the 4th 1739 Blaikhorn
Cow Bult 3d time at Mr R[awlinson's] paid
Read Cow Bult the same day
at same Place not paid
6th Little Spinkt why Bult
at Mr Rawlinsons paid 1s
Bro Edward M– –y [sic] the same Day
22d Blaikhornt Cow Bult
the <2> 4th time at Mr Rawlinson's
paid before
September the 11th Baikhorn [sic] Cow
Boult at Mr Rawlinson's 5th time
with new Bull
November 15th Great Lousey Why
Bult at Mr Rawlinsons
January 23d
1739   Old Spink Cow Buled

[*p. 147*]

October 19th Blaikhorn Cow
bult at Mr Rawlinson's 6th
time

Peter Taylor had two paid
<more> Less Then [*sic*] C Taylor

		li			
Thinn C. 16		212			
Richard 2li more Then [*sic*] C.T.					
Thick ones <20> <10> 20 C		442			
half [of *interlined*] Thick ones Charge			1	17	
Thinn ones C			1	13	6
			3	10	6[216]

January 24th 1739
Debtor to Benjamin Pennington
for Weaving a[s *interlined*] below

	li	s	d	
24 yards A hemp tow Webb	0	3	0	
19 yards of Blankets	0	2	4 1/2	
33 yards of Linn at 4d per yard	0	11	0	0
21 yards of Cotton at 4d per yard		7	0	0
	1	3	4	2

Young Spinkt Cow Bult 12 May
1740 at Mr Rawlinson's

[*p. 148*]

12d 2 quarters per yard Peter Sawrey

3	12	0
1	13	9
1	18	3
	12	0

| Emmy Morise Cheese with Carraige | 0 | 9 | 7 1/2 |

---

216 It is not clear to what this calculation refers.

February 1739 Lent Peter Taylor   10s
by Bief & 2d in Brass   3
more in Hagg when paid Preston   2
Debtor to Peter pro half a peck of B[arley]
peter Debtor to me for half a pecck [sic]
Debtor to Peter for 21li ½ of Chese
at 2d per li
Peter Debtor for Wood & Trennals   li   s   d
to me Halfe of   3   13   5
Marchant Debtor   18li   9s   10d

August Debtor to Benjamin Pennington
for Weaving <Bratt> 35 yards of Linsey
& Bratt aprons 3 yards
Shag 23 yards
26 yards of Harden <26> at 2d½ per yard

                              quarter   Bushell
New Close Bark   112   3
Knott & Farr Hagg &c   173   6
Farr Hagg being about 60 quarter
Coals in Farr & Jane Hagg 40 load

January 24 1740 Peter
Taylor Remains Debtor   11i   13s   9d

[p. 149]

February the 1th 1739 Then received
of Thomas Danson by
Shoemaker Work   3   10
More in Cash   2   11
                                            ─────────
                                            6   1
2d more   1   10
plowing   0   7   6

February 1739 Received more of John Walker   li   s
2d toward Interest of 1738   4   0
Remains behind of that year
7li
March 10 Bushels
of Barley at 6s 6d   <5>3   5
more   3   15

The Account Book of Clement Taylor   135

May 13 1740 Received of John Walker towards Interes [sic] for 1739	4	13	
September <22> 21th 1740 Blaikehorn Cow Bult at Mr Rawlinsons		s	d
more for 29 days Work		19	4
More of John Walker by 8 bushels of Barley	3	16	
more In Cash		8	4
September 10th More half a bushel of Wheat of J Walker			7s
February 2d 1741 Received of John Walker	li 12	s 0	
more 6 pecks of Barly	0	10	6
June the 10th Received more of John Walker by his Son	4	18	6

[*Isabel Taylor*]

Recieed [sic] of John Wallker February 2 11s by the hands of
Edward Taylor 1742
Received Oct 4 6 paid by the same hand

[*p. 150*]

[*Clement Taylor*]

Good friday April the 4th 1740 Disposed of Edward Taylor's <Leg> Money[217]	s	d
To Jane Woodburne	8	0
Elizabeth Soalby	3	0
Dorathy Braithwait	5	0
	16	
the Same time of William Dansons[218] to Jane Danson	4	0

217 See n. 182.
218 William Danson left £5 in trust for the poor of Finsthwaite by will dated 20 August 1729. From 1741 it was amalgamated with the Edward Taylor charity [see n. 182], but before that, as here, the interest was given to members of the Danson family: CRO, WPR 101/W1.

July 10   Nedy Burnes Cow bult [at]
1741   Lawrence Harrisons paid
August 21 Black hornt Cow bult
Mr Rawlinsons paid
30th Water Side Weggey Why Bult
at Mr Rawlinsons paid
Malley went to Kendal
2 weeks before Sent Jamses [sic][219]
September the 2d Watter Side
broad head Black brandt
Why bult at Mr Rawlinson's paid
September 24th Old read Cow belonging
to Water Side bult at L[awrence] Harrison paid
November 24th White Back Cow
Bult at Mr Rawlnson's [sic] paid
December 1th White Back Cow
bult at Mr Rawlinson's 2d time paid
13 March White Backed
Why which Lieth in farr Cow
House Bult at Lawrence Harrisons
paid
February 19th Water Side
Blaik hornt Cow which we have
Bult at Lawrance Harrison's
paid

[*Isabel Taylor*]

October 29
bleck horn Cow baled [sic] at
Risland the seck [sic] time

[*p. 151*]

[*Hand A*][220]

<A Valuation of Water
Side Estate ....
Three Tarn Potts ....
......>

219 St James's day, 25 July. His daughter Mary ('Malley') would have been fourteen years old, but it seems unlikely that she was going into service of any kind.
220 The writer of this hand has not been identified by name, but he appears to be Isobel Taylor's man of business, after the death of her husband. Her son was still only eleven, and, as her own entries on pp. 159, 165, and 181 *sqq* indicate, she herself was not highly literate. The only personal note in what he contributes to the account book is on p. 187, when in 1743 he went to Cartmel to be sworn in as churchwarden, but the list in CRO, WPR 101/W1 only indicates that 'Widow Taylor's servant' served in that year for Charley Crag.

[p. 152]

[Clement Taylor]

December 21th 1740
Then Disbursed of Thomas Strickland
Money[221] as Followeth being
60li Lent at Interest of 2li 10lii [sic]
per annum

		s	d
East Side of Coulton B[eck]		11	5
West Side		7	4
Nibthwaite		12	6
Haverthwaite		4	9
Finsthwaite		6	4
Rusland		7	8
totall	2	10	0

December 1740 laid out
for Sessments and repairs
to the House late belongin
to Margart [sic] Sawrey Deceased[222]

	s	d
To John Cragg for House Door	7	0
for a lock for the same	1	8
To Thomas Pepper for A Band & Gorgans and other Things	0	8
James Rawlinson Master Wage	0	4

221 See n. 177.
222 Margaret Sawrey was buried on 20 September 1738. By will dated 18 October 1734 she left her house to her niece Margaret Braithwaite, with reversion to three trustees, of whom Clement Taylor was one, for the poor inhabitants of Finsthwaite: LRO, DDPd 26/247. Margaret Braithwaite was buried on 15 April 1740. Here, the house is passing into the possession of the trustees, who are doing minor repairs, paid for out of a rent of 15s, the remaining 4s being distributed to four poor women. In 1746 the house was put up for sale by the then trustees, Isabel Taylor, her son Edward, and James Backhouse, and was sold for £25 19s to John Russell of Force Forge, who was bidding for Isabel Taylor. She paid the purchase money on 27 January 1747; for these transactions, see *ibid*. 26/274–6. Edward Taylor bought the house, which stood on the site of the present Green Cottage, from his mother in 1757: *ibid*. 26/290. In 1747 1s was added to the purchase money to round it up to £26, and it was treated as a charity in money like the others, the interest being distributed on Good Fridays from then on: CRO, WPR 101/W1. The house provided a church-warden; James Backhouse served in 1741 for 'the poor House at th' Green'. By 1769 it had been rebuilt: *ibid*.

138 *The Account Book of Clement Taylor*

George Taylor Master Wage and Sessment	0	4	3
Jonathan Wilson <M> Cunstable Sess	0	0	3
to Jane Coward for half a days Work	0	7	
John Walker Poor Sess	0	3	3
	11	0	1

The remaining 4[s] was Devided amongst Jane Danson Jane Woodburn Henry Taylor Wife & Elizabeth Sealby being 12d apeice

[p. 153]

December 1740 Then Disposed of Thomas Strickland Legacie[223] as follows

		s	d
To Isaac Jackson	0	1	6
To Jane Woodburne	0	0	6
To Henry Taylor W[ife]		3	10
Jane Danson		0	6

March 29 1741 Disbursed Edward Taylor's Legacie & William Dansons

		s	d
Jane Woodburne		5	0
Elizabeth Soalby		3	6
Jane Danson		6	6
Henry Taylor		5	0
	1	0	0

Sent [sic] Thomas Day Disbursed Thomas Strickland Gift as Follows for the year 1741

Jane Woodburne	1	2
Elizabeth Soalby	0	6
Henry Taylor	2	0
Isaac Jackson	1	6
Daniel of Nibthwait	1	0
	6	2

223 See nn. 177, 182, 218.

[*p. 154*]

5 Inch <stepe> [within Crown *interlined*] Crown

7 Innch of stepe[224]

Land Tax 14s 7d latter payment
with Bloomer Redding 1741

16th of April 1742 Then Livered
Thirty Sheep to John Cragg[225]
1th 15 Ews and Lams one with
Lam 4 which Had Lost lams
4 Gimer Hogg & 2 Wedder
Hoggs & 4 Wedders
to the Judgment of Thomas
Dixon and Thomas Danson
when retorned to C. Taylor

Wedders   7s
Hogs   5
Ews   5

[*p. 155*]

	s	d	q
December 1740 Account Disbursments for Margaret Sawrey House[226] & and [*sic*] Sessments Martinmas			
To Thomas Jonson for Smithy rent for 1740	0	0	2
To Mr Rawlinson Land Tax for 1740	0	5	0
To James Rawlinson Master Wage & Sessment	0	4	3
To William Coward poor Sess	0	4	0
to Robert Taylor poor Sess for 1741	0	2	0
July 25th to Barney [for 4 days ½ *interlined*] & Antoney 1741 Garnet <Each> 5 days at 1s 2d per day	11	1	

---

224 The meaning of this is not clear.
225 See n. 76.
226 See n. 222.

140   *The Account Book of Clement Taylor*

July paid Robert Atkinson		
27 1741 Master Wage	0	4
to John Coward for		
Latts & Nails	6	1
Jonas Skelding L[and] Tax	2	2
Smithy rent for 1741	2	
Constable Sess	0	3
to Robert Atkinson repairs of		
Church	0	3
Master Wage	4	0
Robert Taylor poor Sess	2	0
Jonas Skelding L[and] Tax	2	2
Master Wage	4	0

[*p. 156*]

[*Edward Taylor*]

Tom Cragg Farm 1756[227]			
taken off from Waterside			
Three Acres in the low			
Side of Dales adjoining	£	s	d
of White Stone	8	00	0
wool Moss & Meadow			
five Roods	0	16	0
Haggs Little and Great	<2>3	00<15>	0
for the Priviledge of			
Sheep going through			
Becking & two Haggs	0	05	0
Tarnhaw	0	02	0
Tom Cragg Share of			
Dales Matthew Meadow			
[*illegible*] Hill Haw			
Little Butt & Great Mea			
dow share & dales End			
Meadow			
Lag Parrock Fairing			
Brow Great and Little	9	12	0
	16	10	0

227 Here the extent of Tom Crag Farm is made clear. Some reorganisation of fields has taken place, but the farm still has its 'dales' in those shared with other farms. The lower part of the entry is badly blotted. The total is *recte* £21 15s.

Newlands Low Moss
& Rough Moss Will
Bridge End & 1/2 of
Great Ellerside
a a [sic] Rood in the Wooll
Moss Meadow
Little Moss wood In the
Room of Will Bridge End
wood
Peslands
T[homas] Huddleston to have the
Peslands this Year But
John Benson is to have
the Price deducted from the
Rent.
Peslands & Little [Butt interlined] to be plowd
and eaten only with Horses
& Sheep for three year for
the falling of the Wood

[p. 157]

[Clement Taylor]

	li	s	
30 december 1741			
Then Borrowed of John			
Coward	19	17	
February 2d 1741 received			
Land rent of Thomas Danson			
by Shoemaker	li		
Work	5	0	
in Cash	1	1	
Received May 29 Received Land rent			
& for 3 days plowing in full	1	1s	
February the 6th 1741 Then			
Received of Thomas Jonson			
toward Land rent	2	2	
May the 12th Then settled			
account with William Coward & he	li	s	d
remains debtor	<4	12	0>
<More a Calf>			
February 21 1742			
Thomas Danson for shoow <m>	ll	s	
-maker work	1	17	
for Land Rent	4	3<0>	

142   *The Account Book of Clement Taylor*

[*Edward Taylor*]

Edward Taylor's Finsthwaite

[*p. 158 is blank*]

[*p. 159*]

[*Clement Taylor*]

Isabel Fell wage for the year 1742 is	2	0
one Shilling given in part [of the Same *interlined*] for Earnest Thomas Thompson Wage is 4li 2d [*sic*] one shilling in part	4	1

[*Isabel Taylor*]

gave to Isabel Fell more
the 21 ten shillings beeing
part of the 28 shillings
which remained from
her wage for 1741
Aug 6 gave to Is[abel] Fell more ten shilling
Thomas Tompson wage for
1743 is four giuenes and
1 shilling more which
he has as ernest 4 4
to T[homas] T[hompson] September 21 5 shillings
Gven [*sic*] to Isabel Fell 8 shillins
Isabel Fell wage for
1743 is 2 paid
gven to Isabel Fell 8s remeans
due [*illegible*]
Thomas Tompson wage
for 1744 £4 7 6
Isabel Fell wages
for 1744 is 2 00
May 12
Debtor to Isabel Fell £4 paid
gave to Isabel Fell july
the 1 1744 2 shillings
more to Isabel Fell a cloak

9 shillings
more to Isabel Fell 18s

[*p. 160*]

[*Edward Taylor*]

Edward Taylor
Finsthwaite
Furness Fells
Lancashire

Edward Taylor
Finsthwaite
Furness Fells
Lancashire
1763

[*p. 161*]

[*Clement Taylor*]

3 of July 1742 Edward Burnes
White fased Cow Bult at Mr
Rawlinson's paid

[*Edward Taylor*]

Valuation of Tom Cragg
Estate as it is at present rented
to John Benson

	£	s	d
Antient Rent	10	1	0
Waterside Share in the Dales	3	0	0
Great Meadow	1	1	0
Wooll Moss Gate		5	0
Wooll Moss Meadow			
Great & Little Haggs			
Tarn Hows			

[p. 162]

[Hand A]

A Valuation of Waterside
Estate vizt

	£	s	d
Three Tarn Potts	4	0	0
Nether End of the Close & Low Field	1	15	
High Field	1	10	0
Hag Scarr	0	10	
Newland Head	0	5	0
Dales	3	0	0
Pincher Croft Dale & Meadow	0	15	0
Great Meadow	0	12	0
Little Drylands	1	00	0
Long Meadow Share	0	8	0
Wool Moss Meadow	0	12	0
Ditto Gail two years in three	0	5	0
Houses Orchards &c	1	0	0
	15	12	0

[Edward Taylor; written along the page]

		s	
Wooll Moss		5	
Wooll Moss Meadow		10	
Miew & Broad Moss		8	
Dales		3	0
Great Meadow		0	10
		4	13
deducted £3 2s from the Antient Rent	1	11	0
	£3	2	00

£	
11	
£3 2	deducted from
———	the Antient Rent £11
<8>7 0	£3 2s
———	
7 18	

[p. 163]

[Another hand, possibly brother Edward Taylor][228]

	ll	s	d
Februarij the 2 day 1742 Thomas Danson			
the ould rent	2	14	0
Two Haggs	2	15	0
Halfe an Ackre medow	0	4	0
Pincher Croft	0	15	0
Tarn Haw	0	2	6
Little Close	0	2	6
	6	13	0

	l	s	d
May the 20 day Remaining part of May day Rent and plowing	1 1	1	0

[Isabel Taylor]

February 3 1743

Then Received of Thomas
Danson toward Land
rent in Cash and Shoos
5 pound 4 shillings
May the 7 1744
then Recived of Thomas Danson
1£ 9s beeing the remaining
part of may day rent. at
the same time recived of
Thomas Danson for 3 days
plowing 7s 6d
February 1 1744 Rceived [sic] of
Thomas Danson in
part for Land rent
5 pound
May 15 1745 then Receved
of Thomas Danson the
the [sic] latter part of
land rent 1£ 9s

[Edward Taylor]
Edward Taylor 1754
1754

May 7th 1754

---

228 This hand is very like Clement Taylor's but he died in November 1742 and cannot therefore have written this entry in February 1743. The similarities suggest that it may be that of his brother Edward.

146   *The Account Book of Clement Taylor*

[*p. 164 is blank*]

[*p. 165*]

April the 13 1743

	Days
John Crage	1

Recived of John Crage
by worke 5 shillings
and 6 pence

John Crage	1

august the ?16

John Crage	3
John Prudance	2

Recived of John Crage
the Land rent for 1742
£15 0s 0d

Recived of John Crage November 10
1743 toward Land rent
£6   5   0

Recived of John Crage
Land rent for 1743
fourteen pound 3s

Received of John Crag february 8
1744 Land rent for
this year £14 3 shillings

<Debtor to John Crag 15s
Paid to J[ohn] Crag by plowing
8s 9d
Remaining debtor to J[ohn] Crag 4 3>
due to J[ohn] Crag 9s 3d

[*p. 166 is blank*]

[*p. 167*]

[*Edward Taylor*]

February 20 1748[229]

	Antony Garnot	5 days
	John Atkinson	5 days
	Thomas Gibson	5 days

229   These entries must refer to work done at Finsthwaite House after Clement Taylor's death; see xxiv.

27	Anthony Garnot	2 days
	John Atkinson	3 days
	Thomas Gibson	3 days
march 28		
	Antony Garnot	1 day
	John Atkinson	2 days
April 29		
	Antony Garnot	3 days
	John Atkinson	1 days
	Thomas Gibson	2 days
may 8		
	Antony Garnot	1 day
	Thomas Gibson	1 day
June 7		
	Antony Garnot	1 day
September		
	Antony Garnet	1 day
[*Hand A*]		
September 30	Antony Garnett	1 Day
Ditto	Thomas Gibson	1 Day
[*Edward Taylor*]		
november	Antony Garnot	1 day
18	Thomas Gibson	1 day
december	Antony Garnot	1 day
[*Hand A*]	Thomas Gibson	1 day
[*Edward Taylor*]		
1749		
February	Antony Garnet	1 day
	Thomas Gibson	1 day
march	George Drinkald	1 day
23	Antony Garnot	1 day & half
	Thomas Gibson	1 day & half
	George Drinkald	1 day & half
[*Hand A*]		
1 May	Thomas Gibson	1 day

[p. 168]

[Edward Taylor]

october 22 1750	Antony garnot	3 days
	Thomas Gibson	3 days
	George Drinkald	3 days

[Hand A]

February 27 1750	Anthony Garnett	2 Days
27 July	Anthony Garnett	1 Day
1751	Thomas Gibson	1 Day

[p. 169]

[Edward Taylor]

February 6 1748	George Park	3 day & half
	James	4 days
	Robert Woodburn	4 days
28	George Park	1 day
march <29> 31	James	1 day
August 2	James	1 Day
September 5	James	2 days
october 5	George Park	3 days
november 28	George Park	3 days
	John Howlm	3 days
December	James Fell	2 days
	John Howlm	2 days

[Hand A]

6 March,	James Fell	<.> 1 Day

[Edward Taylor]

6 july	George Park	2 Day
13	George Park	1 Day

[Hand A]

September 22	George Parke	1 Day
	John Holme	1 Day
23	George Parke	1 Day
	John Holme	1 Day

		D[ays]
March 6 1750		
	Matthew Taylor	2
	John Harrison	2
March 19	M[athew]	1
	J[ohn] Harrison	1
25	M[atthew] Taylor	1
	J[ohn] Harrison	1

[p. 170]

		Days
M[arch] 30	Matthew Taylor	1
	John Harrison	1
April 10	John Harrison	1
20	John Harrison	½ Day
May 10	John Harrison	1
May 17	John Harrison	1
June 12	John Harrison	1

[p. 171]

[*Isabel Taylor*]

	£	s	
John Benson rent for Land due 2 February 1749	10	1	

| august the 15 1750 received of John Benson in full for rent due 2 february last | 10 | 1 | 0 |

[*Hand A*]

February 7th 1750
Received of John Benson	£	s	d
by Cash	6	0	4
by Work	2	12	8
	£8	13	0

In part of Land Rent
Settled and received the Ballance in
full for the Year 1750

[p. 172 is blank]

[p. 173]

[Isabel Taylor]

Let to Matthew Taylor townend house and Land for 1749 the rent	£4	0	0
february 5 1749 Received of Matthew Taylor by the hand of his wife [in part *interlined*]	2	10	0
november 15 Recived of Matthew Taylor in Caish	1	1	0
by work	0	6	0

[Hand A]

January 29 Received of Mathew Taylor the remaining Part of last years Rent	0	3	0
Ditto Received of Mathew Taylor In Cash In part of next Year's Rent 1751	1	0	0

[p. 174 is blank]

[p. 175]

[Isabel Taylor]

	£	s	d
Thomas Danson Land rent	6	8	0
recived of Thomas Danson in part	£5	0	0
february 1 175 [sic] received the remaining part of last year rent	1	8	0
for half of top parrock	0	2	0

[*Hand A*]

Thomas Danson Rent	6	10	0

[*Isabel Taylor*]

february 1 1750 then received of Thomas Danson in part of Land rent	5	0	0

[*Hand A*]

By Cash & Work May 20 received of Thomas Danson the Remaining Part of Rent & Plowing	1	15	0
	£6	15	0
February 4 1752 Received of Thomas Danson			
By Shoemaker Work	3	7	6
By Cash	1	12	6
	5	00	0
Remaining Yet till May Day	1	10	0

[*p. 176*]

[*Hand A*]

Waterside Rent 1752	£11	0	0
5 February Received of Edward Taylor By Cash & By Ballance of Accounts the abovesaid Sum In full for one Year's Rent due 2nd February 1752	£11	0	0

[*p. 177*]

[*Isabel Taylor*]

Thomas Ashburner The Crag Estate[230] 1749 the rent of 8 5 due 2 February

---

230 Charley Crag.

[*Edward Taylor*]
February   £   s   d
2th Receved of Thomas Ashburner
rent Crage Estate   8   5   0
[*Hand A*]
24
December Received of Thomas Ashburner
of Cragg one year's Rent   8   5
Paid also Lime for Repairs   0   5

February 3d 1752
Received of Thomas Ashburner of   £   s
Cragg Rent for the same   8   5
and allowed him for Slate   0   3
and gave him again   0   1

[*p. 178 is blank*]

[*p. 179*]

[*Isabel Taylor*]

for the [*sic*] April 1743
then disbursed to the poor
of Finsthwait the intrest of
40 pound left by Edward Taylor &
Richard Robinson each 20 pound[231]
                                                        s   d
to Henry Taylor   15   0
To Jane Woodburn   8   0
To Elizabeth Soulby   7   0
To Grace Braithwait   2   0

the intrest of 5 pound left by Will Danson

[*George Simpson*]

To Chris[topher] Danson   2s
To William Fell   2

---

[231] Richard Robinson of Waterside left £20 for the poor of Finsthwaite, and £20 to buy books for poor children by will dated 2 February 1741: LRO, DDPd 26/254. For the Edward Taylor and William Danson charities, see nn. 182, 218. All the charities were eventually amalgamated to form one Good Friday charity: *The Public Charities of the Hundred of Lonsdale North of the Sands*, Ulverston, 1852, 50–1.

		s	d
Good Friday 1745			
To Henry Taylor		10	0
To Betty Soulby		5	6
To Jennet Woodburn		5	6
To Grace Braithwaite		5	0
To Robert Leck		4	0
To William Fell		4	0
To Chris[topher] Danson		2	0
	£1	16	0

The Interest of the said Legacies was divided as above for the year 1744

		s	d
Good Friday March 28th 1746 Then distributed to the poor Inhabitants of Finsthwaite viz.			
To Henry Taylor		14	0
To Jennet Woodburne widow		5	6
To Betty Soulby widow		5	6
To Grace Braithwaite Widow		5	0
To William Fell		6	0
	£1	16	0

[*Hand A*]

The Interest of the said Legacies was divided as above for the year 1746			
To Henry Taylor	0	14	0
To William Fell	0	14	0
To Betty Soleby	0	05	0
To Grace B[raithwaite]	0	03	0

[*p. 180 is blank*]

[*p. 181*]

[*Isabel Taylor*]

The account of money laid out by Isabel Taylor

154   *The Account Book of Clement Taylor*

november 14 1742 to the poor as dail at 3[d] apiece at funaral[232]	5	12	6
to T[homas] Danson for beef and butter	1	5	10½
for frute	0	1	4
24 november to Mr Backhouse the creditor side of an acount settled with him	14	18	0¼
to Edward Taylor for a cow november to the revd Mr Lowther for proving the desesed will	4	0	0
	1	19	8
to Dr Fell	0	6	0
to the Revd Mr Simpson for sermon & burial	1	1	0
28 to Gorge Danson for a cow drink	0	4	0
December Miles W for geese	0	3	4
Margret Harrison for cooking	0	5	0
4 Thomas Braithwait and Thomas Willson for hedging	0	5	6
for Tamerings to W[illiam] R[ownson]	0	1	6
for a ham 7 december	0	5	6
Edward Buckles	0	0	6
december 14 for Beef muton and veal Loaf shugar & lemons for punch	0	11	0
for bread at the funeral	0	4	6
4 gallon of Brandy & rum	[blank]		
for the sale of wood	1	4	0

232   Clement Taylor was buried on 14 November 1742. The sum distributed to the poor means that 450 poor people attended to receive their gifts. Funerals were in the nature of a holiday for the poor. At Warton John Lucas remarked of them: 'Nor . . . are the Poor forgotten, but all that come (and great Numbers I have seen upon this Occasion, many whereof would rather go 7 or 8 miles to a Penny-Dole, than earn Six Pence in the Time by a more laudable Industry) are put into some large Barn or Yard, and as they come out receive every one a Penny or more according to the Charity or Circumstances of the Giver . . .': *History of Warton*, ed. Ford and Fuller-Maitland, 24. William Hutton, incumbent of Beetham, recorded that 'My Father's Funeral in 1736 was the last that had a Dole; fourpence a piece to everyone that wou'd come for it': *The Beetham Repository*, ed. Ford, 171. The custom was burdensome to some people. When George Browne of Townend in Troutbeck, Westm., was buried in 1792, a payment of 6d apiece was made 'To the poor of our own town and none else'; only 21 people benefited: S.H. Scott, *A Westmorland Village*, London, 1904, 138.

[p. 182 is blank]

[p. 183]

	£	s	
january 29 1742 to Rager [sic] Jackson for work	0	3	6
to Rowland Lickbarrow for dying	0	7	0
31 to Anthony Garnet for woork	0	19	4
to William Danson for shoes	0	4	0
February 4 to Mary Coward funeral expences	4	4	0
5 to mr Miller for medisons & atendance	8	2	0
11 to William [Satterthwaite *interlined*] for coals & deal	3	<2>11	6
16 to Thomas Pepper for worke	2	9	0
[February 8 *interlined by Hand A*] Alice Anderson [*Hand A*] for Interest	0	15	8 1/2
February 8 Isabel Anderson for Interest[233]	0	15	8 1/2
16 To Mr Simondson for Medicins		[blank]	
21 For Tableing Stones & Expences	0	11	8
March 4 Paid William Massicks for Coaling	0	9	4
March 2nd Paid William Rownson	1	1	0
10 Paid for Stags Grass at Tharfingsty[234]	0	14	0
12 Mr Ashburner for Books for the poor			

233 Alice Williamson of Barrow Fold, Staveley, by will dated 19 September 1728, left money to her nephew William Anderson for the maintenance of his four daughters, among whom were Alice and Isobel. She was buried at Cartmel in 1732 and one of her executors was Richard Robinson. He died in 1741 and here his sister is dealing with the uncompleted executorship. Alice Anderson was baptised on 19 March 1721 at Cartmel, so she would have been 21 in 1742; the legacy was paid in 1744. Alice Williamson's will and inventory are at LRO, DDPd 36/7–8 and the receipts for the legacies are *ibid*. 36/12; *ibid*. 26/250 is a certificate of the baptisms of three of the Anderson daughters, sent to Richard Robinson in January 1740.
234 Thorphinsty, in Cartmel Fell.

Children being a Lega-
cy left by Richard R[obinson]235
Ballance of an Ac-
count with P[eter] Taylor   0   16

[*p. 184 is blank*]

[*p. 185*]

	£	s	d	qr
& Paid him	0	2	1	1/2
March 14 Paid Doctor Croft				
for a Journey	0	18	6	
for a Bottle of Sack	0	02	2	
16 Paid Thomas Barrow				
for Flax & other Things		2	4	
26 Paid James Rigg				
for himself & Man two				
Days	0	1	8	
Paid Mr Simpson for				
Edward Learning	0	4	0	
Paid Henry Taylor for				
getting Stones & other Work	0	3	9	
April 6 Paid Fardinando				
Casson for Calling Sale				
at Waterside	0	5	0	
1 Being Good Friday				
Gave to the Poor of Fins-				
thwaite the Interest of				
£20 given by R[ichard] R[obinson]	0	16	0	
April 30, Paid Reginald				
Grigg & Co for pulling				
down & rebuilding the				
late dwelling House				
at the South End of Clement				
Taylor236	£2	6		
Henry Taylor 8 days				
Work	0	5		
Roger Jackson for				
Serving the Wallers	0	5	3	
William Massicks for Ditto	0	1	6	

[*p. 186 is blank*]

---

235 See n. 231 and below p. 185.
236 For this, see xxiii–xxiv.

[p. 187]

1743
May 3. Paid to Elizabeth Denny for Eating & Drinking at the Commission held there the 9 & 11 April 1743[237]	2	14	0
Blue Shag for Edward Bretches & Mohair	0	4	9
Foure Stone of Hair for Plaister	0	5	0
May 7 Paid Mr Backhouse for a Deal Plank	0	4	0
Paid Mr Backhouse for an Ovid de Tristibus[238]	0	2	6
Some Black Damask for Mending Edward Waistcoat	0	2	3
Paid to Backbarrow Company for 64 Iron Ballisters & four Iron Railes	9	12	2
June 9 1743 Paid at Cartmell at going of Chappel Warding[239]	0	9	10
Paid for being Swore in in December	0	2	0
July 2 Paid Agnes Braithwaite being a Legacy left her by R[ichard] R[obinson] with Interest for 5 Months the Principal being £10[240] 10	9	10	
Expences at Kendal when it was Paid	0	0	8
December 3. Paid for Ticking Buttons Thread Silk Twist & Mohair & Stay Tape for Edward	0	4	0

[p. 188 is blank]

---

237 At the inn at Newby Bridge.
238 Presumably for Edward, who was still being taught in Finsthwaite. No particular edition can be identified.
239 See n. 220.
240 Richard Robinson left £10 each to his cousins, Agnes, Ruth, and Jane, daughters of John Braithwaite, late of Hawkshead Field. Agnes's receipt for her legacy is LRO, DDPd 26/269.

158 *The Account Book of Clement Taylor*

[*p. 189*]

	£	s	d
November 10 1743			
Paid John Cragg for a Coffin[241]	0	13	
more for a Gate	0	2	6
Ditto for Cutting 6 Loads & Seven Sacks of Coals	1	3	0
Ditto for Carriage	0	13	0
Ditto for breaking a Rock Grubbing & felling Ash Birch Wood	0	10	6
another Gate	0	1	6
Paid James Rawlinson for Landing Freestone	0	2	6
January 25 Paid John Corthwaite the Remaining Part of £12 for Rigging, Chimney Pieces Pillars, & Copings for Pallisadoes & Trough as the Account sheweth	7	2	0
January 27. Paid William Coward the Poor Assessment at the Rate of 18 Poor Bills	1	7	9
February 1 Paid Anthony Garnett for 83 Days Work	2	15	4
Paid Ditto at the Same Time for 9 Rood of Wall in the Hagscar at 9d per Rood	0	6	9
Paid Ditto for 42 more in the Hagscar at 8d per Rood	1	<7>8	00
Paid Ditto for Work done at Newby Bridge House[242]	1	7	0
February 7 Paid Benjamin Ayrey for Casting Iron Spit	0	15	1 1/2

241 This was an expensive coffin, and was probably Clement Taylor's own, although if so payment was made a year after he died. His mother's coffin cost only 8s: see n. 247.

242 On 9–10 March 1741 Elizabeth Denny of Cartmel sold 2/5 of a property at Newby Bridge to Clement Taylor and James Backhouse: LRO, DDPd 36/11. This was the inn, now the Swan Hotel. The rest of it belonged to the Robinsons of Newby Bridge, as is made clear in Edward Taylor's own account book, where the rent is detailed: *ibid.* 26/338.

[*p. 190*]

[*Clement Taylor*]

	li	s	d
February the 7th 1740 Then rackoned [with Thomas Jonson *interlined*] & he Remains Debtor	1	15	6
Received Land rent of Thomas Danson by Shooe Maker Work & Cash	5	0	0
June More of Thomas Danson 1741 for plowing & Land rent	1	16	6

[*p. 191*]

[*Hand A*]

<May 1744 ......>

February 4 1743 Paid William Anderson the Interest of Seventeen Pounds Eighteen Shillings & two Pence	0	15	8 1/2
February 6, Paid for Peeling Bark Cutting Coaling & Leading Coals in the Top of Parrock	3	08	02
March 20, Paid to Mr Bare for four yards of <Everlasting> Dimety White & 1 dozen & 1/2 of Buttons for Edward Taylor	0	6	0
May 11, Paid to Thomas Johnson for Cutting Coaling & leading the Coals In Edy Sand Moss Newlands Fairing-Brow, Cutting at 3s 6, Coaling at 4s, and leading at 2d per Load, Paid him In all	9	16	4
June 2, 1744 from Bowth a Quart of Line Seed oyl	0	0	8
White Lead	0	1	4
Spanish Brown 2lb 1/2	0	0	7

& other Things for the Cornice of the House,	0	6	10
Paid William Coward for Serving overseer of Poor for Tom Cragg	0	15	0

[*p. 192*]

March 22 1744 Paid to William Satterthwaite the [Remains *interlined*] of £13 9s 5d In full for the 1/32 Part of a Ship Called the Jane	3	9	5
October 1745 Paid for Advertising Cragg & Spent at the Sale when it was lett[243]	0	13	2
May, 8 1744, Bought of Mr Bare 2 yards 1/2 of Black Everlasting at 9d per yard for Buttons & Twist in all	0	5	10
A pair of Knee Buckles	0	0	3 1/2
A Pocket Book	0	0	8
June 9 1744 A <pair> dozen of Buttons	0	0	6
Paid Mr Hunter for Edward Boarding & Schooling for 36 Weeks[244]	3	3	0
& to the Maid	0	1	0
Gave Mr Hunter for Cockpenny for Edward	0	10	6
Gave to Dr Morton for Edward Taylor	2	2	
August, 10, 1744, Paid Mr Rigg for Medicines	0	5	0
Paid to John Harrison for a Hat for Edward,	0	8	6
Waistcoat Buttons & Diaper Tape	0	0	8

243 This must be Tom Crag, unless the family was acting for Peter Taylor at Charley Crag, who left Finsthwaite about this time.

244 Edward's school is not named, but it was certainly Browedge, where his uncle William and probably also his father were educated. Mr Hunter paid William's bursary in 1721 [p. 9], but has not otherwise been identified.

[p. 193]

Paid for a Book	0	0	8
September 22 Paid for Clark's Essay[245]	0	2	6
Paid James Rigg for Makeing Edward's Cloaths	[blank]		
August 3, 1744 Paid to Reginald Grigg & Company for Ruff-Casting the South-End of the House	1	03	01
Paid to Robert Kendal for Sand	0	04	0
Paid for one Day Working Ground Work at Newby [Bridge *interlined*] House[246]	0	0	10
Paid Mother Taylor's Funeral Expences[247]	14	4	07
Gave Mr Law at the Comission	2	02	00
Paid William Satterthwaite towards 1/32 of a Ship	10	00	0
Paid Alice Anderson her Legacy & Interest[248]	19	12	10 1/2
<...> Paid Robert Birkett Mr Gurnell's Draft <of> on Mr Taylor	2	12	6
February 1 1744 Paid to Thomas Danson for Edward Taylor Shoes	1	3	7
Paid to Mr Sergeant for Edward's Learning to Dance	0	7	0
Gave to Mr Hunter for a Cockpenny for Edward	0	10	6

245 John Clarke (1687–1734), schoolmaster and classicist, was the author of *An Essay on Study, wherein directions are given for the due conduct thereof, and the collection of a Library*, London, 1731 (repr. 1737, and in Dublin, 1736).
246 See n. 242.
247 Clement Taylor's mother, Elizabeth, was buried on 29 April 1744. The payment for her coffin is on p. 194.
248 See n. 233.

[*p. 194*]

	£	s	d	
Paid to Captain Thomas Barrow for Edwards [*sic*] Taylor Boarding		0	10	0
Gave to Edward Taylor for Pocket Money	1	1	0	
2½ yards Shag for Edwards Bretches, Buttons & Mohair	0	5	9	
October 6 1744, Paid to George Stamper for Choosing Dales for Clement Taylor[249]	0	1	6	
<December 14 Paid to William S...>				
January 29 1744 Paid William Anderson for Interest not Due till Candlemas	0	15	8	
February 2; Paid to Sarah Addi<n>son Now & before the Intrest of ten £ for two years	01	6	8½	
February 8 Paid John Cragg for a Coffin	0	8	0	
For Cutting Coalwood 2 Load, Carriage one Load	0	7	0	
	0	2	0	
Paid John Cragg for 42 Days Work done at Waterside	1	10	0	

[*p. 195 is blank*]

[*p. 196*]

[*Clement Taylor*]

	s	d
prisoners & Correction Receipts[250]	6	4
June 12th & 17th Bridges & King's troops	6	<4>8
Master of House of Correction	2	6
12 & <Receipts pro Bridges & publick ... 17	6	8>
at Mid Summer when I paid Bridge Money Staying all Night	5	6
to John Carter	0	6

---

249 See xxiv.
250 Further sheriff's business; see n. 101.

July 31th <Licences> Articles & Acquittances				
Prisoners	1	3	4	
September Ribble Bridge Receipts		3	4	
at Michaelmas Sessions		2	6	
Profit of Rools[251]		6	0	
December 1735 receipts for 4 Warrants		13	4	
<January 14th Spent going to Lancaster Sessions to pay 4 Warrants>		<7>0	0	
profit of 4 Orders			7	0
at Lent Assizes Size Articles & receipts & profit of Roll	1li	6s		

		s		
July Peter Wife	0	8		
	0	8		
June 23 Peter Taylor	0	10		
June 12th Peter Wife	2li	0		
May 18 Peter Taylor	3li	3s		

	li	s	d
April the 28 1736 Peter Taylor	1	1	
William Parke per William Cow[ard]	2	1	1½
peter Taylor	0	10	0

	li	s	d
Peter Taylor	1	3	2
Peter Taylor	2	6	
William Coward	5	5	
Jacob Park	2li	2s	

August 10th Lent Mr Sandys	10li	10s	
September 19 Then Lent Miles Harrison	21	0	
June 25th J[ames] B[ackhouse] Debtor to C T J[ames] B[ackhouse]	19li	3s	

[*miscellaneous calculations on a scrap of paper pinned in here*]

[*p. 197*]

April 15th 1735 1th Sessions

To Mr Edge pro Swearing me	3	0
More Idem pro ?a part G[252]	2	6

---

251 Rolls.
252 The meaning of this is not clear.

164   *The Account Book of Clement Taylor*

Dinner with Justices at Lancaster		2	6
11 persons Treat at Elizabeth Dennyes	1	1	6
to Mr Braithwait pro Order	0	2	6
at 1th Sessions to John Carter	0	1	0
Spent at 1th private Sessions E[lizabeth] Denny's[253]		2	0
Spent at Ulverston & Cartmel in Receiving 40 Warrants		2	0
June 24th When I paid Bridge Money &c & Staying all Night at Lancaster		5	6
at the Same time to John Carter		0	6
July the 15th at Mid Sumer Sessions		5	6
to John Carter		0	6
July 31 Spent in Colecting Warrants & presentments		0	7
August Viewing the High Ways		3	0
at Summer Assizes		10	0
September 23 & at Signing Sess bills being 2 Sessions		3	0
at Michaelmas Sessions		5	6
Spent in Collecting 20 Warrants & sending them out		2	6
<profit of Rolls January 14		7	0>
January 14th Spent in going to Lancaster Sessions		7	0
Spent at Elizabeth Denny's at the Special Sessions		2	6
at Lent Assizes		10	0
Order		1	0

[*pp. 198 and 199 are blank*]

[*p. 200*]

February 2d paid to Walker & 2 Garmens towards Cutting of Knott Wood Equally amongst them	1 3	s 15	
March 2d to Walker when paid Little faire	0	11	

---

253 At the inn at Newby Bridge. Meetings of sessions, when a particular local matter had to be dealt with, were occasionally held in public houses.

William Garman 20 Herrin	0	[blank]	
John Garman 42	0	1	2
Walker 42	0	1	2
Walker ½ Bushel of potatoes	0	2	0
William Garman ½ Bushel potatoes	0	2	0
May [12th *interlined*] in Our House to Kurby Wife	1	6	0
J Walker			
May 23 in Our parler	li	s	
when he paid Work fook[254]	1	2	
Hugh & Antoney 27 days Table at 5d per Day which Walker is to pay	0	11	3
June 2d To William Garman when he paid Bark peelers	li 2	0	
Peter Taylor Barley & Herren	[blank]		
June 16th	li		
To Elizabeth Kirby &c	1	0	
To John Garmen	2	2	
7 of June		s	
To Peter Wife	0	5	0
To Elizabeth Kirby in farr Hagg	0	10	0
John Garman Man Robert 4 days Table	0	1	8
John Walker Men 4 [days *interlined*] Table		1	8
Peter Taylor Wife	0	5s	0

[*p. 201*]

Emmy Moris Cloath for	l	s	d
a Cloak	0	7	0
A quarter of a 108 of Cheese	0	5	4 ½
Peter Taylor the Same	0	5	4 ½
July 29th to Peter Taylor	1	0	0
Emmy 27 pound of Cheese at 2d a pound & half of mine C T and mine a pound more than Peters the whole 108li at 1li 5s <1li <.> 9<½> 0> 1li 7s 9d			
	l	s	
August 16th to Peter Wife	1	1	
to Robert Leck			

254 Folk, the workmen.

on William Garman Account		0	10	
To Emmey by Kurby Wife		0	3	<2> 1
29 to Elizabeth Kurby on John Garmans Account		0	9	8
Peter Taylor a Hoop of wheat		[blank]		
More to Robert Leck on William Garmans Account		0	10	1
September				
27 To Peter Taylor		1	1	0
To Elizabeth Kirby		0	10	0
To William Garman		0	10	6
28 to Peter when his wife to Cart laine [sic]255		1	1	0
October Peter Taylor when he 15 was Carding in our House		3	3	0
To Agnes Dixon to buy beef with		0	10	0
November to Peter Wife when she paid the man that wheeled Wood in		1	8	0
Elizabeth Kirby &c in full		3	7	0
December to Peter when he paid James		2	0	0

[p. 202]

May 8 1734 [illegible]			s	d	
William Coward a Calfe & a quarter to our self besides on the same Calfe			8	2	
2 lam Skinns			0	4	
1 lam Skinn			[blank]		
2 Sheep			10	11	
1 Tup Bowth Fair256			6	10	
Great Tup Blease			8	00	
a Wedder			5	8	
2 stone & a half of Tallow			5	10	
A Sheep			7	5	2
A Sheep			7	2	2
	paid	3li	0	5	

255 See n. 94.
256 See n. 106. For the tup 'Blease', see intro n. 20, xv. The tallow would be for making candles or rushlights.

June 10th 1735 Sheep [&c *interlined*] Sold to
William Coward this year

Weggy Calf	0	8	7 1/2	
July 5th Sturdy Hogg	0	2	11	
September 9th 6 Sheep & a lam	1	8	7	1
October the 27th 4 Sheep	0	16	4	
December Broken L[eg?] Ewe[257]	0	2	10	2
William Coward Debtor	4	10	6	1/4

[*p. 203*]

June the 30th 1735 Then took Measure
of 12 quarter & 1 Bushell [Bark *interlined*] from Elizabeth Kirby in my
Hay loft for John Satterthwait by the
Order of George Muckelt per C.Taylor

	quarter	Bushell
July 11th from Peter Taylor at Finsike	3	1
17 from John Prudance in my Barn	15	2
Last Week [of *interlined*] July from John Prudance in my Barn	4	1
15th of August from John Prudance in Barn	3	4
22 from John Prudance in my Barne	3	4
30th from John Prudance	17	0
Peter Taylor at Finsike	2	2
30 George Braithwait Wife	2	4
September 9th Jane Wood burne	1	4

October the 4th 1735 Then Took
measure of 9 quarter & 3 Bushell of Bark at
Water Side from Richard Robinson
for Marchent Satterthwait per C.T.
15th Then took Measure from Agnes
Dixon in Charley Cragg Barn of
7 quarter & 5 Bushell of Bark for John Russel
by C Taylor

---

257 Two of what would now be called casualty animals were sold in this section, a hogg with sturdy and a ewe with a broken leg. The sum is *recte* £2 19s 4 1/4d, but perhaps other matters were involved.

168   *The Account Book of Clement Taylor*

December the 17th 1735 Then Took
Measure from Thomas Jonson in Town End
Barne by The Order of John
Russel of [*blank*] 35 quarter of
Oke Bark & 2 Barels
per C.Taylor
September 1737 Bark Measured
from Margaret Braithwait in Old
House which Came out of Jolivertree
wood 15 quarter 6 Bushell

[*p. 204*]

January 22d 1733
Then Accounted with Thomas Jonson
About Redding Work

a peck of Wheat		0	1	8
a Chese 1li			1	8
Tobacco			0	6
			3	10
A Chese 9li 3oz			1	3
A Stone of hemp			2	10
	paid		7	11
	Cheese		8	9

Debtor Thomas Jonson pro Coaling
& Cutting Cordwood in
Redding at 4s per load

5 load & 4 Sacks Cutting			19	6
10 load [& 8 Sacks *interlined*] Coaling at 4s per load	2	2	8
Mawing [*sic*] 2 Days		0	1	4
Hay Working 4 days at 4d			1	4
Broad Meadow Fogg mind[258]			1	0
	paid	3	5	10
March 6 days at Well 4th		0	3	0
		3	8	10

Then rackned with Thomas Jonson
& paid him and his Wife pro all
work Done

---

258   The note 'mind' indicates that he was reminding himself to remember something.

[*p. 205*]

	quarter	Bushell
June 27 1739 Then John Walker Measured Bark to Marchant Wife in Hayloft	20	6
The Same Day from Elizabeth Kirby & Dixon at Town End	6	0
July 10th More in George Old House Measured by C Taylor by Order of Merchant	<. . . .> 13	3
to from [*sic*] Emmy Morris	18	4
August 29th from John Garman	32	1
<Peter Taylor for a Hoop of W[heat]> Elizabeth Kirby more	04	3
William Garman by Elizabeth Kirby	22	5
to more 4d	0	4
Kirby Wife	45	2
Peter Taylor	8	6

[*p. 206*]

Account of money I paid Mary & Roger toward 1733		
Roger 1 stone &c of wool at	6s	
Roger a Shift &c 3 yards 1/2		
Mary when she went to Doctor	2	0
August [Mary *interlined*] a Smock Cloth 2 yards 1/2	5	0
More to Mary at Esthwait	1	0
more a Calf Skinn Mary		
March 12 a bottle of Dafey	1	3
18 Roger Jackson a Napkin	0	10

Miles Harrison Knot	tuns	
Timber	<500>	504 1/2
Bark Quarters		600
Coals		80

The price 1<7>78li
at 10 Bushell of Bark of the tunn

170   *The Account Book of Clement Taylor*

		l	s	
2d June To Roger		2	2	
paid Mary Singleton		1	0	
More pro Mr Branthwait		0	18	
being in full for her wage for 1733				
June Roger A Napkin			1s	2d

[*p. 207 is blank*]

[*p. 208*]

	quarter	Bushell		
June the 30th 1733 Account of Bark Mesured by John Satterthwait				
Imprimis by Joseph Pull & J[ames] Danson	14	0		
July 26 by Joseph Pull & Peter T[aylor] in Mathew Barn	19	1		
The Same Day In Jonathan Barn per Joseph Pull & Peter T[aylor]	6	4		
The Same Day per H[enry] Crosdall	9	2		
August 15th In William Coward Barn per Edward Barwick	13	5		
In Jonathan Barn per P[eter] T[aylor] & Joseph Pull	07	4		
the Same Day In Matthew Barn per Joseph Pull & P[eter] Taylor	13	6		
29th per Edward Barwick		15	4	
September Edward Barwick	1	2		
4				
24th by John Pruday in Thomas Danson Cowhouse	<4>5	6		
November by Margaret Braithwait	5	7		
3d James Danson	27	3		
Thomas Jonson	8	4		

	li	s	d
January 24th 1733 Then Received of John Satterthwait in part for Redding Bark	21	0	0
February 2d Received of The Same at Bouth per Son Clement Test Christopher Taylor	7	5	0

More 12li of Soape
More B[randy] 2 gallon & 3 quarts
& <better> pint A Gill [*sic*]

		li	s
May 16 Received More of The above said 6 Moiders & of his Wife 10 Gunies		8 10	2 10
July 20 Received of Marchant Satterthwaite		10	0

[p. 209]

N 2 May 1732			
N 3 June 1732	147	B 3	
N 4 July 1732		18	
April 1732		45	
June 1733		66	3
September 1732			
August 1732			
October 1732		Maychel Bottle	
November 1732		holds near	
December 1732[259]		5 quarts	

	quarter	Bushell
July Then Took Measure from Peter Taylor in My Barn of George Muckelt Bark per Marchant Saterthwait Order per me Clement Taylor	8	4
of Richard Robinson <6>	6	4
of John Robinson	24	2
of John Prudey in our barn	5	0
of Peter Taylor	20	1
of George Braithwaite	15	0
of John Prudey at Sinder hill	6	6
John Prudey in Stable	11	1
	66 quarters	4 Bushels[260]

	l	s	d
June 23 1733 Account of what I Sold William Coward This year			
A Calf	0	8	9
A Sheep Skin December		1	0
July 7th A Lam	0	3	4
a Sheep Skin December		1	2

259 It is not clear to what these dates and notes refer.
260 *recte* 97 quarters and 2 bushels.

172 *The Account Book of Clement Taylor*

October 2d a tupp	0	4	4
a Sheep Skin	0	0	8
a Calf	0	7	0
November 2 Sheep & a Skin		8	6
3 Sheep		12	0
1 Sheep		7	2
[*at side*] Belly Liver		6	6

September 20th 1733			
to Thomas Jonson pro tobacco	0	0	6
More a Peck of Wheat			
More per Agnes Dixon	0	5	<0>6
October 2d To Peter Taylor Wife		10	0
9 To Edward Barwick		2	0
15 To Edward Barwick		<5>2	6
16th To Peter Taylor		10	0
27th To Edward Barwick a peck			
of Malt			
November to Jennet woodburn		15	0
12 to Edward Barwick		9	6
18 to Peter Taylor pro <1> 2 Sheet			
of parchment & one of paper		3	10 ¹/₂
peter a Cheese 9li 1oz			
Jonson A Cheese 9li 3oz			
December 2d to Peter Taylor		10	0
4 paid Agnes Dixon		4	5
Jonson a Ston of Hemp			
paid Henry Crosdale			
pro leading 4 quarter B[ark]	0	3s	0
12 Henry Crosdale in full	0	12	
Jane Woodburne			
for Leading Coals & Bark			
7 load 7 sack			
Bark 11 quarter 7 Bushel		16	4
December When Margaret Braithwait			
paid to Peter Taylor		13	0
December 16 paid Jonson W[ife] not paid		09	11
if she calle for it next Weddensday			

[*p. 211*]

May 4th 1733 Disbursed to Peter Taylor
towards Cutting Coalwood & peeling Bark
in Lending Redding as below

	li	s	d
Imprimis To John Pruday by Peter Order when John Went to Carlile	0	10	0

11th To Edward Barwick Towards paying for Bief &c	0	11	0
June 12 paid Peter Taylor in part in Redding	8	0	0
18 paid Peter pro 2 Sheet of paper	0	1	3
21th To [sic] for proving John Will[261]	0	8	6
Expences of J[ames] B[ackhouse] & C. T.	0	2	0
31th paid Henry Croasdale per his wife	0	10	0
July 7th paid Peter Taylor 19li of Cheese at 1s 3d per li		[blank]	
Thomas Jonson a Cheese 11li			
11 paid Edward Barwick per the hand of Joseph Pull	0	4s	0
<To the Same> On the same account to [sic]			
To Robert Harrison	0	1	0
July paid Edward Barwick per they [sic] hands of John & Samuel Coward for felling wood	0	1	10
August to Henry Crosdall per the 5th the hand of Thomas Danson	1	1	0
29th To Edward Barwick at Matthews spent	0	0	4
Henry Stewardson &	0	<1>0	11
Henry Taylor Each one Day			11
7th To Edward Barwick	1	1	0
To Edward Barwick per J[oseph] P[ull] pro Chopping Bark	0	0	10
September 10 paid Edward Barwick for Bark peeling and Leading & 6 Days work in full being what remained behind	0	2	6
at the Said Time Gave Edward Barwick toward Wood Cutting	0	2	6

261 John Taylor of Charley Crag [see 241, *sub* Taylor, John, collier] made his will on 8 April 1732. He left all his property to Clement Taylor and James Backhouse, in trust to sell it and pay the interest on the sum raised to his mother Alice for her lifetime, provided that her parish pension of 12d a week was continued. After her death the capital was to be divided between his two brothers and three sisters, and his brother Peter was to be allowed to buy the house at Charley Crag for £50: LRO, DDPd 26/234. The house was sold to Peter Taylor on 15 January 1734: *ibid.* 26/236. The probate accounts are *ibid.* 26/233. John Taylor owned only his work tools, valued at 6s 8d, a chest and a table (3s 6d), a horse (£2 5s), some clothes, and the money in his purse (£1 2s), and he had £5 owing to him as 'book debts'. The family spent 9s on 'veal &c for the Funeral'. Alice's parish allowance is mentioned on p. 121; see also n. 188.

[p. 212]

April 1733 Expences <on> about Redding Wood

Spent at Mathew's[262] when wood was bout	0	1	6
Spent at Mathews when I design'd to Fest Bark peeling &c	0	1	2
June 12 Sent Bark peelers 2 Duzen [sic]	0	2	0
Spent at Matthews at other times	0	0	4
Spent at Mathews when Bark Chopp'd	0	0	2
31 Spent at the Same when Measured Bark to Satterthwait 1th time	0	1	0
July 26th Spent at Mathew's 2d time	0	1	0
August 5 Spent at Mathews 3 time	0	1	0
29 Spent at Mathews 4 time	0	0	8
November Spent at 2 Sundry times	0	0	4

January 16th To Peter Taylor
by Mr Dodson pro Writing
Deed 2s 6d & bond 6d[263]   03s

[p. 213]

Lancashire[264] By Virtue of a Roll under the hands & Seals of his Majisties Justices of the Peace & Quorum made at the General Quarter Sessions of the peace held at Lancaster in and for the said County the 3d Day of October Last past You are required to Collect Levy & gather within your Divisions the Sume of Seven Shillings & Eight pence farthing being your <being> proportion of 32li 10s (togather [sic] with your Charges of the said Roll) Charged upon this hundred for Conv<a>eying of Vagrants & thereof make Payment to me at the House of Alice Benson Widow

262 Matthew is Matthew Taylor of Town End [see 241], whose wife Phyllis clearly brewed beer for sale.
263 Probably the deed for the sale of Charley Crag, 15 January 1734: LRO, DDPd 26/236. Deeds were often supported by a bond, but this one does not survive.
264 Copies of orders from the High Constable of Lonsdale Ward to the parish constables of Colton. Clement Taylor served as constable in 1732: CRO, BPR 17/C2/1. On the duties of the high and petty constables, see M.A. Logie, 'Benjamin Browne of Troutbeck, High Constable of Kendal Ward', *CW2*, 1971, 75–89.

in Ulverstone on Thursday the 22d Day
of February Instant here of fail not
Given Under my Hand the fifth Day
of February 1732
    R.S C[hief] Constable

| To the Constables | paid per C Taylor | 7s | 8d | 1qr |
| of C[olto]n | Receipt pro the same | 0 | 2 | 00 |

Lancashire By Virtue of an Order made by
his Majesty's Justices of the peace & Quorum
at the last General Quarter Sessions of
the Peace held at Lancaster in & for the said
County You are required to Collect levy
& gather within [your *interlined*] Parish the Sume of four
Shillings & four pence charged Upon
you for the relief of the poor prisoners
in Lancaster Cast<e>le And Thereof make
payment to me at the house of Alice
Bensons [*sic*] Widow in Ulverstone on
Thursday the twenty Second Day of February
Instant hereof fail not Given Under
my hand The fifth Day of February 1732

To The C[onstables] of C[olton]	R.S C[hief] Constable			
Paid per C Taylor		4s	4d	0q
Receipt		0	2	0

Sperits of Salvelateley[265]

[*p. 214*]

Lancaster In Answer to the Articles Sent us by
March the High Constable we whose names are
10th   Subscribed [we answer <..> *interlined*] present
1732

First, That no Felonies have been
Comitted in our <Township> Constablewicks Since the
last Assizes
Item, That No Vagabonds have been appre-
hended or did aney Escap to our knowledge
Item, Watch when required duly kept
Item, No Popish recusants

265 Sal volatile.

Item, No Decay of Houses, Tillage is
well performed
Item, No Unlicenced Malsters
Item, No Unlicenced Ale Houses
Item, Ale House keepers keep good orders
Item, No Engrossers, Forestallers or
Regrators
Item, Our Highways are in good Repair
Item, Our Poor are well provided for
Item, No Common Drunkards or
Swearers

paid 1s C[lement] T[aylor]
                              C[onstables] of C[olton]
                G[eorge] D[rinkell]

Lancashire By Virtue of an Order from the
Receiver General for the Said County you are
required to give Due Notice to the
Collectors of the Land Tax & window
Money within your Divisions to pay the
two latter half yearly payments of the
Said Duties to the Said Receiver General
Or his Deputy at the House of Mr Roger
Woodburne in Ulverstone on Wedensday
The fourth Day of April Next
Hereof fail not Given Under my hand
the twelfth Day of March 1732

To the Constables   R.S   C[hief] Constable
of Colton

[p. 215]

Lancashire to wit you are hereby required
& Commanded to make a true Presentment
In fair Writing Under your hands to Every
article here in contained & the Same
return <..> unto me in your own proper person
on Thursday the last Day of July at the
House of James Cowper Innholder in
Ulverstone between the Hours of ten
& twelve in the forenoon Clement Taylor
Chief Constable[266]

---

266 This might imply that Clement Taylor was High (Chief) Constable, but he was not.

[*p. 216*]

An Assessment Laid for the
Constable of Finsthwait Haverthwait
& Rusland for the year 1733[267]

			s	d	
John Walker			1	0	q
John Rawlinson Husbandman			0	6	3
Arthur Benson			1	4	3
John Rawlinson Smith			0	8	2
Mr James Maychell			1	9	0
<Occupiers of> Richard Nuby			0	0	2
Occupiers of Richard Rawlinson Lands			0	0	1
Miles Walker Younger			0	10	2
Jonah Skeldin			0	3	2
Richard Postlethwait			0	11	2
Margaret Bornes			0	0	3
Richard Simpson			0	9	0
Occupiers of Bray-Dale			0	9	0
Joseph Penny			0	3	3
Occupiers of James Walker Lands			0	2	3
Edward Walker			0	3	0
James Backhouse & Clement Taylor			0	3	0
George Taylor			0	9	3
Margaret Sawrey			0	0	3
William Danson			0	0	3
Richard Robinson			1	6	0
Clement Taylor	2d	2½qrs	2	9	3
James Backhouse	3	¾qrs	1	6	3
Christopher Taylor			0	6	2
George Taylor	3d	1½qrs	1	4	2
Henry Taylor	9d		2	0	3
Widdow Denny			0	3	0
Miles Harrison	10½d		<0>1	0	0
Robert Taylor			1	1	2
George Braithwaite	2¼qrs		1	8	1
William Spence Elersid			0	1	2
Samuel Robinson			0	1	2
Occupiers of James Walker			0	0	3

267 As parish constable, Clement Taylor would have been responsible for collecting the money. The first fourteen names are from Haverthwaite, the next fourteen from Finsthwaite, Stott Park, and Newby Bridge north of the river, and the remainder from Rusland. The 'Meeting house' mentioned towards the end is the Quaker meeting house at Rook How, built for the Swarthmoor monthly meeting in 1725: D.M. Butler, *Quaker Meeting Houses of the Lake Counties*, Friends Historical Society, 1978, 137–40, 142. The sum is *recte* 43s 10½d.

178 *The Account Book of Clement Taylor*

[*p. 217*]

	s	d	q
Richard Simpson	0	0	3
Peter Taylor	0	0	3
Robert Scales	2	5	2
John Scales	0	4	0
Thomas Walker	1	<6>5	0
Robert Wilson	0	4	2
Richard Corker	0	1	2
* mind Short[268]			
Occupiers of Clement* Taylor	0	8	1
George Bank	0	9	3
Robert Taylor	1	1	2
Rowland Wilson	0	9	3
Robert Atkinson	1	0	2
John Wilson Bar	0	4	1
John Wilson Smith	0	0	2
George Drinkall	0	10	2
Mr William Rawlinson	2	10	2
William Ormady	1	7	1
Widdow Strickland	0	2	0
Thomas Dixon	0	1	1
Thomas Strickland	0	11	3
Widdow Bailif	0	1	0
Rowland Taylor	1	1	0
Thomas Satterthwaite	0	3	0
Meeting house	0	2	1
William Strickland, Whit Stock		6	0
Richard Corker	0	2	0
John Russell	0	0	2
John Torner	0	0	2
	25	0	

Assessed 3 poor bills by
Robert Taylor of Crosslands
Clement Taylor being Constable
This bill is not refused paying
by any

---

268 He is reminding himself that not all the 8¼d had been paid, not that the other Clement Taylor was deranged.

[p. 218]

	House of Correction			poor prisoners in LC[269]		
	s	d		s	d	
Urswick	3	9		8	8	
Kirkby Ire[leth]	3	5	1/2	8	8	
Pennington	1	1	1	8	8	
Leece	3	7	2			
Ulverstone	3	0	3	3	0	
Broughton in F[urness]	3	0	3			
Conistone	0	9	3	1	6	
Torver	0	9	3	1	6	
Osmotherley	0	9	3	1	6	
Blawith	0	6		1	6	
Lowick	1	0		1	6	
Egton & Newland	0	7	2	1	6	
Mansriggs	0	2		1	0	
Aldingham	3	5	2	8	8	
Holker	3	7	1	4	10	2
Alithwaite	2	3		3	1	
Broughton in Cart[mel]	3	8		5	0	2
Dalton	3	3		8	8	
Hawkshead	1	11	2	4	4	
Coulton	1	3	2	4	1	
in all 2li	2s	3	1	3li 18		

Poor Prisoners in Lancaster Castle

	s	d	
Holker Parthway[270] for Prisoners	4	10	1/2
Alithwaite	3	1	0
Broughton in Cartmell	5	0	1/2
	13	0	0

[p. 219]

Land Sold by Mr Henry Taylor & Trustees[271]
as Followeth & Smithy rent & poor

---

269 L[ancaster] C[astle]. The total for the poor prisoners is *recte* £3 17s 9d.
270 'Parthway' is quite clear, but its meaning is not.
271 See nn. 194, 196. The prices paid by the various purchasers of Henry Taylor's land appears at the left, with the amount of bloomsmithy rent owed by each of them, followed by the allocation of poor rate at what appears to be 5 1/2 farthings per £100. But Myles Harrison paid over £1400 for his part of the property and yet is assessed at only 3 1/2d. So 'H' cannot mean Hundred.

bill also at the rate of 5q & a ¹/₂ per H

li	s	d		li	s	d	
1403	12	0	Miles Harrison	0	1	7	
93	3		George Braithwait	0	0	1 ¹/₂	
387	14	8	Clement Taylor	0	0	5	
146	1	8	James Backhouse	0	0	2	
467	1	8	George Taylor	0	0	6 ¹/₂	
and Remained to Lending				0	2	2	
		in all			5	0	

Poor bill Taken with the abovesaid
Lands as followeth

	d	q	H[alf]
Miles Harrison at a poor bill	3	2	
George Braithwait	0	0	³/₄
Clement Taylor 3	0		
James Backhouse	0	1	¹/₄

Poor bill taken of Henry Taylor
as followeth

	d	q	Half
Miles Harison	3	2	
George Braithwait	0	0	³/₄
Clement Taylor	0	3	¹/₂
James Backhouse	0	1	¹/₄
George Taylor	1	0	¹/₂

| Remained to Lending | 3 | 0 | |

[*p. 220 is blank*]

[*p. 221*]

March Tusday 3d 1740 Then
a Why bult at Thomas Walkers
from Watterside
18th Thicknecked Why bult
at Thomas Walkers. Wedensday
White Backt Why Bult
at Lawrance Harrisons
March 13th 1741 which Laid in farr
Cowhouse paid Lawarance [*sic*]

[*p. 222*]

[*Isabel Taylor*]

How many Sheep was put to the fell at Clipping 1744
26 Wedders
28 Ews
16 Hogs

[*p. 223*]

[*Clement Taylor*]

December 1732
A renunciation Need not be on
Stamp [*sic*]272
The [*sic*] Shu'd both be attested by Dorothy
Wife of Edward Kellet whereby her
Consent will be testified
becase the tuition wo'd've belong'd
to her with[out *interlined*] a will
The Intended tutors or Gardions
when the [*sic*] are made Such, must
give bond to the Court to be
Accountable for all that Comes to
their hands, & Joseph Taylor
being also <one of the> a trustee may Draw
the money belonging to the Minor
and Sign an Acknowledgement
To the other Trustees that he has
Received it for the Minor's Use
& So the [*sic*] will need no other Security
The bond to be given to the
Court & the Acknowledgement where
the money is being Sufficient
   James Holme
    proctor

[*p. 224 is blank*]

---

272 i.e. on stamped paper: see n. 91. We are not told whose children would have come under the guardianship of Dorothy Kellett, who was the wife of the woodmonger, Edward Kellett: see 232.

[p. 225]

Coals	loads	sacks
Henry Croasdales	5	3
& a Sack <O> of his own wood wet being made of sapps <one>		1 sack
Thomas Jonson	5	4
Edward Barwick	9	9
Peter Taylor	32	3
	<3>42	0

Coals	load	Sacks
Thomas Dixon	13	<3>2
CT	13	1
J[ane] Woodburn	7	7
Richard Robinson	1	<10>8
Peter Taylor	8	6
Thomas Johnson	8	5
	32	7[273]

Bridge Bark	quarter	Bushel
7 Thomas Jonson	20	7
7 Peter Taylor	20	1
7½ Thomas Dixon	13 <4>	2

[p. 226]

April 15th 1732 Edward Taylor Account[274] of what was Spent at Dalton when we went to pay Law & Brandwood Children	0	6	11
Gave Brandwoods Children towards their Jorney	0	15	0
A Journey to Kendal to Desire Mr Wilson to Come to Dalton to pay Brandwood & Law Spent	0	2s	0
April 19th paid Edward Taylor when he paid pro malt Making	2	0	0

---

273 The sums are *recte* fifty-two loads and eight sacks, and fifty-two loads and five sacks, if there were twelve sacks to the load.
274 For pp. 226–30, see Appendix.

20 Spent at Ulverston when I paid James Fell pro Bief	0	<1>0	9
at the same time paid Fell for 22li [at 3d 2q per li *interlined*] Beif had for Hathornthwait funeral	0	6	5
paid Richard Law	150	0	0
paid Brandwoods	50	0	0
May 13th paid Mr Wilson towards Henry Barwick bond	0	1	0
Spent that day at Kendal	0	2	3
14 George Dodson Acknowledged himself Debtor to Edward Taylor & also promised to pay to him pro the executorship of John Hathornthwait Will 26li [17s *interlined*] & Interest for the same for one year 3 months & 2 weeks			
16th a Journey to Kendal about George Dodson Suit	0 <4>3	0	
(1s) & a New Mortgage spent more [J C *interlined*] Lost		1	0
Spent at Bouth with Mr Dodson In inquiring about G[eorge] Dodson Bond		0	4d
27 paid Edward Taylor per my Wife		1	10
The same Day To Edward when he was to send a retainer to Mr Holme proctor		0	10
June 1th A Journey to Lancaster 1s to advise with Mr Holme spent		0	3

John Brandwoods ?C-tin-C

[*p. 227*]

April 15 1732
John Sedon of Heton in the parish
of Dean near Boulton le Moors

		old
April 15th 1732	Thomas Brandwood	18
yet unpaid	in May next	
& to be paid	Mary Brandwood	16
when the come	16th May next	
to age of	Ann Brandwood	12
21 years	in June next	
	John Brandwood hath seal'd	

April Received [*as interlined*] below of Brother Edward Account			
1732 Imprimis of Mr Wilson	150		
April 15 of Mr Peny Elder	050		
28th more of Mr Penny per the hands of Mr Sandys	200		
paid Edward A[ccount] Colanel Wilson Money	200		
May 2 paid Edward Taylor Cononel [*sic*] money in the presence [of *interlined*] his Wife & ant Emey which I sepose J[ames] Bacchouse had to keep or take Care of			
Received of Mr Maychel	100li		

[*p. 228*]

August 17th A Journey to Lancaster about the Chancarey Bill & on the Account of Referance with Abrahams Spent on the Journey	0	15	3
21th Spent when James Bacchouse & I went to Newton in Order to pay Hathornwait Legacie	0	2	6
September the 7th Letter from York	0	0	4
16th paid John Hathornwhait	134li	15s	
19 a Journey to Borrow to advise with Mr Fenwick[275]			
Gave him [for *interlined*] a fie	1	1	0
Spent on the Journey	0	1	0
29 Spent with Mr Holme at Lancaster fair[276]	0	1	9
October 7 Journey to Lancaster & in Kendal to Advise with Mr Wilson Mr Holme went to Kendal with me to Suport the will Expences on the Journey pro [*sic*] with Mr W[ilson] Mr Holme & my self	0	6	0
15th a Journey to Swarthmoor Spent			4d
18th Spent at Nuby Bridge when Sir Thomas Mr Sandys & Mr Rawlinson & abrahams Mr Maychel & others met on the account of Referance		14s	

---

[275] Robert Fenwick (1688–1750) of Burrow House, near Kirkby Lonsdale, King's Sergeant in the Duchy Court at Lancaster, and MP for Lancaster 1734–46; see *CW2*, 1936, 9, 11–12.

[276] Lancaster had four yearly fairs; this was evidently the one held in September.

27 at Ulverston at the Correction Cort with Mr Holme	0	0	6
November 2 A Journey to Kendall to advise with Mr Wilson & Mr Holme about a prohibition about Hathornwhat Effects Spent with Mr Wilson & Holme & on the Journey		2s	6d
10th to Mr Rawlinson's Servants		2	0
13 to Mr Sandys Servants		2	0
December 1th 2 letters		0	6

[*p. 229*]

December 4th 1732[277]
Spent on the Account of a Referance
with Mr Abrahams at Nuby bridge
Mr Knipe Mr Sandys
Mr Harison Mr Maychel
Mr Wilson beinging [*sic*]
there & others & also E[dward] T[aylor]
this being the Charge of <of>
two Meetings per them

Spent at Nuby brigde [*sic*]		<2>1 li	<2> 1s
Spent	1	1	
To Mr Knipe	1	11	6
a Letter from Preston	0	0	4
To R[ichard] R[obinson] for York and Lancaster Letters		[*blank*]	
February 23 a letter from Lancaster	0	0	1
23 to [Brother *interlined*] William Taylor on Edward Account of Interest	6	0	0
To Edward when he went to York	15	16	0
To Edward Taylor [of *interlined*] Mr Penny Money J[ames] Backhouse keeps	126	0	0
March 26 a Journey to Kurby 1733 Lonsdale to mr Fenwicks[278]	0	<2>3	<4>0
To Brother William on his Account	6	0	0
Spent in Goeing from Lancaster to Kendal being all night		s	d
James Backhouse & my self		3	6

277 This entry straggles about the page as though the writer was drunk. The meeting had evidently been a convivial one.
278 See n. 275.

186   *The Account Book of Clement Taylor*

Spent with Wilson when we put in our answers	0	1	0
<January> February Spent at Bouth with J[ames] Rownson about Refferance	0	1	0

[*p. 230*]

June 1th Sent Mr Wilson	li	s	d
1732 to pay Oliver Brandwood with	12	10	0
5th To Betty Kellet when she went to Send to buy Corn for Edward	2	0	0
15 paid John Seden & John Brandwood on the Infants Children Account	37 li	10s	
more to the Same Interest pro 2 Months <being> due on the Same		6	
Sent a Guney with Mr Wilson to London to take advice with	1	1	0
My Expences on the Journey to Lancaster	0	2	0
15th to Mr Harrison pro Copeying Denisonce Agreement	0	1	0
21 To Thomas Fisher pro a Waist Coat & Furniture to the Same	0	11	1
Expences on the Journey about James Fell	0	0	10
January & June Letters from York	0	0	8
June 8th To William Taylor for 3 retainers at York	1	1	0
a Journey to Ulverston with Mr Maychel to J[ames] Fell's Spent	0	1	6
a Journey to preston to appear against Abrahams	0	9	1
To Mr Gibson a retainer	0	5	0
July 15 when I went to Kendal to see Mr Wilson when he Came from London & to se how the Case Stud		1	0
August 8th a Journey to Ulverston when I Went too se how matters Stud with Abrahams Hathornthwait & Den[ison]	0	1	0
13 a Journey to Preston to Consult with Mr Gibson the Answer to the Chancery Bill & Payment of Farington &c	0	6	0

[*p. 231*]

April 28 1732
Disbursed on the Account of John Taylor[279]
Deceased & at his Funeral

Imprimis to Henry Croasdal	0	2	0	
To John Coward pro Coffin & Winding Sheet	0	11	6	
27th May To Mr Harrison pro Funerall Sermon	0	10	0	
June 16th paid Betty her wage Emey[280] Being present	0	15	0	
20th paid Thomas Strickland what remained behind on Slate account	0	1	6	
July 23d To William Walker for Wheat Bread had at funerall	0	7	4 1/2	
August 2d paid Thomas Dixon Wife & A.D.[281] per the hands of Elizabeth Taylor for Butter & Milk had pro John Taylor deceased the summe of	0	3	0	
To Edward Rigg poor Sess	0	0	3	
Rowland Taylor Master Wage	0	0	<4>8	
Robert Capland Constable Sess	0	0	0	2
John Coward a Napkin	0	0	<.>7	
Thomas Pepper	0	2	6	
Edward Rigg poor Sess	0	0	2	
<William Coward			4d>	
John Coward 3li prunes	0	1	0	
To Justices for Going off	0	1	0	
February 23d paid Peter Taylor	1	4	0	

James Backhouse William Coward
& E[dward] Taylor Betty & her Mother being present
& Henry his Brother also vide Peter paper
Jonas Skelding 1d Master Wage Church Sess
John Rawlinson L[and] Sess 1d

[*p. 232*]

February 9th 1731 Account of Money laid out for Brother William Taylor as follows	li	s	d	q
Imprimis two Charr potts[282]	0	1	3	0

---

279 See n. 261.
280 His sister-in-law Emma, wife of his brother Edward.
281 A.D. is unidentified.
282 See n. 77.

Ditto 4 duzen of Charrs at 5s per duzen	1	0	0	0
Ceasoning for the Same				
Mace 1oz qr	0	1	10	2
Cloves 1 & 1/2	0	1	1	2
Sinenon 1 & 1/2	0	1	1	2
Black peper	0	0	3	0
Carriage to Davintry at 2d per li W[eight] 29li	0	5	0	0
	1	10	7	2

[p. 233]

June Lent Thomas Strickland		17s	6d
1732 Received 6d of the Same on William Taylor account			
August 13th Lent Thomas Strickland by the hand of Samuel	10li		
Accounted to Ben Airey			
75 Guineas	78	15s	
1/2 Gu[i]nea	0	10	6
Silver & Copper		1	7
to Mr Maychel	79	7	1
Part of Henry Barwicks <Money>			
Mr Maychel Debtor	3	18	
paid in part	2	10	
Remains Debtor	1	8	

[p. 234]

May the 1th 1731
Sarah Fell 2 days bearing peats
July working hay 1 d[ay]
10 that week – two working hay
17 that week 4 1/2 W[orking] hay
25th that Week 3 W[orking] Hay
August 1th Last W[eek] 4 1/2 W[orking] Hay
4th this Week 2 W[orking] Hay
14 this W[eek] 2 Shearing Bigg
September 23d 1 day in Garding

20 trees 73 foot ¹/₂
Cheese 16s 5d¹/₂
Knott Coles 170
Bark 385

G[reat] Field Bark 90 quarter
Coals 18 load

parrackfould
& head of Field
Bark   45<0> quarter 12<10> li
Coals   45<0> load   33<2>   15
        ─────────────────────────
                 45<0>

[*A paper pinned in at foot with miscellaneous calculations on the back of the following:*]

21 June 1733
Received of Mr Harrison, Robert Taylor, John Case,   li   s   d
Mr Clement Taylor & James Backhouse the Sum of   9   6   0
nine pounds six shillings in full of my
Bills formerly sent & of all Demands
            by Me
                    Charles Lambert[283]

[*p. 235*]

February 13th 1730 John Walker	5 days
& his man at Stairs[284]	5
20th 2d Week Each	6
6th Jackey Window Seats &c	6
August 7th Jackey Edging	
boards	4
14th John & Jackey Each	
about Lying parler floor	6
September 18 Jackey <5>	
at W[indow] Seats & Garret Doors	5

283 Charles Lambert of Lancaster was the lawyer concerned in the dispute with Robert Bateman: see n. 154.
284 John Walker and Jackey are working on the new house: see xxiii.

190   *The Account Book of Clement Taylor*

Jackey 25 September that W[eek]
at Window Seats & Edging
Loft floor to Wall   6

Ocober 2 that Week John W[alker]
& Jackey Each
at parler Cornish   5
9 John Walker & Jackey
Each Mind J[ohn] W[alker]   5   ½
29 John W[alker] Coulering Door top   1   0
November 20th that Week John Walker
& Jackey Each   6
in making Beddstocks &
a Little Table

80ty D[ay]s 2.3.4[285]

[*p. 236*]

		li	s	
February 1739 paid John Taylor Towards Woodcutting &c				
1th at Candlmas		1	10	
To Leonard Kendal		0	2	6
a hoop of Beans				
a lock		0	1	
To Peter Nuby \<on\> his Account		0	2	1
May 8th a pair of H'es[286]		0	\<8\>	8
16th when he Bough [*sic*] Henry Cloase paid as we went to Chapel			5	0
to repairs of Church		0	0	3
to preest wage[287]		0	4	
June 14th Ditto when he paid J[ohn] Coward		2 li	2	0
June 23d when he paid Thomas Braithwait for Bark P[eeling]		0	10	0
more at Midsummer [27li *interlined*] of Chese and Carraige		0	4	7
To Miles Taylor a hoop of peas on John Account		0	1	0
July 4th To George Braithwait Wife when she paid \<Biggins\> Mr Taylor for Miller & Webster		0	5	10

285 The total number of days worked is *recte* 89, but 80 days at 4d a day is £2 3s 4d.
286 This word is unexplained.
287 The vicar's salary. The survival of the word 'priest' in the Lake District is interesting.

October paid John when he rackned with George & Wife		1	14	
9th when he paid John Coward		1	1	
November 3 to J[ohn] Taylor when he sent to Ulverston Oats		0	10	
5th To Margaret Braithwait on the Account of Coals		0	10	1
Hagg Fogg		0	3	6
Chese at Michaelmas		0	11	6
diescordium				3d
Idem more 3[d]		0	0	3
at Candlemas		5	1	0
March 21th paid him in full		1	14	11

[p. 237]

February 1729 Account of money
Laid out for Brother William Taylor

	li	s	d	
12 hoops of Cockles	0	3	0	
3 Caggs paid for to H[288]	0	2	6	
an ounce & a half of Mace	0	2	4	
an ounce of Cloves	0	0	9	
2 ounce of White peper	0	0	6	
Ranie ginger	0	0	1	
Carriage of 3 Caggs weighed 31li to Farthingstone	0	4	0	

January the 20th [1730 *interlined*] A Cagg of Cockles
For Mrs Holbeck

	li	s	d	
4 hopes of Cockles	0	1	0	
1 ounce of White peper	0	0	3	
1/2 an ounce of Mace	0	0	9	
1/2 an ounce of Cloves	0	0	4 1/2	
White Ginger	0	0	1	2
Cage [*sic*]	0		10	0
Carrage to Davintry	0	1	6	

February 6th [1730 *interlined*] Sent Brother William per Mr
James Greehow [*sic*] Carier   64 li
to him pro Carriage of the Same   00   7   6

---

288 Kegs. 'H' is probably Henry Croasdale: see 228. Mrs Holbeck below was presumably a neighbour of William Taylor's in Northamptonshire who had ordered some cockles; *cf* n. 60.

[p. 238]

		s	d
June the 14th 1731 paid for my Servant Margaret Burket pro a bottel of Daffey	0	1	3
October Then Lent Margaret 29 when she sent to Kendall for Cloth with Roger	0	1	0
February when her Father was not well	0	12s	0

Received of Margaret all the above
Except for a Daffey Bottel

February 21th 1731 Received of Richard
Atkinson for 28 Weeks being
all that was due till the above
said day pro the Mentainance
of her Child from William Braithwait
at 8d per week per me C T which said
sum I paid to her[289]

[p. 239]

		s	d	q
May 1730 Account of Meat had of Edward Burnes This year Imprimis a Neck of Veal		0	8	0
another second time		0	[blank]	
June Saturday 20th a Neck of Veal		[blank]		
the 27th a Neck of Veal		[blank]		
Saturday July the 4th 1/2 quarter Veal		[blank]		
Saturday 11th a hind quarter Lamb		[blank]		
Saturday 18th a hind quarter Mutton	0	1	6	
Saturday 25th a hind M[utton]	0	1	0	
Saturday 31th a hind quarter M[utton]		[blank]		
Saturday August 8 a hind quarter M[utton]	0	1	2	
Saturday August 22d a hind quarter Mutton		[blank]		
Saturday 29 a Hind quarter		1s	3d	
Saturday September 5th a hind quarter		[blank]		
Saturday October 10th a hind quarter		1	11	
Saturday 17th a hind quarter		1	0	
Saturday 24 A hind quarter		1	0	
Saturday December 5th a hind quarter of veal		2	6	

[289] The baptism of Margaret Birkett's child has so far not been traced. The entry on p. 103 indicates that it was a daughter.

for Killing a Calf		1	0	
12 Saturday a Fore quarter of Mutton		1	0	
a pluck				
23 a forequarter Veal		2	10	
a Swine quarter		9	3	
paid Edward Burnes in full	1	12	0[290]	
& remain Debtor 10s				
Received in part per George of Jamies[291]	0	2	5	

[p. 240]

May 17 1729 Account of what meat				
Clement Taylor had of Edward Burnes	l	s	d	q
1th a Neck of Veal	0	0	9	0
June a fore quarter of Veal	0	2	4	0
12 a neck of veal	0	0	8	
Miles Harrison had it				
<17 Tuesday 2 quarter veal>	0	0	0	
20th A hind quarter Lam	0	1	2	
27 ½ quarter Veal		0	0	8
July 5th 2 quarters of Mutton	0	2	4	
Edward Burnes had a Calfe				
13 August Mutton & a quarter Lam		2	4	
19 a quarter Mutton		1s	6	
26 a Hind quarter Mutton		1	1	
29 half a quarter Veal		0	7	
August				
3d a hind quarter Mutton		1	10	
9 a hind quarter Mutton		1	8	
16th a hind quarter Mutton		0	11	
23d a hind quarter Mutton		1	4	
29th a hind quarter		1s	0d	
½ quarter Tup Mutton		0	10	
September 6th a hind quarter Mutton		1	4	
13th a Legg of Mutten		0	7	
20th a Legg of Mutton		0	8	
28 a quarter Mutton		0	10	
October the 4th A Legg of Mutton		0	8	
11th a Loine of Mutton		0	7	<7>1
18 a Loyne of Mutton		0	<7>6	½
total paid	1li	5s	4d	

290 The total is *recte* £1 6s 1d but the extra 5s 11d may be for the items for which no price was given.
291 George Braithwaite, son of James, called 'of Jamies' to distinguish him from other George Braithwaites; see 226.

194 *The Account Book of Clement Taylor*

[*p. 241*]

A Single pore bill [sessed *interlined*] for Finsthwait
Haverthwait & Rusland [May *interlined*] A.D 1729[292]

	s	d	q
Myles Walker	0	4	
John Rawlinson	0	2	1
Alen Parke	0	3	
Mr John Maychel	0	11	
Arthur Benson	0	5	3
Robert Rigg	0	3	3
Jonah Skelding	0	1	1
Richard Postlethwait	0	4	
Richard Simpson	0	3	3
Margaret Bornes	0	0	1
James Walker	0	0	3
Occupiers of Braydel	0	3	
Joseph Penny	0	1	1
Edward Walker	0	1	
Clement Taylor & J[ames] Backhouse		0	1
George Taylor	0	3	1
Widdow Sawrey	0	0	1
William Danson	0	0	1
Richard Robinson	0	6	
Clement Taylor	0	11	<1/2>1
James Backhouse	0	6	1
Christhopher [*sic*] Taylor	0	2	1
Mr Henry Taylor	0	8	1/2
Thomas Denny	0	1	
Myles Harrison	0	4	
<Robert & George Taylor>	0	10	1
George Braithwaite	0	6	3
Occupiers E[dward] T[aylor] for Elersid	0	0	2
R. Simpson of High Cragg	0	0	1
James Walker	0	0	1
Samuel Robinson	0	0	1/2
John Taylor <alias Peter>	0	0	1
Robert Taylor	0	4	2
George Taylor	0	5	2

[292] The first fourteen names are from Haverthwaite, the next thirteen from Finsthwaite, and the remainder from Rusland; see also n. 267.

[p. 242]

	s	d	q
Robert Scales	0	9	2
Jonathan Wilson	0	0	2
John Scales	0	1	
William Taylor	0	5	2
Clement Taylor	0	5	1
Robert Wilson	0	1	1
George Bank	0	3	1
Robert Atkinson	0	3	3
Robert Taylor	0	4	
Robert Taylor more for E[dward] T[aylor] Land	0	0	2
Rowland Wilson	0	3	
John Wilson	0	1	1
Myles Drinkalt	0	3	2
Mr Abraham Rawlinson	0	11	2
Reginald Strickland	0	6	2
William Strickland	0	0	3
Widdow Strickland Sike	0	0	1
Thomas Strickland	0	4	
Widdow Bailif Light H[ow]	0	1	
John Taylor	0	5	1
Thomas Satterthwait	0	1	
William Strickland Whitstock-hall	0	2	
Richard Corker	0	0	3
John Russell	0	0	1
Occupiers New Meeting House	0	1	

George Taylor Overseer for ano 1728 Thomas Rigg Constable

[p. 243]

A Single poor bill for Rusland may 1729 from William Taylor

		d	q	
Robert Scales <...> <d q 2>		9	<.>3	<1/2>2
John Scales		<.>1	<.>1	3
Jonathan Wilson		<.>1	<.>0	
William Taylor	5d 2q	5	2 <1/4>1/2	
Clement Taylor	3d 1q	<4	3	2/4>

Robert Wilson	1<1><2>	<1
George Banke	3	0
Robert Taylor	4	<1>2
Robert Atkinson	<3>4	<.>0
Rowland Wilson	3	<.>1
John Wilson	1	1
John Wilson Smith	0	0
Mr Rawlinson	11	2
Reginald Strickland	6	2
John Turner	0	0
Robert Strickland Sike	0	1
William Strickland Sike	0	3
Thomas Strickland Light How	3	3
John Bailif Light How	0	1
John Taylor	4	1
Thomas Satterthwait	1	0
-hall		
William Strickland Whit Stock	1	3
Richard Corker	0	2
John Russel	0	0
New Meeting House	0	3
Myles Drinkall	3	2
Richard Corker Takes of Clement Taylor for Dick how 2q at a poor bill		
Robert Scales	[blank]	

[p. 244]

Account of money Laid out
& Expences about Chapel & buy
Land

	[s	d]
Imprimis To James Greenwood	0	5
To a Letter from Governors[293]	0	5
To Westmorland [i.e. *interlined*] Sigsweck	1	0
To Bolton Head & Slatborn	4	9
April 7th To preston Carier pro 2 letters	2	
1727 In Going to Garsdale	3	6½
January the paid John Postlethwait per 14 the hand of Joseph Penny	2	6

293 i.e. of Queen Anne's Bounty; for this, see nn. 105, 144, 166. When land was being bought for the church, property in Sedgwick, Westm., at Bolton Head, near Gosforth, Cumb., and at Slaidburn, WR Yorks., was also being considered.

The Account Book of Clement Taylor 197

		s	d	q
1731 Debtor to Edward Burnes for meat Imprimis Neck of Veal		0	11	0
a quarter Lam		1	1	0
July 17th a Neck of veal				
Received of George Jamies[294]		2s	5d	
on E[dward] Burnes Account				

Debtor to James Danson for meat
Imprimis a fore quarter Mutton
a hind quarter Mutton
A Legg

	s	d
1 Sheep Cark[295]	3	2
2 Sheep C	2	6
3 Sheep C	2	4
3 heads & 3 P[luck]	0	6
Suet in 3 sheep 12li	2	9
3 Skinns	2	0
4th Sheep	5	8
one Calfe	9	8
2 Sheep Skins	2	7

1	11	2

[p. 245]

head	4	Garsdale	2	6	
Tripe	6	at Kendall	0	8	
feet	2	a Show	0	4 1/2	
Tripes	8				
hide	5s 9<.>				
	6 8				

1732
July 28 Sold to William Coward
before this time

	li	s	d	
A Wedder	0	13	0	
A Calfe	0	10	8	
a Sheep Skinn	0	1	0	
August a Tup	0	6		
8 Sheep & a Skinn	1	19	1	2
November 27 Two Sheep	0	10	11	

---

294 See n. 291.
295 Carcase; 'P' below is probably for 'pluck'.

198 The Account Book of Clement Taylor

		[blank]	
two dael [sic] planks			
January 19 A Wedder	0	6	11
<3 kins [sic] more>			
February the 5th a Wedder Cand[lemas]	0	6	4
5 <a> Skin of the same	0	6	10 1/2
12th a wedder	0	7	7
	5	<6>8	5
for William Coward Labour		8	6
his Book	5	3	8 1/2
William Debtor pro 2 Dales	0	2	4
Ballance due to William		1	4
more per G[eorge] Braithwait		5	0
February 12th paid William Ballance		6	4
1732 Received of William For White Stirk	1	10	6

[p. 246]

September 1725 Debtor to
James Danson for 6 dayes
Sarveing Slaters & Scything
Rubaige about New House
19 James Danson More Sarrowing
Slaters at Back Side of New
House 6 Dayes
25 more 3 Dayes Bearing
peats of [sic] & Geting Sand
29 more one day Geting Sand
October
10   more 3 dayes Shearing
17th   <1> 2 dayes Shearing
          1 day Threshing & Sarving to beamfilling
          1 day Drissing In New House Rubbige
          1 day Salveing hoggs
October
23   2 dayes Salveing Sheep
28   1 day Salving
November 6th 6 dayes Salving Sheep
14th   2 dayes Threshing
          1 day Salving Sheep
<December> 1 day Threshing

2   December
    1 day Geting Stone in Green
    Slack
    2 Dayes Threshing Oats
    1 day Scailing rubbaige at Back [Door *interlined*]
    1 day faling[296] appletrees & ashes pro Lime
    Kill
22 1 day falling ashes & Cross-cutting
    of them
27 1 day Looking wedders & Smitting
    Ews
January 1th 1 day Looking Sheep
4   1 day fetching hoggs
    in out of Knoat &c
8   2 dayes Leading Lime Stone
    1 day Leading rubbaige into
    Little Garth
    1 day Leading rubbaige
    1 day Getting Stones in Walker B[row]

[*p. 247*]

18 2 dayes Leading rubbige
February 5 2 dayes one at Mill [*torn*]
            of them <at>
of Edward Account 3 dayes
12 2 dayes riveing wood pro Kill
19 6 dayes dressing Ground work
25th 6 dayes Leading Lime Stons
March 5th 6 dayes plowing & leading lime Stons
12 4 dayes plowing &c
19 6 dayes plowings
26 6 dayes Leading Stones &c
April 2d 5 dayes at Slate & plow
9th 5$^{1/2}$ at plow, Sand & Leading Stones
15 6 plowing Leading Stons & Geting [Sand *interlined*]
24 6 days Leading Stons
29 6 days Leading Maner &c
8 6 day plowing & Slat & Stons
15 6 days Graving peats leading Slate &c

10$^{1/2}$
1<2>11$^{1/2}$

296   Felling.

	s	d[297]				
2	3	8				
0	2	0	4	16	4	
			3	0	0	
2	5	8	2	10	0	
0	6	0		6	8	
4	7	6				
4	10	0	10	13	0	
11	9	2				
10	13	0				
	16	2				
pece of wood	1s					
	17s	2d Due to J[ames] Danson
	1	6
	18	8

[*p. 248*]

Account of Money Disbursed

	li	s	
To Walers May 1725			
To Edward Parke	4	0	
To Robert Addison	1	0	0
John Nuby	0	16	0
To James Walker pro 19 dayes work	0	9	6
gratis 6d			
To Rownson Taylor	0	3	0
To John Nuby	0	9	0
May To Jacob Park \<in part\>	1	0	0
15 To Peter Taylor	0	4	0
To Thomas of Myles is	0	3	0
To Edward Barwick for 7 dayes work	0	3	6
To Rownson pro 8 dayes	0	4	0
June			
02 for 19 pair of Gloves[298]	0	9	6

297 These are the calculations for what was owed to James Danson.
298 For gifts of gloves to workmen, *cf* Fell, *op. cit.*, 297.

August To Jacob Parke		0	10	6	
6 To James Walker		0	15	0	
To Rownson Taylor		0	3	0	
Robert Addison		0	8	0	
James Taylor		2	2	0	
James Walker		0	1	0	

September   To John Sawrey & George
15   of High Nibthwait
for Leading 104 load of
Slate from Coniston to
Finsthwait being 4 boat load   2   8   0
More to George of Lords for
Leading 8 load from Coniston
Waterhead to my house[299]   0   6   8
To James Taylor of Nibthwait leading
6 load from Coniston to my house   5   0

li   s   d

[p. 249]

19 paid Robert Adinson for dressing & Lyeing Slate on the New House	0	8s	6	
October				
10 To Old Henry Crank 4 dayes		[blank]		
to young Henry Crank 4 dayes at 4d per day		[blank]		
October				
28 John Walker 31 days	1	0	6	
Holme 42	1	6	8	
Solamon 85	<1>2	<2>9	4	
Wilson 58	1	9	0	
Pert 16 dayes	0	8	0	
330	9	7	6[300]	

29 To Rownson Taylor for Serving Limers at 6d per day	0	7	0
December 31th to Cranks	1	4	2
Samuel Towers	1	<7>8	0
Leonard Parke	0	10	0

[299] The slate would have come from the quarries at Tilberthwaite. It was loaded onto boats at Coniston Waterhead and taken down to the southern end of the lake, from where local men brought it to Finsthwaite by road.

[300] The number of days is *recte* 232, or 240 if the Cranks' time is added, and the sum *recte* £6 13s 6d, or £7 4s 10d if payments to Robert Addison and the Cranks are included.

James Taylor	1	7	0
peter Taylor 7 dayes	0	3	6
Smithworke near	4	0	0
2d February paid Jacob Park	3	2	<1>0
Rownson Taylor for 3 days			
Blending lime & and	0	1	6
more to the Same for washing			
Sand 3 dayes		1	6
August			
23 to Rownson	0	6	0
October			
11th To Rownson pro	in full		
26 day work	0	13	0
paid in full To Cranks pro Plais-	1	19	8
tering Gave	0	0	5½

[p. 250]

April 4th 1730 John Walker & Man
Each 5 dayes at Staires
2 Week J[ohn] Walker 3 days
his man Jack 5 days
Ditto 6 pecks of Barley
20 yards Linn at 1s 3d per yard
May 15th J[ohn] Walker & his man Jack
Each 4 days at Stairs head &
Side boards to Staires
June 23 J[ohn] Walker Jackey & J[ames] Leece Each
2 days at bed teaster[301]
July 2d John Walker 2 days at Bed
John & Jack Each 5 days at Stair head
Henry Taylor alias dickies[302]
2 days bearing peats at F[ar] M[oss]
more 2 days at Far Moss
Margaret Braithwait alias Dolies 1 day
John Taylor House 14 foot deep
& 31 foot Long Consider drissing[303]

April 30th 1730 Jane Woodburne
One day Bearing peats at F[ar] M[oss]

301 Tester. James Leece was a builder, so it is possible that the bed was being fixed into the wall.
302 Henry, son of Richard Taylor; see n. 165 and 240. For 'Dolies' below, see n. 181.
303 'Drissing' in this case must mean pointing or roughcoasting. The house in question is Charley Crag, which Clement Taylor had bought in 1718 from John Taylor's widow, Jennet: LRO, DDPd 26/206. The entry refers across to the work done in 1726 on p. 251.

September Jane more 1 day Shearing hay
December Jane 3 days Spinning flanel

May 8th–9th
Sarah Fell & her Son Each a day
bearing peats <(minde footing ..)>
May 29 Sarah 1 [day *interlined*] Louking in Garding
June 25th Sarah 2 days Working hay
More half a day that week

July 4th Sarah 4 days working hay pow[304]
    11th that week 2 days
    18 that week 3 <1/2>0
    25 that week 2
See on the over Leave side

[*p. 251*]

Account of Worke done at Townend [Barn *interlined*]

February 19	paid James Taylor	6 dayes	G[round] Wark		
1725	James Danson	6			
	Edward parke	6			
	paid Leonard Park	6	one Wateday[305]		
	paid George Braithwait	1			
	Our Edward				
	John of Wattersid	2			
25	Leonard Parke	6 dayes at [Crag *interlined*]			
paid	for Side of House				
paid	James Taylor	4 days at Cragg			
April 29	paid Rownson	4 days washing sand			
June 2th	to Cranks for Ruffcasting		1	s	
1726	House		<.>3	2	
at the Same time To Rownson			0	6	6d
To Edward parke			3	14	6
September 18 to Rownson			0	2	6

March 30th 1730 Sarah Fell
1 day & 2 half days in Garding
William Fell 1 day Harrowing in Field
Sar[ah] Fell 1 day Harrowing in Hag
& Green Slack

---

304 Hay in the meadows near Rusland Pool. The cross-reference below is to p. 251 where the account
     with Sarah Fell is continued.
305 Perhaps wet day is meant.

April 2 days Filling Mainer
May S[arah] Fell [half *interlined*] a day footing peats
July 29 S[arah] Fell 1 [day *interlined*] & a half working hay
August 8 Sarah 2 days working [hay *interlined*]
25th
Sarah Fell 1 day Shearning [*sic*] bigg
September 1 day Shearing Hagg
another day Shearing In field
24th one day Working in Garding
December Sarah 5 [days *interlined*] spining flanel

[*p. 252*]

The Smithy rent of Finsthwaite
and Stot parke pro the year 1713

	li	s	d	
Robert Taylor	0	3	6	0
George Braithwaite	0	2	7	2
Myles Harrison	0	1	1	0
Mr John Taylor	0	5	2	0
Christopher Taylor	0	1	6	0
Robert Taylor pro Chap[man House]		0	2	3
John Taylor	0	1	6	2
Clement Taylor	0	2	10	<2>3
Robert Sawrey	0	0	11	0
Richard Robinson	0	2	7	1
George Taylor	0	1	<1>0	<1>2
George Braithwait	0	0	1	2
Genet Dixon	0	0	2	2
vidua John Adinson	0	0	2	0
James Taylor	0	0	4	2
vidua Edward Taylor	0	0	0	2
Edward Nuby	0	0	0	2
Baldra moss	0	0	1	0
John Maychell	0	0	0	1
James Walker	0	0	5	2
of Mart [*sic*] & John Sawrey pro parrack[306]			0	2

Smithy Rent			
Finsthwait	1	4	4
Haverthwait	0	16	10
Rusland	1	13	0
rent in all	3	14	2

306 This line is a later insertion.

			d	q
1718				
paid at a single poor [bill *interlined*]			11	1 1/2
more pro Bloomer R[idding]			0	2
payment in all			11	3 1/2
Land Sess at 3s per li		12s	8	
Bloomer Riddin		00	6	1/3
October 1th 1724 Land Sess				
pro Finsthwait & Townend at 2s				
al paid 8s 6d 2q				

[*p. 253*]

[*at side*] a S[ingle] p[oor] Bill

		s	d	
A Single poor Bill				
for Haverthwait Finsthwait & Rusland	0	15	0	
Nibthwait	0	10	0	
a single poor Bill the East Side C[olton] Beck	0	8	4	
the West Side C[olton] Beck		6	8	
	2	0	0	
Smithy rent bill[307]				
Robert Taylor		3	6	
George Braithwaite		2	10	
Lawrance Harrison		1	0	
John Taylor Lending		5	4 1/2	
Henry Elertson		1	6	
Robert Atkinson pro Chap[man House]		0	3	
Edward Taylor		2	11 1/2	
Robert Sawrey		0	4 1/2	
Richard Robinson		2		
George Taylor		1	2	
Charley Cragg		0	1 1/2	
George Braithwait		0	2 1/2	
Jennet Dixon		0	2 1/2	
James Taylor		0	8	ob qr
James Adinson		0	2	
Elerside		0	0 1/2	
Abraham Rawlinson		0	1	
Edward Nuby		0	0 1/2	
John Maychel		0	0	qr

[307] This smithy rental is undated, but it was made before John Taylor of Landing died in 1723.

[p. 254]

	s	d	q
Smithy rent pro 1731			
George Braithwait	2	7	2
Robert Taylor & George	3	8	3
Miles Harrison	1	1	
Mr Henry Taylor	5	0	
James Dixon	0	2	
Christopher Taylor	1	6	
James Backhouse	1	6	2
Clement Taylor	3	<.>4	2
John Taylor <payes in part of C Taylor's>		1	
Margaret Sawrey	0	2	
Richard Robinson	2	8	1
William Danson	0	0	2
Margaret Braithwait	0	0	1
George Taylor	1	0	2
Thomas & George Braithwait	0	1	
Samuel Robinson	0	2	2
Widdow Denny	0	2	
William Spence pro Elerside	0	0	2
Richard Simpson	0	1	2
Richard Postlethwait	0	1	2
Baldramoss	0	1	
Mr John Maychel	0	0	1
Thomas Walker alias R[ichard] Robinson	0	5	2

Colector C T	1li	4s	4d

[p. 255]

The Master Wage pro
Finsthwait Haverthwait & Rusland pro
1722[308]

	s	d
Myles Walker	1	8
John Rawlinson	0	4
Thomas Bornes	0	4
Arthur Benson alias J[ohn] R[awlinson]	1	0
Stephen Rawlinson	0	10
Richard Nuby	0	4
John Maychell	2	6
John Robinson	0	4
Robert Rigge	0	8

308 For the school at Colton, see n. 31. The first thirteen names are from Haverthwaite, the next seventeen from Finsthwaite, and the remainder from Rusland.

Jona Skelding	0	10
Richard Postlethwaite	0	8
Edward Nuby	0	8
John Bornes	0	4
James Dixon	0	4
Thomas & George Braithwaite	0	4
George Taylor	0	8
Richard Robinson	0	8
Robert Sawrey	0	4
Old Jennet Taylor C. T.	0	4
Clement Taylor	0	6
James Taylor C. T. payes	0	4
Cobbyes C. T. payes	1	0
John Taylor	0	6
Christopher Taylor	0	4
Myles Harrison	0	8
George Braithwaite	1	0
Robert & George Taylor	1	10
Mr John Taylor	1	8
Thomas Denny	0	4
Sinderhill	[blank]	

[p. 256]

	s	d
Robert Scales	0	8
John Scales	1	0
George Maychell	0	6
William Taylor	1	0
Clement Taylor	0	10
Robert Wilson	0	4
George Bank	0	6
Robert Taylor	0	6
Bailif & Margaret Walker	0	4
Robert Atkinson	0	8
Rowland Wilson	0	4
Elizabeth Bailif	0	4
John Wilson	0	4
John Wilson Smith	0	4
Myles Drinkell	0	8
Mr Abraham Rawlinson	1	6
Robert Atkinson of Dope	0	4
Reginald Strickland	1	2
William Strickland	0	4
Thomas Strickland	0	4

Thomas Strickland   0   6
John Bailif   0   6
John Taylor   0   4
Thomas Satterthwait   0   4

Richard Nuby Churchwarden

A receipt how to make
Inke
1th   8 ounces of blew galls
          4 ounces of Gumm
(Ether)   4 ounce of Copperas
2 or   4 ounce of Lofe Suger
          1 pint of [white wine *interlined*] Vinegar
          2 quarts of Rainwater

[*p. 257*]

A List of what persons were
Sworne together at Hawskhead
Ano Domini 1723[309]

Agnes Garner of Bordridge–[Windermear *interlined*]
George Towers of Conistone
Clement Taylor of Finsthwait
William Braithwaite fould in Sawrey
William Nicholson Hanickin
John Braithwait Satterhow
Richard Robinson Waterside
John Taylor Joliver tree
Robert Taylor Stotparke
Myles Harrison Stotpark
John Robinson Arnside
Elizabeth Robinson Arnside
Edward Kellet Counsey
Rowland Wilson Crosslands
William Braithwait Law Satterhow
William Braithwait Lain Head Sawrey
Edward Braithwait Hawkshead
George Banke Crosslands
William Braithwait Sawrey Infra
Thomas Strickland Light How
Thomas Satterthwaite Whait Moss

309   No indication of why they were 'sworne together' is given. They are all relatively prosperous landowners, mainly from High Furness; the presence of three women is interesting.

John Bailif Light How
Robert Rigge Sawrey Infra
John Hutchinson Sawrey Infra
Mary Wilson Sawrey Infra
John Dixon Sawrey Extra
John Braithwait of peper in Sawrey
William Walker Daleparke
Robert Atkinson Crosslands
Robert Taylor Crosslands
Jonathan Fisher Sawrey Extra
Myles Sawrey Coniston Waterhead
Number 32

[*p. 258*]

	days	day
July 5th 1730 Thomas Masicks		1/2
2d Week	2	0
17th 3 Week	1	0

Peter Wife 2 days shearing
Agnes Dixon half a day shearing
Grace one day shearing
G[race] another

July
Isabel Dixon one day & 2 half days
          days
25 that week 2
30 that week 1
August 5th 1 day Shearing bigg backside
September 7 2 days Shearing oats G & H
one Day Shearing in M[yles] Field

on St. Thomas Day devided to they
poor Labrours of Finsthwait which
being their peyment deue of <60li> the Intrest
of 60li for 2 years due at the
abovesaid day 1731[310]

	s	d
To Sarah Fell Widdaw	1	6
To George Braithwait	1	6
To Thomas Braithwait	1	6
To Jane Woodburne	1	0

Devid [*sic*] per C T being Thomas Strickland
Gift per his will

310 St Thomas the Apostle, 21 December; for the Thomas Strickland charity, see n. 177.

[p. 259]

June	1727 <Work> at pertition[311]				
2	John Walker	5	0	dayes	
week	John Holme	6	0		
	John Wilson	6	0		

3 week at pertition

John Walker	4	0		
Holme	4	0	June	
Wilson	4	0		

1th week I have not the Account of Walker work

John Walker	5		
J[ohn] H[olme]	5		29th June
J[ohn] Wilson	5		

July 21 John Holme	5	
John Wilson	5	

John Walker	3	
John Holme	6	July 29th
John Wilson	6	

August	John Holme	1 day	1/2
12th	John Walker	5	1/2
	John Holme	6	0

19	John Walker	6	0	Expenses
September	John Walker	3		
3d	John Holme	4		
John Wilson		4		

9th	John Walker	4 1/2
	John Wilson	4 1/2
	John Holme	6

24	John Walker	5
	John Wilson	6
	John Holme	3
November	John Walker	6
	John Holme	6
	John Wilson	6

311 These entries refer to work in the new house; see xxiii.

Margaret Braithwait 1 day working [hay *interlined*]
august M[argaret] B[raithwait] more 1/2 day working hay
2 days shearing off potates

[*p. 260*]

July 1th 1727
Sold William Coward 9 wedders

For			2	8	0
More a Tup			0	8	0
More a Wedder			0	7	0
More Great Cow Calf			0	10	0
September 2 wedders			0	8	0
5 Sheep Skins			0	2	0
	C T	total	4	03	0
August 12 a quarter of Mutton about			0	1	0
19 a quarter of Mutton			0	1	2
27 a leg of Mutton			0	1	0
September a quarter of Mutton			0	1	0
9th a quarter of Mutton			0	1	2

January 1727
Meat had of William Cowhird

since June Last			0	19	3
for peeling 16 1/2 quarter of					
Bark in Thomas Hagg Coppy					
Comes to			1	13	6
for Cutting 3 load 1/2 of					
Coals at 2s 6d per load			0	8	9
	William C[oward]	total	3	1	6
debtor to C T as above			4	3	0
Due to William Coward			3	1	6
Ballance due to W[illiam] C[oward]			1	1	6
More a Ceslap[312]			0	0	6
Behind of Beif			0	1	0
paid per C T					

---

312 The word is perfectly clear, but its meaning is unknown.

212 *The Account Book of Clement Taylor*

February 21 Then bought of Thomas Hall
for Chappel
Blackwell Second hand in
Eight Voloms³¹³ for   1   14   6

[*p. 261*]

June 1726 Meat Had of William
Coward
2 [hind *interlined*] quarters of Lam about   01   6
a quarter Mutton [J T *interlined*] Sheep   01   0
July a quarter of Veal of our own Calf   1   8
a quarter of Mutton of Edward sheep   1   0
A Calf head   0   4
a Sheep Innmeat & 2 pound Suit³¹⁴   0   6 1/2

William Coward Had a Calf   10   0

July William Coward Had 2 Ews   12   0

of William Coward a Legg of Mutton   0   8
A Sheep In Meat   0
31th a Legg of Mutton   [*blank*]
August a hind quarter of Mutton   8
17th a quarter Mutton   1   2
23   quarter of Muten   1   2
   2li 1/2 of Suet at 2d 1/2   0   6   1q
Sold A Tupp to William C[oward]   [*blank*]
27th a Hind quarter Mutton about   0   8   0
September 10th a Legg of Mutton   6   0
14th a quarter of Mutten   0   11   0
18 a Legg of Mutten   0   6   0
a Sheep head pro Rownson   0   1   1/2
a Sheep had from bouth pro Rownson   [*blank*]

October a legg of Mutton   [*blank*]

William Cowhird had My wife Why Calf   8   6
February 1726 accounted with the above

---

313 Offspring Blackall or Blackhall (1654–1716), bishop of Exeter, author of sermons and pamphlets. His name is given correctly in the churchwardens' account book: 'Paid to Mr Hall for Blackall's Sermons 8 Volumes £1 14 6': CRO, WPR 101/W1.
314 Suet; 'inmeat' may mean offal.

said upon all Accompts to this day
Meat had of William Coward Since 1 June

		s	d
1727			
a quarter Mutton about		1	2
a quarter & 1/2 of veal		2	9
a leg of Tup Mutton		0	7d
Received in part for Sheep	2li	0	0
a Calf head & 2 Gang of Calf feet		[blank]	
July a Legg of Tup Mutton	0	1	1
24 a quarter Mutton	0	1	4
30 a quarter Mutton	0	1	0
Bought at Bouth a quarter Mutton	0	1	0

[*p. 262*]

To The Reverend Mr Taylor
Vicar [of *interlined*] Long Buckby to be left
at The post-house in Daventry
Northamptonshire
These

	li
1 pott weyd	15 1/2
1 pott	12 1/2[315]

[*p. 263*]

November the 6 1715
Account of Number of Sheep at the time
Imprimis   75 Wedders
Item   82 Ews
Item   68 hoggs

October 1th 1718   [*miscellaneous calculations at side*]
hogs   59
Ews   [*blank*]
Wedders   [*blank*]

March 26 1720
Account of Sheep <with lam>
Ews lamtt & with lam   96
hoggs   51

---

315 *cf* n. 77.

Wedders   67
Geld Ews   02

Aprill 20th 1720 Account of
lams gelded   41
Imprimis [illegible]   39 all lived
October 29 1720 Account of Sheep Salved
Hoggs   62
Wedders   54
More Wedder twinters   09 & bad on [sic]
Ews   101   November
More fouer Tups   004   82 Ews
                              ---   61 hoggs
                              230   9 w[edder] twinters
of the said Number 4 roten Ews

November 1720
Sold 10 Wedders   <10>10   0
one Wedder Died   01   0
one hogg Dyed   01   0
kilt 3 Ews   3   0
Sold 16 Ews   16   0
one Ewe Died in Myles Field   01   0
3 Ews Dead   3   0
3 Ews Dead   3   0
3 hoggs Ditto   3   0

Aprill 1721
Ews with lams when we turned them   53   0
More 5 In Dispute   5   0
More 12 Gend [sic][316] Ews   12   0
More 2 with lam   02   0
More 2 Geld Ews   02   0

[p. 264]

November the 1th 1721 Account of Number
of Sheep
Wedders put to Height   48   0
Wedder twinters in Knott   27   0
Old wedders in Knott   03   0
Ews put to Tupp   74   0
Gimmer twinters in Hagg   05   0

316   Gelt.

one Wedder twinter in Hagg	01	0
Two tainted Ews		
Broken Legged Wedder twinter		
Hoggs	37	0
Two Tipps[317]	02	0

Ews Dead one in New Cloas	
Hoggs Dead	4

Aprill Sheep Sold to Henry Samson

		[s	d]
1722			
Imprimis two Geld Ews		8	0
paid Item 3 wedders		18	0
Item <3> 4 Hoggs		12	0
Item one Wedder		04	0

October Sold to Edward Bland 16 gimmers

Sheep Salved This year 1722
October

28 1722 Wedders put to Height	60	0
Wedder Twinters	03	
Ews put To Tup	72	
Hoggs Salved	40	
Tup twinters	02	
Aggy Tup[318]	01	
Borrowed Thomas Rigg Tup	00	
More Wedders	02	
More Wedder twinters	3	
one Wedder more	1	

Stogs[319] & Deyed	3	0

[p. 265]

Sheep Salved in 1723		
1th Ews	68	0
Wedders	61	0
Wedder twinters	11	0
Hoggs	39	0
tups	02	0
	181	

317 Tups.
318 Children were frequently left a lamb in a godparent's will, and Clement's daughter Agnes was probably the owner of this tup. She was only three, so it seems unlikely to have been her pet lamb.
319 This word is no longer recognised.

216 *The Account Book of Clement Taylor*

Sheep Salved 1724
Ews   75
Wedders about   80   about
hoggs   44   dead 2
Tups   02

Sheep Salved Anno 1725

		li	s
Top of Parrack Wood			
120 quarter of Bark		50	0
33 tunn of timber		43	0
20 load of Coales		18	0
		111	0

[*miscellaneous calculations at foot*]

[*p. 266*]

[*miscellaneous calculations at head*]

Aprill the 16th 1715[320]

account of Sheep Livered from
Mr. John Taylor to John Coward
pro the Use of Mr. Robert Ridgway
Imprimis   77 Ews
                21 Wedders
                07 rams
                37 hoggs

        in all   142

November Meat had of William Cowhird This
1725   year in all   15   5
a Sheep Carcass at
Child's funerall[321]   4   6

---

320 *cf* n. 76. This is the farm at Plum Green [now Rose Cottage], the home of Henry Taylor's family until they removed to Landing before the death of his grandfather George in 1684. The old Plum Green house was retained and divided in two, a new one being created from its downhouse; see n. 194. Robert Ridgway has not been identified, and his part in the transaction is mysterious, as John Coward was the tenant.
321 See n. 103.

a quarter of Veal which
went to Jolivertree pro
present

1725
William Cowhird Bout Sheep
& a Calfe which Came to
this year   1   4   6

a receipt pro a Swelling in a
women's brest
hongrey water 3d per ounce
Spirits of Lavander 6d per ounce
use a little of the Spirits of Lavander
mixt with the other

[*George Simpson: loose paper inserted*]

For Robert Leck's Son a Spelling Book
& a Testament. For H. Taylor's Son
Horn Book & 2 Primers. For his
Daughter Emme a Bible; <a>2 Common
prayer Books; The pious country Parishoner[322]

[*another hand*]

Taylor   Eliz Taylor
Eliz Taylor   Elizabeth
                              Taylor

[*p. i: the dorse of the front endpaper which was originally stuck onto the cover; miscellaneous accounts and scribbles by Edward Taylor, of which the following are legible examples*]

paid the above

3.17
   4
―――
4. 1 the Rent
of M[ary] Danson Farm

[322] William, son of Robert Leck, was baptised 17 September 1738; Thomas, son of Henry Taylor, was baptised 22 February 1741; Emme, daughter of Henry Taylor, was baptised 17 September 1738. The seventh edition of *The Pious Country Parishioner*, an anonymous work in eight recorded editions, was first published in 1736. These may be books for poor children being paid for out of Richard Robinson's legacy: see n. 231.

2.3 per Dozen

1756

Edward Taylor Finsthwaite
    Furness Fells
per Caxton Bag Lancashire

Edward Taylor Finsthwaite
    Furness Fells
      Lancashire

[*p. ii: original front endpaper, gradually covered with miscellaneous notes and calculations by Clement Taylor:*]

The Several raisures being first made
in presentia nostrum J Dixon Bond
Testa. C.T.

a Messenger

a Messenger will come to Graithwait per this
pa<q>cquet

Interlined

	days
Clement	2 mowing
	1 shearing
	1 salving

of Wedders 2 days

William son of [Edward *interlined*] Taylor
baptised May 22 1700
per Thomas Taylor Minister
of Coulton

C Taylor L[and] & window tax
at 2s per half year 7s 6d
    1730

March 11th & November 11 Nusepaper
from Kendall per Jeramiah
Huddarst [*sic*] 1731

6th October Lewcastell [*sic*]³²³
paper Quarter End

[*p. iii: originally left blank, but with notes similar to those on p. ii:*]

1717 C.T Debtor [*torn*]   16s

Margaret	Taylor			40	0
More				20	0
more	lieu in Stead			02	
More	Dower widdow right			03	0
More	[*Illegible*]			02	0
		day		21	0
				88	0
William Taylor			1	9	0
				Clement	
	Clement			20	0

Jane Woodburn

January 13 1729 look for   per day³²⁴
                        days
Old Nick   2
Ladd Henry Junior   2

Old Henry	3				
William	3	days first week ?haring day			
Young Nick	3				
Rownson	2	1th week one of old			
William	6				
Henry	6	2d week		depen	
Nick Junior	6	September 10		Depen	
boy Henry Junior	6				
Rownson	6	paid Rownson 2s 6d part			
Rownson	2	September 18			
September	23 Rownson	5			
	30 Rownson	3	N Elder	11d =	74d
			Nick Junior	17 9	11
October	Nick	6	Old William	9 6	
8	Henry	6	Henry Elder	16 10	8
	Nick Junior	6	Henry Younger	16 4	4

323 An error for Newcastle; see n. 214.
324 These are payments for plastering in the new house.

Henry Junior	6				
Rownson	5		1	18	3
Rownson	2				

	Chapel	
Nick	2	Bn 27<8> November
Henry Elder	2	White Loves had
Nick Junior	2	of William Walker 4
Henry younger	2	
		3 halfpenny Loves

Candle before C

[*p. iv: dorse of p. iii*]

Mr Ros[sk]kell	1s	6d per quarter[325]
Mr Rowlandson	2s	6d
Mr Hunter		
Cockpeny Comes to	2s	6d

1 9 6

Edward Danson Farm			
ancient	2	14	
Haggs	3	00	
pull Middow	0	12	
pincha Croft	0	15	
Top of Parrack		2	he hath not 1727
Tarnhaw		4	
	li	s	d
Fearr Hagg & Long Myr	1	0	0
E[dward] D[anson] Rent 1729	7	5	0

head 5d tongue 5d tripes & feet 1s

January the 18
1734
price of
Coals & piggs

[*inside back cover; the back endpaper is missing*]

1754 [*twice*]; Edward Taylor [*three times*]

325 Payments to Browedge School, probably for William Taylor.

APPENDIX

JOHN HATHORNTHWAITE'S WILL

One series of entries in the account book takes us away from Finsthwaite and into a wider world and another religious faith. Pp. 226-30, and one entry on p. 123 are concerned with the will of a Quaker yeoman, John Hathornthwaite of Sandside in Kirkby Ireleth, who died on 13 April 1731 and was buried on the 16th in the Friends' burial ground at Sunbrick, near Ulverston.[1] One of his executors was Clement Taylor's brother Edward, who, when a problem arose over the executorship, clearly asked for his brother's help. What Edward's connection with Hathornthwaite was is not made clear.

In his will, dated 12 April 1731, John Hathornthwaite left £100 each to the (unnamed) children of his late brother James, £100 each to his cousin John Denison and his sister Sarah Denison, £20 each to the children of his cousin William Denison, and £10 to the new meeting house at Rookhow.[2]

John, James, and Sarah Hathornthwaite were the children of William Hathornthwaite who died on 22 April 1700 and was buried at Sunbrick on the 24th. John was probably born in 1653, the son of William and his first wife Elizabeth,[3] and seems to have been unmarried. Sarah married William Denison, a grocer at Dalton-in-Furness and apparently a non-Quaker. Their children were baptised at Dalton church, and William was buried there on 20 October 1740. His wife, who affirmed instead of taking the oath when she proved his will and was buried 'at Sepulchre' on 11 December 1748,[4] evidently remained true to the faith in which she had been brought up.

William and Sarah Denison had two sons, William and John, and three daughters, Elizabeth, Sarah, and Jane. William became an innkeeper in Ulverston and died in 1756. John was still alive in 1741 when his sister Jane made her will, and is the cousin John mentioned in John Hathornthwaite's will. Elizabeth married James Crane of Ormskirk at Croston, Lancs., in 1721, and although Sarah's marriage to Thomas Farrington has not been traced their son Thomas was baptised at Croston in 1743. Jane remained in Dalton and kept some kind of shop there (its contents are mentioned in her probate inventory). She died in 1755.

James Hathornthwaite married Bridget Cowell in or about 1674. His burial has not been traced, but she was buried at Ulverston on 2 March 1700 from Arrad Foot. The male Hathornthwaites of this generation seem to have allowed their Quakerism to sit lightly upon them. James and Bridget were said to have been married by a 'Preist of Baal',[5] presumably an Anglican clergyman, and John apparently

---

1 *CW2*, 1906, 277.
2 LRO, DDPd 32/1; the probate copy is *ibid.* 32/3. For Rook How meeting house, see n. 267.
3 *The Household Account Book of Sarah Fell of Swarthmoor Hall*, ed. N. Penney, Cambridge, 1920, 531.
4 Her burial is not recorded at either Sunbrick or Swarthmoor, but is noted in the register at Dalton.
5 *The Household Account Book of Sarah Fell*, 545.

permitted shocking irregularities at his father's funeral in 1700.[6] James and Bridget had at least four children who were known to be alive after their uncle John's death. John lived at Newton-in-Furness; Elizabeth had married Richard Law of Blackburn; Sarah married an innkeeper from Bolton-le-Moors, John Brandwood, who died in 1729; the whereabouts of Dorothy were unknown. Only John and Elizabeth were found immediately after their uncle died, but it emerged shortly afterwards that Sarah Brandwood must have been dead as her children succeeded to her claim upon his estate.

When Edward Taylor and his fellow-executor, Daniel Abraham of Swarthmoor Hall,[7] came to prove John Hathornthwaite's will, the question arose of how many of James Hathornthwaite's children there might be in all, none having been named precisely, and how the executors might protect themselves from claims made by any others who might appear in the future. Daniel Abraham seems to have taken a different view of the matter than Edward Taylor did, and so a 'Referance' took place between them.

An arrangement was made in May 1731,[8] whereby the two executors agreed to pay increased legacies to John Hathornthwaite, Elizabeth and Richard Law, William Denison, his daughters Elizabeth Crane, Sarah Farrington, and Jane Denison, and his son William,[9] and to the six children of Sarah Brandwood, John, Oliver, Elizabeth, Sarah, Richard, and Ann. There was some doubt in Clement Taylor's mind about these children, as the list on p. 227 mentions only four of them, two of whom do not appear on the list in the agreement of May 1731. That said that it was uncertain whether any other children of James Hathornthwaite were living when his brother died, but that the testator might have thought that there were and that they might subsequently appear. So the legacies were increased by sums of £50 to John Hathornthwaite, the Laws, and the Cranes, £20 to William Denison senior, and £100 to the Brandwood children. In return, those legatees agreed to indemnify the executors against claims from any other relation who might appear in the future. In particular, they agreed that they would pay Dorothy Hathornthwaite if she were to make a claim upon her uncle's estate.

By this agreement, therefore, the executors were able to retain what remained of John Hathornthwaite's personal estate after the legacies were paid. Richard Law received his wife's increased legacy of £150 in April 1732 [p. 226], so he was evidently satisfied, and part of the Brandwood children's money was paid at the same time. But Daniel Abraham was apparently not content, for Clement Taylor records meetings with lawyers and others over the matter in the late summer of 1732. John Hathornthwaite was paid in September [p. 228],[10] but the negotiations dragged on, although William Denison senior made a formal renunciation of any

---

6   *ibid.* 531.
7   Daniel, son of John Abraham of Manchester, grocer, married Rachel, daughter of Judge Thomas Fell of Swarthmoor Hall, on 7 March 1683, and so became the son-in-law of Margaret and George Fox. Clement Taylor always called him 'Abrahams'.
8   LRO, DDPd 32/2.
9   Curiously, the agreement does not mention John Denison, who was named as a legatee in the will.
10   His quitclaim for £150 is *ibid.* 26/232.

claim he might have against the executors in January 1733.[11] The following November Thomas Farrington of Croston acknowledged a payment of £50.[12] Daniel Abraham died in December 1732 and was buried at Swarthmoor on the 27th. His part of the executorship would have passed to his son John, and the matter was evidently not immediately settled.[13] As late as March 1735 Edward Taylor 'Waited for Abraham with a designe to devide H money' [p. 123], and in September 1735 John Abraham wrote to him proposing arrangements to pay the money owed to William Denison junior and urging him to be 'att Ulverston next market Day without fail'.[14]

What happened in the end is not made clear from the account book, but presumably the agreement of 1731 was adhered to, and all the legacies paid. George Dodson [p. 226] was presumably a debtor of John Hathornthwaite's. John Sedon of Deane [pp. 227, 230] was probably the guardian of such of the Brandwood children who were still minors.

---

11 *ibid.* 32/4.
12 *ibid.* 26/235.
13 John Abraham may already have been involved. On 17 August 1732 Edward and Clement Taylor drew up a bond to him for £50 to abide by an arbitration in an unspecified matter by Myles Sandys and William Rawlinson: CRO, BD/HJ/89, bundle 4, no. 3. No mention of any such arbitration appears in the account book, but both Sandys and Rawlinson are mentioned, and Clement Taylor paid money to their servants in November 1732 [p. 228].
14 LRO, DDPd 26/243a.

BIOGRAPHICAL INDEX

Clement Taylor mentions a great number of people in his account book. It is possible to identify many of them, though for some the available detail is disproportionate to their importance in his life. Some major figures, on the other hand, cannot be properly identified, like John Walker, the joiner who worked on the new house, who cannot be distinguished among a number of local John Walkers. There are also other John Taylors, apart from those included here, and the same is true of other names. I have not given details for everyone mentioned in the bloomsmithy rentals and similar lists, but all Finsthwaite residents appear in the list below. Some other names in the book are explained in footnotes to the text.

Dates of baptisms, marriages, and burials are from the Finsthwaite parish registers unless otherwise indicated; wills and administrations are from the series of Richmond wills in LRO, WRW/F and marriage bonds from LRO, ARR 11. Dates from Quaker registers have been modernised, *e.g.* 2nd month is rendered as April.

Addison, Frances	widow of John Addison of Newby Bridge, borrower (bur. 26.5.1712 Hawkshead); the original loan of £60 was made by Edward Taylor, father of Clement; Sarah Addison, lender in 1744, was her daughter
Atkinson, Robert	of Over Kellet, Westm., stone merchant; bap. 10 Dec. 1682 Over Kellet; children bap. at Over Kellet 1714–27; bur. 6.4.1737 Over Kellet
Ayrey, Benjamin	agent, or company secretary, at the Backbarrow Co. from *c.*1714, and widely respected; d. 28 Aug. 1750, bur. at Height meeting house: Cartmel Quaker reg.; partner in the Glengarry venture 1727; see A. Fell, *The Early Iron Industry of Furness and District*, Ulverston, 1908, 303–4, 350; in his will, 26 Aug. 1750, he provided for his brothers and sister and their children, and mentioned his 'Library of Books' and some prized furniture
Backhouse, James	bap. 11 June 1695 Crosthwaite, Westm.; mar. Mary Gurnell (*q.v.*), 29 May 1729; children bap. 1729–32; bur. 14 Mar. 1762; wife bur. 30 Oct. 1744; through marriage he came to live at his wife's house at Jolliver Tree, and was probably responsible for building the new one next door to it, very much in the style of Clement Taylor's; a prime mover in

establishing the church and school at Finsthwaite, and an important figure in local shipping circles, and in the iron industry; partner in the Newland Co. and in the Lorne furnace; churchwarden for both houses at Jolliver Tree 1736–7, and for Green Cottage 1741; his only son died at the age of 20 in 1752, two daughters having died in infancy, and he brought a nephew to live in Finsthwaite as the heir to most of his very considerable property there

Banke, George — of Crosslands, Rusland; bur. 5 Feb. 1775 Rusland (Colton reg.); overseer 1720, constable 1740

Barwick, Edward — carpenter; gained settlement in Finsthwaite 15 April 1715 from Hawkshead 'for his better Advancement in his Trade': CRO, BPR 17/Ol/3; children bap. at Colton, Cartmel, and Finsthwaite 1715–31; bur. 5 April 1734; wife Margaret bur. 28 Oct. 1733; lived at Stott Park, Finsyke, and Sinderhill; administration granted to principal creditors 1734

Barwick, Henry — of Aynsome and Cartmel, borrower; bap. 24 May 1683 Cartmel; children bap. at Cartmel 1727–30; bur. 10 Jan. 1767 Cartmel; some involvement in the sale of the wood from Partingtree

Benson, John — tenant of Tom Crag c. 1750–91; mar. Jane Benson, 5 June 1745; children bap. 1746-56; bur. 10 May 1795; wife bur. 5 Jan. 1791

Bland, Edward — stocktaker at the Backbarrow Co. 1715: CRO, BDX 295/2; bought sheep from Clement Taylor; occ. 1727 in dispute at Browedge school: *CW2*, 1972, 221

Blendall, John — of Cark, miller; mar. Margaret Green, 14 Dec. 1729 Cartmel; children bap. at Cartmel 1730–34; bur. 26 Oct. 1734 Cartmel; gave evidence in dispute about peat rights, c.1739: LRO, DDPd 26/333

Braithwaite, Dorothy 'Dolie' — wife of Thomas Braithwaite of Town End (*q.v.*); bur. 25 Aug. 1743; received charity money 1732–40

Braithwaite, George — of Kendal, dyer; Quaker; established dyeing and drysaltery business in Kendal 1711: E.J. Satterthwaite, *Records of the Friends' Burial Ground at Colthouse*, Ambleside, 1914, 29

Biographical Index

Braithwaite, George — of Stott Park; bap. 31 Oct. 1671 Warton, son of William Braithwaite of Carnforth and Stott Park; mar. Deborah French, 29 Oct. 1709 Bolton-le-Sands; bur. 5 Sept. 1761, aged 91; wife bur. 22 Sept. 1769; dissenter, associated with both the Baptist church at Tottlebank and the Unitarian chapel in Kendal, and therefore contributed only to the school at Finsthwaite, not to the church; churchwarden at Colton 1745, constable 1706, overseer 1719

Braithwaite, George 'of Jamies' — of Town End, labourer and woodcutter; son of James Braithwaite; mar. 1) Margaret Walker, 21 Nov. 1721 Colton; 1st wife bur. 18 Aug. 1721 Colton; mar. 2) Grace (*q.v.*); bur. 11 April 1739; with brothers Thomas (*q.v.*) and William sold most or all of the land inherited from their father 1707–15: LRO, DDPd 26/176-80, 196; received charity money 1730–37

Braithwaite, Grace — 2nd wife of George Braithwaite of Town End (*q.v.*); bur. 27 Feb. 1763, of Plum Green; received parish pension from Colton, and funeral expenses: CRO, BPR 17/C2/1

Braithwaite, Margaret — da. of Thomas Braithwaite (*q.v.*) of Town End; bur. 15 April 1740; will 13 April 1740, apparently written in her own hand, bequeathed all property to her mother Dorothy (*q.v.*) for life, then to her uncle Robert Sharp of Cartmel Fell, and his younger daughter 'Barty Bonaz', and some gifts of money, including 'a Ginney & a halfe' to the vicar, John Harrison (*q.v.*), and 2s each to Clement Taylor and James Backhouse (*q.v.*); her inventory lists only money and clothes (£2 18s 6d), household goods (£1 16s 6d), and money owing (£22), but for her inheritance from her aunt, Margaret Sawrey, see n. 221

Braithwaite, Thomas — of Town End, woodcutter and labourer; son of James Braithwaite, and brother of George (*q.v.*) and William; mar. Dorothy Sharp, 22 June 1696 Hawkshead; bur. 27 Jan. 1732; for sales of land in Finsthwaite, see George Braithwaite of Town End

Burns, Edward — of Bouth, yeoman and butcher; bap. 12 Dec. 1688 Colton; mar. Alice Scales, 1 June 1712 Colton; children bap. at Colton 1713–31; not bur. Colton;

	wife bur. 14 Feb. 1764 Colton; financial disaster implied in will, 28 Oct. 1731, proved 1734, which left all property to be sold for payment of debts, the residue for support of wife and children, and personal estate under £5
Case, John	of Northscale, Walney; bap. 9 May 1704 Dalton; mar. Elizabeth Cowpland, 14 Jan. 1728; children bap. at Dalton 1729–40; bur. 28 Sept. 1766 Dalton; wife bur. 4 Dec. 1760 Dalton; involved in dispute with the vicar of Colton (see n. 154), although not resident in Finsthwaite
Chamney, Francis	of Stock, borrower; mar. Elizabeth Scotson, 9 April 1710 Colton; children bap. at Colton 1711–27; bur. 2 July 1767 Colton; lessee of Stoney Hazel forge 1718 Fell, *op.cit.*, 202; overseer and constable at Colton
Chapman, William	of Old Hall, Bouth; son of Thomas Chapman (bur. 1713 Colton) and wife Barbara Sandys (bur. 1712 Colton), who owned Chapman House, Finsthwaite; mar. Jennett Fell (of Daltongate, Ulverston), 1708 (bond); children bap. at Colton 1710–24; bur. 5 April 1757 Colton; wife bur. 21 Aug. 1759 Colton; churchwarden and overseer at Colton
Collinson, William	maker of sheriff's uniform 1725; probably of Market Place, Ulverston, and bur. 10 Feb. 1761 Ulverston
Coupland, James	of Parkamoor, borrower; d. 1724; dissenter, not bur. at Colton; churchwarden and overseer at Colton
Coupland, Robert	of Parkamoor, borrower; mar. Ann Richardson of Firbank, Westm., 1729 (bond); d. 1733; dissenter, not bur. at Colton; churchwarden, overseer, and constable at Colton
Coward, John	tenant of Henry Taylor of Landing (*q.v.*) at Plum Green; 1st wife Barbara bur. 9 Mar. 1726; mar. 2) Margaret Satterthwaite of Hawkshead, widow, 1728 (bond); bur. 8 July 1741, of Hazel How, Satterthwaite; father of William Coward (*q.v.*)
Coward, William	butcher and workman, son of John Coward (*q.v.*); mar. Ellen Bank, 20 May 1719 Colton; children bap.

at Colton and Finsthwaite 1720–37; lived at Plum Green, Landing, and Chapman House; ? overseer for Tom Crag 1743, but appears to have left Finsthwaite by 1741 as he was of 'Stockbrandreth', near Esthwaite in his father's will

Cragge, John — tenant of Waterside; mar. Anne Ridgeway of Satterthwaite, 17 Feb. 1742; son William bap. 23 Jan. 1743; ? bur. 16 Aug. 1765 Cartmel; probably son of James Cragg of Waterside, shoemaker (bur. 4 Aug. 1746)

Crank, Nicholas — of Ulverston, plasterer; worked at the church and on Clement Taylor's own house; ? bap. 3 Mar. 1678 Urswick; bur. 11 Nov. 1760 Ulverston; Henry Crank and Henry Crank junior were clearly connected, but their exact relationship has not been established

Croasdale, Henry — joiner and cooper; bap. 24 Mar. 1695 Waddington, WR Yorks.; mar. Eleanor Stockdale 6 Oct. 1722 Cartmel; children bap at Cartmel and Finsthwaite 1723–39; bur. 3 Sept. 1770; wife bur. 1 Feb. 1763; settlement certificate from Waddington to Colton 1724: CRO, BPR 17/Ol/9; lived at Fiddler Hall, Landing, Staveley, Plum Green, Chapman House, and Charley Crag; the first of a long line of woodcutters, joiners, coopers, and labourers in Finsthwaite, the last of whom still lived there in the present century; churchwarden at Colton 1757

Crossfield, Richard — of Seatle, woodmonger; bap. 28 Dec. 1682 Cartmel; mar. 1) Janet Pow, 12 Oct. 1703 Cartmel; 1st wife bur. 16 Sept. 1704 Cartmel; mar. 2) Elizabeth Muckelt, 19 Jan. 1713 Cartmel; children bap. at Cartmel 1704, 1713–21; bur. 7 May 1739 Cartmel

Danson, Christopher — son of James Danson (*q.v.*); bap. 12 Sept. 1716 Cartmel; bur. 15 Feb. 1799; unmarried; received charity money 1743

Danson, Edward — weaver and tenant of Cobby House; bap. 19 Aug. 1655 Cartmel; mar. Alice Addison 1684 (bond); children bap. at Colton 1685–8; bur. 16 Mar. 1730; wife bur. 23 Nov. 1752; lived also at Stott Park; his inventory mentions his 'shop' and he had an unusually large herd of cattle valued at £17 15s.

Danson, James	son of Edward Danson (*q.v.*); bap. 15 May 1688 Colton; 1st wife Sarah bur. 29 Dec. 1719 Colton; mar. 2) Jennett Burns, 16.12.1733; children bap. at Colton and Cartmel 1712–19; bur. 7 Mar. 1740; tenant, but of Stott Park at death; overseer 1729; received charity money; wife mar. 2) William Fell (see Richard Fell) 5 June 1742
Danson, Thomas	shoemaker and tenant of Cobby House; eldest son of Edward Danson (*q.v.*); mar. Mary Bankes of Grizedale, widow 1746 (bond); bur. 12 May 1754; wife bur. 8 May 1788; a prosperous man with goods valued at nearly £300 at death, including almost £200 lent on security and over £53 owing for book and other debts; his 'shop' contained, besides a stock of leather, seats and a table
Danson, William	shoemaker and beekeeper; son of Edward Danson (*q.v.*); bap. 22 Dec. 1685 Colton; unmarried; bur. 9 Sept. 1729; perhaps lived at Town End; left a new pair of boots to Clement Taylor; his will and inventory reveal hives of bees in at least four different parts of the village, leather valued at £22 10s, with 'rosin' and wooden heels, but no farm stock; for his bequest to the poor, see n. 218
Denny, Thomas	blacksmith and innkeeper at Newby Bridge; bap. 14 Nov. 1688 Cartmel; children bap. at Colton 1716–23; bur. 8 Sept. 1729; his wife Elizabeth continued to keep the inn after his death, but was of Cartmel when she sold property at Newby Bridge in 1741: LRO, DDPd 36/11 (see n. 242)
Drinkall, George	of Rusland, son of Myles Drinkall (*q.v.*); bap. 9 Nov. 1705 Colton; mar. 1) Esther Dodgson, 22 April 1731 Colton; 1st wife bur. 4 April 1733 Colton; mar. 2) Hannah Atkinson, 7 June 1739 Ulverston; co-founder of Lowwood furnace 1747; freeman of Lancaster 1745–6; deacon at Tottlebank Baptist church; bur. 23 Jan. 1789 Tottlebank; 2nd wife bur. 8 June 1801 Tottlebank; overseer and constable at Colton
Drinkall, Myles	of Rusland; mar. Mary Taylor, 24 Aug. 1704 Colton; dissenter; churchwarden and overseer at Colton

230 *Biographical Index*

Fallows, Randall	of Far Sawrey, collier, associated with Cunsey forge; 'a Cheshire-man', possibly coming to Cunsey with Richard Ford (*q.v.*); mar. Elizabeth Hobson, 29 June 1713 Hawkshead; children bap. at Hawkshead 1714–29
Fell, Richard	husbandman and labourer, of Town End; mar. Sarah Atkinson, 25 Dec. 1711 Ulverston; five children, of whom the three younger were bap. at Colton 1718–22; bur. 21 Oct. 1729; origin uncertain, but of Coniston at mar. and the first member of an extended family which survived in Finsthwaite until the present century; his wife remained there for some years after his death but was not bur. in the parish; da. Agnes and son William (see James Danson) received charity money
Fisher, Henry	chairmaker, of Cartmel; children bap. at Cartmel 1754–6
Ford, Richard	ironmaster; b. 1697 Middlewich, Ches.; manager at Cunsey forge 1722–35, and built furnaces at Nibthwaite and Newland; mar. Elizabeth Bordley, 10 July 1725 Hawkshead; children bap. at Hawkshead 1728–39; bur. 18 Sept. 1757 (Ulverston); ancestor of the Knott family of Monk Coniston
Garman, William	workman; perhaps the William German who mar. Sarah Harrison, 15 May 1725 Cartmel; children bap. at Cartmel Fell 1725–8; ? brother of the John German of Addyfield who bap. a da. at Cartmel Fell 1726
Garnett, Anthony	of Staveley, workman; mar. Anne Pennington, 19 June 1737 Cartmel; children bap. at Cartmel 1738–50; bur. 19 Dec. 1788; wife bur. 2 April 1778
Goad, James	perhaps the James Goad of Allithwaite bur. 18 Jan. 1750 Cartmel, 'drown'd or kill'd by a fall at Lindale'
Grigg, Reginald	of Walker Ground, builder and waller; mar. Margaret Atkinson, 14 April 1719 Hawkshead; children bap. at Hawkshead 1726–40; bur. 19 Feb. 1754 Hawkshead
Gurnell, Mary	da. of Sarah Taylor of Jolliver Tree (*q.v.*); bap. 13 Aug. 1690 Colton; mar. 1) Robert Gurnell of Spooner Close, Cartmel Fell, 1715 (bond); son John bap. 12

Biographical Index 231

June 1715 Heversham and d. 1733; 1st husband bur. 31 Aug. 1725; mar. 2) James Backhouse (*q.v.*); Robert Gurnell was a Quaker, ejected by Swarthmoor meeting 3 May 1715 on his mar. to a non-member; his considerable personal estate, valued at over £600, passed to his widow and her 2nd husband on the death of his son; in 1729 the property at Jolliver Tree was placed in trust for the son and for James Backhouse: LRO, DDTy 2/2/3

Hall, Thomas — of Cartmel, grocer and ironmonger; mar. Elizabeth, niece of William Stout, the Lancaster merchant, 1719; children bap. at Cartmel 1720–22; bur. 25 Mar. 1733 Cartmel; Stout, who went to settle his affairs, said that 'As he grew straitned, he fell to drinking brandy or spirrits, which shortned his days; and she was indolant and thoughtles': *The Autobiography of William Stout of Lancaster, 1655-1752*, Chetham Soc., 3rd ser., xiv, 1967, 211

Harrison, John — incumbent of Finsthwaite 1725–41 (schoolmaster from 1724); bap. 17 Jan. 1702 Isel, Cumb.; educated at Hawkshead school; incumbent at Hawkshead from 1741; bur. 25 Oct. 1761 Hawkshead; unmarried; author of an article in *Philosophical Transactions of the Royal Society* about the movement of water on Windermere, 1756, but other MSS he ordered to be destroyed by his executors; see LRO, DDCh 37/51, clergy bundle, Finsthwaite

Harrison, Lawrence — of Stott Park and Landing; son of Myles Harrison (*q.v.*), bap. 13 Jan. 1714 Colton; mar. Elizabeth Denison; children bap. 1742–50; bur. 17 May 1765; wife bur. 24 Oct. 1780; bought Landing estate from Henry Taylor (*q.v.*) 1737 and moved there, but churchwarden for Stott Park 1755–6; churchwarden for Landing at Colton 1751, constable 1744

Harrison, Myles — eldest son of Lawrence Harrison of Blakeholm, Cartmel, cooper, who bought Low Stott Park in 1669 (CRO, WD/AG/ Box 64/4), and was bur. 8 Oct. 1732; bap. 31 July 1678 Cartmel; mar. 1) Isobel, da. of Robert Taylor of Dalepark, 12 Nov. 1711 Hawkshead; 2) Agnes Walker, widow, 6 June 1731 Cartmel; children bap. at Colton and Finsthwaite 1712–27; bur.

232 *Biographical Index*

	18 June 1740; 1st wife bur. 28 Aug. 1727; 2nd wife's bur. not found; a prime mover in establishing Finsthwaite church and school; churchwarden 1726–7, and at Colton 1723
Harrison, Richard	of Monk Coniston; bap. 26 Sept. 1676 Hawkshead; mar. Agnes Scales, 29 June 1704 Hawkshead; children bap. at Hawkshead 1705–21; bur. 1 Oct. 1761 Hawkshead; da. Catherine mar. William, son of Richard Ford (*q.v.*)
Hirdson, William	of Oxen Park, borrower; mar. Annas Rawnson, 24 Nov. 1683 Colton; children bap. at Colton 1685–1701; bur. 2 Dec. 1728 Colton
Holme, John	workman; ? of Backbarrow and mar. Agnes Kellett, 22 Dec. 1730 Colton; children bap. at Colton 1731–44; bur. 16 June 1745 Colton; wife bur. 11 Mar. 1751 Colton
Huddleston, Thomas	tenant at Town End till 1779; of Millom, Cumb. at mar. to Sarah. da. of Richard Fell (*q.v.*), 4 June 1750; children bap. 1751–63
Jackson, Isaac	poor labourer; children bap. at Colton 1726-35, but received Finsthwaite charity money 1733–40; bur. 16 June 1773 Colton
Jackson, Roger	servant 1729–42; husbandman of Allithwaite at mar. to Elizabeth Rigge, 19 May 1755, but no children bap. at Cartmel or Finsthwaite
Johnson, Thomas	workman and farm tenant at Town End; 1st wife Alice bur. 7 June 1747; mar. 2) Agnes Carter, 24 July 1748; bur. 6 Mar. 1765; bought a house, now Rose Cottage, Town End, 1739: LRO, DDPd 26/249
Keen, Arthur	of Nibthwaite and Bouth, collier; mar. Jane Addison, 23 June 1696 Colton; children bap. at Colton 1698–1709, 1718; bur. 2 May 1729 Colton
Kellett, Edward	of Satterthwaite, woodmonger; bur. 30 May 1756 Hawkshead; wife Dorothy bur. 20 Dec. 1759 Hawkshead, of Far Sawrey, where they had close connections; wife probably da. of Benjamin Taylor of Sawrey and bap. 16 April 1701 Hawkshead

Biographical Index 233

Kirby, Richard	workman; children bap. at Colton 1719–26, from Hay Bridge and Tottlebank; bur. 14 Feb. 1754, of Plum Green
Kitchin, Richard	dyer; mar. Agnes Satterthwaite, 30 Nov. 1724 Colton; children bap. at Colton 1725–34; wife bur. 4 Dec. 1735 Colton, of Little Dicks
Langram, John	of Coniston, slater; bur. 10 May 1726 Coniston
Leck, Robert	bap. 10 April 1714 Cartmel; mar. Margaret Johnson, 24 May 1738 Hawkshead; children bap. 1739–51 from Chapman House, Stott Park, and Town End; churchwarden for houses at Town End and Elinghearth 1747–51; received charity money; Hawkshead register enters names incorrectly at mar. but confirmed in bond
Leece, James	of Booth, builder; bap. 12 Feb. 1688 Colton; bond for maintenance of child by Elizabeth Jackson 1714: CRO, BPR 17/O2/3
Leece, John	of Booth, maltster; bur. 5 Jan. 1747 Colton; churchwarden, constable, and overseer at Colton
Leeming, Ralph	workman; bur. 6 September 1734, of Stott Park
Lickbarrow, Rowland	of Backbarrow, dyer; bap. 23 Sept. 1690 Cartmel, son of William Lickbarrow (*q.v.*); children bap. at Cartmel 1723–38; bur. 28 May 1761 Cartmel
Lickbarrow, William	of Backbarrow, dyer and tenant of land; children bap. at Cartmel 1688–1703; bur. 20 July 1730 Cartmel; bankrupt 1727: *CW2*, 1972, 221
Machell, John	of Hollow Oak, ironmaster; bap. 19 Mar. 1678 Cartmel; mar. Elizabeth Walker, 18 May 1704 Pennington and inherited Hollow Oak through her; bur. 12 Sept. 1750 Cartmel, of Aynsome; one of the four founders of the Backbarrow Co.
Marr, Christopher	of Speelbank, borrower; mar. Jane Burns, 14 Oct. 1680 Cartmel; will proved 1732 but not bur. at Cartmel; paid his interest through Thomas Denny (*q.v.*)

Massicks, Thomas	workman; probably brother of William Massicks (*q.v.*)
Massicks, William	collier; mar. Agnes Wilson, 5 Jan. 1743; bur. 20 Dec. 1790; wife bur. 6 Mar. 1789; of Charley Crag at mar. but moved to Browedge before returning to Finsthwaite where he bought Rose Cottage, Town End in 1758, having previously held a mortgage on it: LRO, DDPd 26/288, 291
Millerson, Thomas	of Ulverston; mar. Jane Fell, 9 Nov. 1707 Ulverston; bur. 27 Feb. 1763 Ulverston; appears in connection with the delivery of letters
Morris, Emmy	da. of Richard Taylor of Finsyke (*q.v.*); bap. 1 Dec. 1707 Colton; mar. John Morris, forgeman, 28 April 1739; children bap. 1741–8; bur. 12 Jan. 1749, of Sinderhill; son Richard bur. 1 Aug. 1777 from the poorhouse at Colton, and both he and his father had payments from the overseers: CRO, BPR 17/C2/1
Muckelt, George	of Kents Bank, woodmonger; bap. 7 Mar. 1688 Cartmel; mar. Grace Carter of Grange, 5 Nov. 1720 Cartmel; children bap. at Cartmel 1721–9
Newby, Richard	of Haverthwaite, swillmaker; ? mar. Margaret Dodgson, 6 June 1686 Colton; bur. 29 Sept. 1734 Colton; will (19 Aug. 1734) included a bequest of £10, the interest of which was to go to a school 'to be kept within Haverthwaite to teach youth the English or Latin Tongue', but no school was founded there until the 19th century; uncle of the wives of James Twisaday and Richard Kitchin (*q.v.*)
Noble, Matthew	of Crag, Egton-cum-Newland, ropemaker; bap. 12 Aug. 1677 Ulverston; children bap. at Ulverston 1711–26; bur. 9 April 1745 Ulverston; see intro., n. 77
Ormandy, Jane	servant 1723–30; ? bap. 31.1.1703 Ulverston, da. of William Ormandy
Park, Jacob	waller; ? bap. 31 Dec. 1704 Torver; mar. Elizabeth Coward 24 May 1729; da. Elizabeth bap. 7 Mar. 1730; bur. 21 Sept. 1735; of Jolliver Tree at mar., and

	Landing at death; he left his da. £120, out of a personal estate of £220; brother of William Park (*q.v.*) and perhaps of Edward Park
Park, William	of Nibthwaite, waller; ? bap. 7 Feb. 1703 Torver; mar. Elizabeth Redhead 10 Feb. 1734 Colton; da. bap. at Colton 1747; bur. 9 Dec. 1753 Colton; wife bur. 28 Oct. 1758 Colton; brother and executor of Jacob Park (*q.v.*)
Pennington, Benjamin	weaver; bap. 20 May 1696 Colton; mar. Dorothy Christopherson, 25 Feb. 1722 Colton; bur. 1 April 1775 Colton, of Bandrakehead
Pennington, Garnet	of Cowridding, borrower; children bap. at Colton 1689–97; bur. 5 Oct. 1727 Colton; churchwarden and overseer at Colton
Pennington, Paul	of Low Longmire, mariner and borrower; bap. 20 May 1694 Colton; mar. Agnes Benson of Mansriggs, 23 May 1736 Ulverston; children bap. at Colton 1737–45, including Isaac (1745–1817) who became President of St John's College, Cambridge; bur. 23 April 1770 Colton; overseer and constable at Colton
Pepper, Thomas	of Newby Bridge, blacksmith; bur. 3 May 1765
Postlethwaite, Richard	of Abbots Reading; bap. 1 July 1693 Colton; mar. Sarah Mason, 11 Dec. 1721 Cartmel; children bap. at Colton 1721–30; bur. 14 Aug. 1787 Colton; wife bur. 25 Dec 1773 Colton; overseer and constable at Colton
Prudence, John	of Town End, carpenter; bur. 10 Mar. 1748; wife Sarah bur. 26 March 1771; occupier of Dorothy Braithwaite's house (*q.v.*) after her death: LRO, DDPd 26/272; da. Agnes received charity money 1732
Rawlinson, Abraham	of Rusland Hall, merchant in Lancaster, and MP; Quaker and trustee of Colthouse meeting house; b. 1666; mar. Elizabeth Beck of Low Wray, 1695; d. 1737; brother of Thomas and William Rawlinson (*q.v.*); inherited Rusland Hall under will of his grandfather, William Rawlinson (1606–80): L. Cunliffe, *The Rawlinsons of Furness*, Kendal, 1978, 30-31, 43

236 *Biographical Index*

Rawlinson, Thomas	of Low Graythwaite, lender; 1679–1739; partner in the Glengarry venture
Rawlinson, William	of Low Graythwaite, co-founder of the Backbarrow Co.; b. 1664; mar. Mary Goldney; bur. 18 Aug. 1734 Colthouse
Rigg, Edward	bap. 9 June 1683 Hawkshead; mar. Ann Dodgson, 21 Feb. 1721 Swarthmoor; bur. 28 Aug. 1770 Colthouse; associated with Abraham Rawlinson (*q.v.*) at Rusland Hall, where he was perhaps farm manager, but of High Wray at death
Rigge, Richard	of Force Mill, borrower; bur. 2 Jan. 1738 Hawkshead
Robinson, John	of Newby Bridge; bap. 23 Nov. 1704 Cartmel; mar. Emma, da. of John Machell (*q.v.*), 4 Sept. 1735 Colton; bur. 30 Aug. 1788 Cartmel; wife bur. 17 May 1791 Cartmel; no children; property passed to wife's brother Thomas, founder of family of Machell of Newby Bridge
Robinson, Richard	of Waterside; grandson of Richard Taylor (bur. 14 Jan. 1706 Hawkshead), the last of the Taylors of Waterside; b. *c.*1680; bur. 10 Feb. 1741; brother-in-law of Clement Taylor, and a prime mover in establishing the church and school at Finsthwaite; churchwarden at Colton 1706, 1739, constable 1718, overseer 1701, 1736; left Waterside to Clement Taylor, who was charged with the payment of legacies, including £200 to his niece Rebecca Stout (see Leonard Stout); for his charity, see n. 231
Roskell, Robert	master at Browedge school 1702–16, and at Cartmel 1716-24; mar. Agnes Kilner, 7 June 1720 Cartmel
Rowlandson, James	buyer of sheep; perhaps of Foxfield, Cartmel Fell, and bur. 23 Nay 1723 Cartmel
Rowlandson, James	master at Browedge school, but for longer than is indicated in *CW2*, 1972, 219n; then curate of Firbank, Westm.
Rownson, William	of Bouth, shopkeeper and glazier; bap. 9 Aug. 1685 Colton; 1st wife Elizabeth bur. 10 Sept. 1715 Colton;

mar. 2) Sarah Benson, 7 Dec. 1718 Colton; children bap. at Colton 1715, 1720–32; bur. 30 Oct. 1760 Colton; his will revealed that he had recently built and let a new house in Bouth, which was left to his wife, with peat for her firing and room in the barn in which to store it; his inventory lists goods in the shop and warehouse, glazier's tools, and 'Ould Lead', and a very high value was placed on his furniture; his total personal estate was £507; churchwarden, constable, and overseer at Colton

Russell, John — of Force Forge, buyer of bark and later grocer (LRO, DDPd 26/338); bap. 17 Dec. 1704 Colton; mar. Margaret Rownson, 26 Dec. 1732 Colton; bur. 18 June 1788 Colton; wife bur. 26 Oct. 1745 Colton

Sandys, Myles — of Graythwaite; bap. 20 June 1696 Hawkshead; mar. Isabel Penny, 20 July 1717; children bap. at Hawkshead 1718–36; bur. 9 May 1766 Hawkshead; wife bur. 30 April 1748 Hawkshead; succeeded to Graythwaite estate 1716 on death of grandfather Myles Sandys; sheriff of Lancs. 1725

Satterthwaite, John — merchant, and always so described by Clement Taylor; of Satterthwaite at baps of two eldest children at Hawkshead 1716–18, and may then have become a Quaker; not bur. Hawkshead or Ulverston, but of Penny Bridge at death; will (15 Sept. 1738) provided for wife Rachel, six daughters, and son William, and in it he called himself 'merchant'; son William continued to trade with Isabel Taylor

Satterthwaite, William — tailor; ? mercer of Hawkshead at death, and bur.14.10.1757 Hawkshead

Sawrey, Robert — shoemaker and tenant of land; mar. Margaret Braithwaite (sister of Thomas and George Braiththwaite, q.v.), 24 May 1687 Colton; bur. 22 May 1724 Hawkshead; lived at Green Cottage (see n. 221); churchwarden at Colton 1703, overseer 1722; wife b. c.1652 at Town End, in Westmorland 1672–7, returning to service at Waterside before they married: LRO, DDPd 26/226; wife bur. 20 Sept. 1738

Scales, John	of Grizedale, borrower: LRO, DDPd 26/248; bur. 28 August 1732 Hawkshead
Scales, Robert	of Thwaite Head; bur. 23 Mar. 1771 Rusland, aged 84 (Colton reg.); constable 1710
Scotson, Thomas	of Abbot Park, borrower; bur. 7 Oct. 1751 Colton; churchwarden, constable, and overseer at Colton
Simpson, George	incumbent of Finsthwaite 1741–78; bap. 30 June 1718 Aldingham; mar. 1) Agnes, da. of Christopher Taylor of Plum Green (*q.v.*), 14 August 1742; children bap. 1743–50; 1st wife bur. 2 Dec. 1750; mar. 2) Margaret, widow of Robert Taylor of High Stott Park (*q.v.*), 15 Nov. 1773; bur. 8 July 1778; 2nd wife bur. 18 April 1786; see LRO, DDCh 37/51, clergy bundle, Finsthwaite
Singleton, Mary	servant 1732–3; possibly niece of John Harrison (*q.v.*). who named her in his will
Soulby, Elizabeth	poor widow, receiving charity payments 1733–43; bur. 30 April 1747
Stamper, George	of Roger Ridding; bur. 23 May 1756 Rusland (Colton reg.); overseer at Colton
Stout, Leonard	1704–89, merchant in Lancaster, nephew of William Stout; mar. Rebecca Robinson, niece of Richard Robinson (*q.v.*), 26 Jan. 1734; wife brought up as dissenter and bap. 14 April 1733, aged 22; Isabel Taylor and her son Edward each invested £100 with him 1759: LRO, DDPd 26/338
Strickland, Thomas	of Iconthwaite, lender; for his charity, see n. 177
Taylor, Adam	of Hawkshead; bap. 5 Oct. 1684 Hawkshead; mar. Alice Dodgson, 28 July 1722 Hawkshead; da. bap. at Hawkshead 1723; wife bur. 24 July 1724 Hawkshead; perhaps the Adam Taylor, innkeeper, mentioned in 1760 at final proof of will of Sarah Tayor of Jolliver Tree (*q.v.*), but not bur. at Hawkshead
Taylor, Benjamin	of Hardcragg, Browedge; bap. 17 July 1673 Cartmel; mar. 1702 (note in Cartmel reg.); children bap. at

Cartmel 1703–12; bur. 12 April 1757 Cartmel, aged 82; wife Alice bur. 5 Sept. 1760 Cartmel, aged 85; his precise relationship to Clement Taylor is unclear, but he was possibly grandson of an Edward Taylor of Sinderhill and his father William (?1641–1701) gave the site for Browedge school (*CW2* 1972, 223); brother of Clement and William Taylor of Hardcragg, and Margaret Taylor (*q.v.*)

Taylor, Christopher — of Plum Green (Nook House, now Whitegate); ? bap. 5 Sept. 1688 Colton; bur. 20 Dec. 1749; wife Jennet bur. 28 May 1753; for only da. Agnes bap. 18 Nov. 1715 Colton, see George Simpson; churchwarden 1734; churchwarden, constable, and overseer at Colton

Taylor, Clement — of Hardcragg; bap. 12 Nov. 1668 Cartmel; bur. 2 Oct. 1745; lived at Jolliver Tree in the 1720s; described in his lifetime as yeoman, he was labourer in his undated will which bore an armorial seal; his inventory revealed very considerable wealth, as he had over £1000 'lent on security', although his personal possessions were only clothes and money (£6), three chests and a box (l0s), and 'One Crow or Gavelock' (2s); brother of Benjamin and William Taylor of Hardcragg, and Margaret Taylor (*q.v.*)

Taylor, Edward — of Craikside, borrower; born at Jolliver Tree, son of William Taylor (bur. 16 Feb. 1689 Hawkshead); bur. 4 June 1729 Colton; brother-in-law of Sarah Taylor (*q.v.*), and uncle of Mary Gurnell (*q.v.*); for his charity, see n. 182

Taylor, Edward — brother of Clement Taylor; bap. 23 May 1691 Colton; mar. Emma Walker, 16 Feb. 1719 Old Hutton, Westm.; children bap. at Colton and Finsthwaite 1724–7; bur. 9 May 1770; of Town Head, Staveley, in the 1740s; leased Waterside 1752 till death; will witnessed by the so-called 'Finsthwaite Princess', Clementina Douglas, and her companion James Douglas, who were lodgers in his house; wife bur. 11 July 1781

Taylor, Elizabeth 'alias Dickies' — da. of Richard Taylor of Finsyke (*q.v.*); bap. 23 Nov. 1712 Colton; bur. 23 Nov. 1775; sister of Peter and twin sister of Henry Taylor (*q.v.*); received charity money 1733–7

Biographical Index

Taylor, Elkanah — of Greetysyke, Ulverston; mar. Margaret Gawith, 16 Dec. 1727 Ulverston; children bap. at Ulverston 1728–54; bur. 8 Jan. 1759 Ulverston

Taylor, George — of Chapman House; bap. 9 March 1708 Colton, son of Robert Taylor of Stott Park (*q.v.*); bur. 7 Aug. 1758 Hawkshead; churchwarden 1733, 1735

Taylor, George — of Finsyke and Elinghearth; mar. Elizabeth Newby, 19 June 1720 Colton; one da. bap. 25 Jan. 1734, other children not bap.; bur. 30 April 1744 Tottlebank; wife bur. 25 March 1741 Colton; Baptist, so contributed only to the school at Finsthwaite, not to the church; constable 1738, overseer 1737

Taylor, Henry 'alias Dickies' — son of Richard Taylor of Finsyke (*q.v.*); bap. 23 Nov. 1712 Colton; mar. Elizabeth Denny, 2 June 1736; children bap. 1736–44; not bur. at Finsthwaite, but of Sinderhill 21 Feb. 1746 at bur. of wife; previously at Nook House and Charley Crag; received charity money until death of wife; churchwarden for Sinderhill 1740–1; brother of Peter and Elizabeth Taylor, and of Emmy Morris (*q.v.*)

Taylor, Henry — of Landing, later Kendal; bap. 7 May 1699 Colton; mar. Sarah Sympson, 20 Jan. 1722 Kendal; children bap. at Kendal and Cartmel 1722–31; bur. 28 Oct. 1737 Kendal; wife bur. 7 July 1738 Kendal; donor of the site of Finsthwaite church 1724, but an unreliable character; for his bankruptcy and sale of land, see nn. 194, 196; churchwarden 1726; churchwarden at Colton 1726–27

Taylor, James — sold Tom Crag 1713 (see xviii), but remained in Finsthwaite as workman until at least 1727; mar. Ellen Moore, 27 Sept. 1708 Colton; not bur. at either Finsthwaite or Colton; widow bur. 14 Dec. 1738 Colton

Taylor, Jane 'Old Jennet' — of Charley Crag; widow of John Taylor, husbandman and collier (bur. 2 April 1718 Colton); b. *c.* 1637; bur. 5 Mar. 1728; mother of John Taylor of Dublin (*q.v.*), Jane, wife of William Woodburn (*q.v.*), and others

Biographical Index 241

Taylor, John	of Charley Crag, collier, son of Richard Taylor of Finsyke (*q.v.*); bap. 4 Oct. 1702 Colton; bur. 28 April 1732; for his will, see n. 261; brother of Peter, Henry, and Elizabeth Taylor, and of Emmy Morris (*q.v.*)
Taylor, John	of Craikside, borrower; born at Jolliver Tree, son of William Taylor (bur. 16 Feb. 1689 Hawkshead); mar. Jane Satterthwaite, widow, 1704 (bond); he and his wife bur. 6 and 8 Aug. 1723 Colton; gave £500 for endowment of Finsthwaite school: *CW2*, 1984, 134; brother of Edward Taylor of Craikside and brother-in-law of Sarah Taylor (*q.v.*)
Taylor, John	of Dublin, son of Jane Taylor of Charley Crag (*q.v.*); bap. 17 April 1678 Colton; to Dublin by 1718 where he was a coachman: LRO, DDPd 26/207
Taylor, John	of Jolliver Tree; bap. 16 July 1694 Colton; bur. 6 Dec. 1724 Hawkshead; son of Sarah Taylor and brother of Mary Gurnell (*q.v.*); constable at Colton
Taylor, Margaret	lender; sister of Benjamin, Clement, and William Taylor of Hardcragg (*q.v.*); bap. 14 March 1671 Cartmel; bur. 28 October 1727; for her bequest to the school at Finsthwaite, see n. 146
Taylor, Matthew	tenant of Town End Farm 1749–61: LRO, DDPd 26/338; children bap. 1730–44 at Crosthwaite, Westm., and at Finsthwaite 1750–6; neither he nor wife Phyllis bur. in Finsthwaite
Taylor, Myles	miller; ? of Beckside and bur. 2 Sept. 1747 Colton
Taylor, Peter	of Finsyke and Charley Crag, son of Richard Taylor of Finsyke (*q.v.*); bap. 22 May 1700 Colton; mar. Anne Massicks, 30 Mar. 1730; children bap. 1731–44; bur. 13 Dec. 1749, of Trundlebrow, Browedge; wife bur. 6 April 1767; bought Charley Crag 1734: LRO, DDPd 26/326; brother of Henry and Elizabeth Taylor, and of Emmy Morris (*q.v.*)
Taylor, Richard	of Finsyke, collier; ? son of Peter Taylor of Waterside (bur. 10 June 1683 Colton); children bap. at Colton 1700–12; bur. 15 May 1724 Colton; wife Alice bur. 12 Feb. 1735; father of Henry, Peter, and Elizabeth Taylor, and of Emmy Morris (*q.v.*)

Biographical Index

Taylor, Robert	of High Stott Park; bap. 12 Mar. 1703 Colton; mar. Margaret Woodburne, 22 Mar. 1728 Ulverston; children bap. 1729–43; bur. 6 April 1772; wife mar. 2) George Simpson (*q.v.*); prime mover in establishing Finsthwaite church and school; churchwarden 1729–30, 1757; churchwarden at Colton 1733, constable 1751, overseer 1725; father of George Taylor of Chapman House (*q.v.*)
Taylor, Robert	of Crosslands; bur. 23 Jan. 1757 Hawkshead
Taylor, Rowland	of Thwaite Moss; bur. 17 May 1759 Rusland (Colton reg.)
Taylor, Sarah	of Jolliver Tree, widow of Christopher Taylor (bur. 27 April 1712 Hawkshead); née Newby, mar. 14 Jan. 1686 Colton; bur. 1 Dec. 1744; mother of Mary Gurnell and John Taylor of Jolliver Tree (*q.v.*)
Taylor, William	brother of Clement Taylor; bap. 22 May 1700 Colton; educated at Browedge School and The Queen's College, Oxford (BA 1724); deacon 1726, priest 1728; mar. Elizabeth Butler, 15 Oct. 1726 Fawsley, Northants.; from 1726 curate of Farthingstone, Northants., vicar of long Buckby, Northants.; d. 23 May 1738; wife mar. 2) Revd David Pratt of Blakesley, Northants.
Taylor, William	of Hardcragg, servant to Clement Taylor 1719–24; bap. 2 July 1684 Cartmel; bur. 11 Jan. 1741 Cartmel; da. Sarah (bap. 23 May 1736 Cartmel) was executrix to her uncle Clement Taylor of Hardcragg (*q.v.*); brother of Benjamin Taylor of Hardcragg and Margaret Taylor (*q.v.*)
Twisaday, James	of Thwaite Moss, carpenter; mar. Isabel Satterthwaite, 10 June 1726 Colton; son bap. at Colton 1728; bur. 10 Jan. 1737 Colton; wife bur. 14 Jan. 1778 Rusland (Colton reg.); wife was niece of Richard Newby (*q.v.*)
Wainhouse, Rowland	of Cartmel, mercer; bap. 26 Aug. 1695 Cartmel; mar. 1) Eleanor Braithwaite, 12 Nov. 1718 Cartmel; mar. 2) Dorothy Medcalf, 21 Feb. 1722 Cartmel; 1st wife bur. 2 Mar. 1720 Cartmel; child bap. 1722 Cartmel; bur. 6 Jan. 1770 (Cartmel), 'old and poor'

Biographical Index 243

Wainman, Thomas	mar. Ruth Brownrigg, 8 Nov. 1719 Colton; children bap. at Colton 1721–3; bur. 9 April 1746 Ulverston, of Finsthwaite, pauper
Walker, Edward	fuller; perhaps the Edward Walker of Bouth (bur. 20 April 1728 Colton), who left to his wife, among other bequests, 'Six Earthen bottles to be Choosen out of all the quantity of Bottles I have'
Walker, James	of Elinghearth, husbandman; mar. Isobel Newby, 22 Jan. 1685 Colton; children bap. at Colton 1688–98; bur. 27 May 1729; wife bur. 4 April 1749
Wilkinson, John	of Bouth, blacksmith; children bap. at Colton 1718–27; 1st wife Eleanor bur. 30 Mar. 1728 Colton; mar. 2) Jane Noble, 1 Dec. 1728 Colton; children of 2nd mar. bap. at Colton 1729–44; settlement certificate from Egton 1719: CRO, BPR 17/O1/8
Wilson, Anthony	of High Wray; bap. 18 May 1683 Hawkshead; mar. Dorothy Benson, 8 July 1702 Colthouse; children b. 1704–15; bur. 24 June 1755 Colthouse; wife bur. 25 July 1755 Colthouse; partner in Invergarry furnace 1727 (Fell, *op.cit.*, 350), but here associated with Cunsey forge
Wilson, Edmund	of Near Sawrey, grocer; from Gillbank, Eskdale, Cumb.; bur. 1 May 1730 Hawkshead; wife Jane bur. 14 Feb. 1730 Hawkshead; he left money for the schoolmaster of Eskdale, and his inventory lists, among other things, 'Some grosserie warre'
Woodburn, William	collier and tenant of Charley Grag; mar. Jane (Jennet), da. of Jane Taylor of Charley Crag (*q.v.*) 20 June 1698 Colton; children bap. at Colton 1699–1717; bur. 1 Feb. 1730; wife bur. 15 Feb. 1748; wife received charity money 1729–38

GLOSSARY

Aloes	a bitter medicine from the juice of plants of the genus *aloe*
Bark	probably cinchona bark, or Jesuits' bark, used as a febrifuge
Beamfilling	making up the tops of walls between the rafters
Bedstocks	the back and front parts of a bed between which the rungs or cross-staves were laid
Bermods hat	perhaps a straw hat
Beverage	money to buy a drink, given at the conclusion of a bargain
Bigg	barley
Boddoming	bottoming, replacing the mesh of a riddle
Boss	probably a cask or leather bottle
Brant	brindled or brown
Brat	an apron
Bready	possibly broad-backed
Bull Alminick	Bole Armoniac, corruption of Bole Armenian, a pale red earth from Armenia, used medicinally, both for humans and animals, *e.g.* against diarrhoea, and in tooth powder
Bun meal	probably a fine meal for making bunloaf or cake
Burnt alum	dried sulphate of ammonia and potassium, used medicinally
Bushel	a dry measure of eight gallons or four pecks; see also Quarter
Caf	chaff; see also Chaff bed
Cage	keg
Calamaniah	calamanco, a shiny woollen material, striped or checked in brilliant colours; a calamanco cat is a tortoishell cat

Cam	stones laid on edge as the top stage of a dry-stone wall
Cambric	fine linen or cotton cloth
Cammey	awry, ill-tempered
Carding	preparing wool for spinning; see Woolcards
Cattels	chattels
Chaff bed	a palliasse or mattress of harden (*q.v.*) filled with chaff
Clog	a stout shoe with a leather upper and a wooden sole shod with iron
Clogg	a measure of wood, here a trunk cut into boards
Coals, Coles	charcoal; coaling is making charcoal; hence coalwood: see also Collier
Cockpenny	the fee paid to a schoolmaster at Shrovetide
Collier	a charcoal-burner
Copperas	proto-sulphate of iron or ferrous sulphate ($FeSO_4$), green vitriol, used in dyeing, tanning, or making ink
Coppey	a small field or coppice; of a cow, headstrong
Cord	a measure of cut wood, especially for fuel; hence cordwood
Correction court	the archdeacon's court, in which ecclesiastical cases, including testamentary disputes, were conducted
Crook	a shepherd's stick
Cumberland cloth	a cotton cloth used for shifts and shirts
Daffey bottle	The Revd Thomas Daffey (d. 1680), rector of Harby and Redmile, Leics., invented an 'Elixir Salutis', a tonic here provided for young women; it was advertised in Kendal in 1736: J.D. Marshall, *Kendal 1661–1801*, Kendal, 1975, 58
Dail	dole, a share, especially of land but sometimes of money

Dale	deal, softwood timber, usually imported
Daywork	of peat or bracken, as much as could be cut in a day
Diaper tape	linen or linen and cotton tape with a self-pattern
Diescardium	diascordium, a medicine made from the dried leaves of *teucrium scordium* (germander), and other herbs
Dimity	cotton cloth woven with raised stripes or figures
Dismission	discharge from service
Dister	dyer
Draget	cloth made of a mixture of wool and flax, or of wool and silk, or wool and cotton, and not necessarily coarse
Dragons blood	a red gum or resin from the palm, *calamus draco*, or the dragon-tree, *dracaena draco*
Drissing	dressing or preparing
Drop	the plate covering a keyhole
Dyke	a wall, of stone or earth
Earnest	money given to seal a bargain or to servants when they were hired
Ell	a measure of cloth, forty-five inches
Engrossers	with forestallers and regrators, persons hoarding goods, usually grain, in the hope that scarcity would raise their price
Everlasting	a hard-wearing cloth
Ewe	a breeding female sheep
Fest	to bind by agreement or contract
Firehouse	usually the main heated room in a house, but also used of the house itself
Floorings	flooring nails

Fogg	second-crop hay
Footing	placing cut peats on end to dry out
Forestallers	see Engrossers
Freestone	fine-grained sand- or limestone
Frock	a coat with long skirts
Furniture	of a coat, the trimmings and buttons
Gall	the oak-apple, used in making ink
Gang	a set, here a set of calves' feet
Garth	enclosed land round a building, here the churchyard
Geld	gelt, barren
Gimmer	a yearling ewe
Girthwood	wood suitable for making a girder or beam
Gorgan	gorgeon, the iron pin fixed in a gatepost from which the gate is hung
Grassing	grazing
Grave	to dig peat
Grubb	to dig out
Harden	a coarse fabric woven from the hards of flax or hemp
Hartshorn	an aqueous solution of ammonia, used in smelling salts
Heart latts	laths made from the heartwood of trees, upon which roof slates were hung
Hogg	a sheep, male or female, before its first shearing
Holland	a linen fabric
Hoop	a dry measure, varying from one quarter of a peck to four pecks

Hungary water	a distillation of rosemary flowers infused in rectified spirits of wine
Jack	a liquid measure of a quarter or half pint
Kill	kiln, usually for burning lime
Latt	lath
Leading	carting
Leah, Ley	a scythe; see also Stub ley
Linn	linen
Linsty	linsey-wolsey, cloth woven from a mixture of wool and flax
Liver	to deliver, hand over
Load	of charcoal, twelve sacks
Louking	weeding
Lousey	uncertain; of a cow it can mean that it shows signs of having milk in the udder, but perhaps just difficult
Lowse	loose; of a letter, to pay for it on delivery
Manner, Mainer	manure
Marchant	merchant, here always used of John Satterthwaite: see 237
Meat	food generally
Metridate	a powder, containing a large variety of ingredients, usually taken in treacle or honey against poison or infectious disease
Milling	fulling cloth
Mograhs hat	Mogra is Arabian jasmine, here possibly a hat trimmed with it
Mohair	properly a watered cloth woven from goat-hair, but in the eighteenth century very often a silk imitation

Moider	moidore, a gold coin from Portugal, in current use in England in this period, of the value of 27s; for an example of its use in 1739, see C. Torr, *Small Talk at Wreyland*, Cambridge, 1923, 24
Moss	a peat moss
Napkin	a neckerchief
Painted	of a napkin, printed or coloured
Pallisados	palisades, ornamental fencing, here apparently of stone
Parrick	parrock, a small enclosure or field
Peck	a dry measure, a quarter of a bushel or two gallons
Percion	Persian, a thin silk material
Pick	pitch
Pigg	a pig of smelted iron
Pitt, Pitstead	the flat earth platform upon which charcoal was made
Pluck	the heart, liver, and lungs of a sheep; see also Tripes
Plugg	plug, the iron wedge driven between two others (the feathers) when splitting rock
Plumm	a lead weight for a sash window
Potter	a hawker of earthenware
Pow	a pole; also pool, as in Rusland Pool
Principle trees	trees large enough to provide principal rafters
Quarter	a dry measure of eight bushels, or a linear measure of nine inches, a quarter of a yard
Referance	reference, referring a dispute for arbitration
Regrators	see Engrossers

250   *Glossary*

Rib	a purlin
Riggin	rigging, the ridge-stones of a roof
Riving	splitting, especially of wood
Sack	white wine from Spain and the Canary Islands
Sal volatile	a solution of ammonium carbonate used as a restorative
Sale bill	the announcement of a public sale
Salving	the practice of rubbing a mixture of Stockholm tar and butter into a sheep's fleece in the late autumn, in order to make the fleece more weatherproof in winter
Sapps, Sap latts	laths from the outer wood of a tree, used to support plaster on internal walls and always covered over
Sarrow	to serve or supply
Scale	to spread about
Scift	to shift or move
Scotch stuff	cloth bought from a Scotchman; see 21, n. 46
Seaves	sieves, rushes for making rushlights
Sess	assessment, *e.g.* for poor rate
Shag	cloth with a velvet nap on one side, usually worsted but sometimes silk
Shaloune	shalloon, a closely-woven woollen material, often used for linings
Shearing	reaping
Shop	a workshop; but *cf* shop goods, bought goods
Skins	leather breeches
Smithy rent	bloomsmithy rent; in 1565 the High Furness bloomsmithies were abolished by royal decree and the £20 rent previously paid to the Crown by the lessees was divided among the customary tenants in the area, so that each property paid a small portion of it

Smitting	marking a sheep with red ruddle as a mark of ownership
Spar	a rafter to which slate-bearing laths are nailed
Spinkt	spotted
Stag	a young unbroken horse
Stancher	stanchion, the upright iron bar set between the mullions of a window
Stay tape	perhaps a hat-string
Stee	a ladder
Stirring	ploughing, often for a second time, or of fallow land
Stub ley	perhaps a hedging tool
Sturdy	*coenurosis* or gid, a brain disease in sheep which causes the animal to move round in circles
Sweeptree	uncertain, but probably a tree so shaped as to be suitable for making the curved struts for a roof truss
Swill	an oval basket made of woven strips of oak suspended from a hazel frame, widely made in the Furness area; hence swillwood, wood for making swills; a side-swill may be one designed to be hung from the shoulder so as to leave the hands free, *e.g.* for sowing seed
Table	board and lodging
Tabling stone	stone used to create a horizontal projecting course on a building
Tamarings	tamarind, the fruit of *tamarindus indica*, usually used as a relish
Tease	to raise the nap on cloth
Test	witnessed by
Tester	a bed canopy
Thick	a strong cloth made from a mixture of wool and cotton, but mostly cotton

252 Glossary

Ticking	a strong linen or cotton cloth used for bed-ticks or mattress covers
Torn	to act as attorney, or in place of another
Tow	fibre of hemp or flax prepared for spinning
Trail	to cart or drag
Trennal	treenail, a wooden pin or peg
Tripes	the innards of a sheep; *cf* Pluck
Tup	a breeding ram
Twinter	a sheep which has lived through two winters, about one and a half years old
Walk	to full cloth
Waller	a mason
Weatherboard	probably stone set over windows to protect them from the weather; in a Lake District context it is unlikely to mean wood for covering whole walls
Webb	a length of cloth
Wedder	wether, a castrated ram kept for wool and meat
Weggey	with horns unequally elevated
Whole	uncertain, but probably to quarry flags
Why	a heiffer
Womble	wimble, a tool for boring holes, here in stone when blasting
Woolcards	instruments with iron teeth to tease or separate threads of wool, hemp, etc., always used in pairs; also a frame with teasel heads set in it for raising the nap on cloth, but the first meaning is more likely here
Yeat	a gate

BIBLIOGRAPHY

1 Manuscript sources.

The Lancashire Record Office in Preston houses the archives from Finsthwaite House (DDPd). I have also made use of material from the deposits of Machell of Penny Bridge (DDMc), Sandys of Graythwaite (DDSa), Townley of Townhead (DDTy), and Archibald of Rusland (DDAr).

Most wills, administrations, and probate inventories are in the records of the archdeaconry of Richmond: LRO, WRW/F and WRW/K. Some survive only in the deposits mentioned above.

Local parish registers and other parish archives have been deposited in the Cumbria Record Office in Kendal (Hawkshead, Cartmel, Cartmel Fell, Crosthwaite, and Finsthwaite) or Barrow-in-Furness (Colton and Ulverston), but except in the case of Cartmel after 1723 they have been printed. Details will be found in section 2 below.

The Finsthwaite churchwardens' account book is CRO, WPR 101/W1.

Quaker registers for Swarthmoor and Cartmel (Height meeting house) are on microfilm at the Cumbria Record Office in Barrow.

2 Printed sources.

a) parish registers:

The Registers of the Parish Church of Cartmel: Part I 1559–1661, ed. H. Brierley, Lancashire Parish Register Society, 28, 1907; Part II 1660–1723, ed. R. Dickinson, 96, 1957

The Registers of Colton Parish Church, ed. A.A. Williams and J.P. Burns, Kendal and London, 1891

Registers of Crosthwaite-cum-Lyth, ed. J.F. Haswell, Penrith, 1935

The Registers of Finsthwaite 1725–1840, ed. A.C.J. Jones and J. Martin, Lancashire Parish Register Society, 135, 1993

The Oldest Register Book of the Parish of Hawkshead 1568–1704, ed. H.S. Cowper, London, 1897

The Second Register Book of the Parish of Hawkshead 1705–1787, ed. K. and G.O.G. Leonard, Hawkshead, [1968]

The Registers of Ulverston Parish Church, ed. C.W. Bardsley and L.R. Ayre, Ulverston, 1881

b) general works; only the main works of reference are listed here; other books and articles will be found in the various footnotes:

Bouch, C.M.L., and Jones, G.P., *The Lake Counties 1500–1830*, Manchester, 1961

Denyer, S., *Traditional Buildings and Life in the Lake District*, London, 1991

Fell, A., *The Early Iron Industry of Furness and District*, Ulverston, 1908

Kirby, R.H. *et al.* (eds), *The Rural Deanery of Cartmel*, Ulverston, 1892

Marshall, J.D., *Furness and the Industrial Revolution*, Barrow-in-Furness, 1958

The Public Charities of the Hundred of Lonsdale North of the Sands, Ulverston, 1852

Rollinson, W., *Life and Tradition in the Lake District*, London, 1974

Stockdale, J., *Annals of Cartmel*, 1872, repr. Beckermet, 1978

West, T., *The Antiquities of Furness*, ed. W. Close, Ulverston, 1805

INDEX

Place-names not ascribed to a particular county are in Lancashire as it existed before the Local Government Act of 1972. Personal names have been given some identification wherever possible, but this has proved difficult in some cases. The entries for John Coward, for instance, a name which appears in three different contexts, may refer to the same man. Unid. = unidentified.

Abrahams, Daniel, of Swarthmoor, 113, 184, 185, 186, 222–3; John, of Swarthmoor, 223
Addison (Adinson), Frances, of Newby Bridge, 8, 204, 224; James, of Newby Bridge, 20n, 205; Robert, slater, xxiii, 200, 201; Sarah, 116, 224
Aldingham, 179
ale licence, 71
Allithwaite, 179, 232
Anderson, Alice, 155, 161; Isabel, 155; William, 155n, 159, 162
Armer, Solomon, waller, xxiii, 67, 201
assessments: by constable, 18, 49, 107, 130, 138, 140, 177–8, 187; land tax, xxvi, 14, 15, 17, 19, 55, 63, 79, 129, 138, 139, 140, 187, 205, 218; poor rate, 14, 19, 28, 33, 129, 130, 138, 139, 140, 158, 179–80, 187, 194–6, 205; window tax, xxvi, 17, 20, 63, 68, 79, 129, 218; see also Colton, school rate
Ashburner family, of High Stott Park, xiin; Agnes, 70; Thomas, of Charley Crag, 151–2
Askew, Adam, MD, of Kendal, 14, 15
Askrigg, NR Yorks., xxvi, 56
Atkinson, John, woodmonger, 23, 38, 42, 44, 45, 46, 49, 51, 53, 54; John, workman, 146, 147; R. (unid.), 96; Richard, of Over Kellet, stone merchant, xxxi, 49, 224; Richard (unid.), 192; Robert, of Cark, xiii, xxxin; Robert, of Crosslands, 57, 140, 178, 195, 196, 205, 207, 209; Robert, of Dope, 207; William, 23, 54; Dr, 15
Ayrey, Benjamin, of Backbarrow Co., xviiin, 102, 105, 107, 158, 188, 224
Ayside, 104

Backbarrow, 64, 74, 78; Company, xvn, xviii, xix, xxiii, xxiv, 129n, 157, 236
Backhouse, Edward, 56; James, of Jolliver Tree, xxiv, 78, 83, 85, 89, 90, 91, 92, 96, 105, 107, 110, 119n, 124, 125, 130, 132, 137n, 154, 157, 158n, 163, 173, 177, 179, 184, 185, 187, 189, 194, 206, 224–5; Mary, see Gurnell

Bailif, Elizabeth, of Light How, 178, 195, 207; John, of Light How, 196, 208, 209
Bainbridge, John, ore-dealer, 22
Banke, George, of Crosslands, 84, 178, 195, 196, 207, 225
Bare, Mr, mercer, 159, 160
bark, xvi, xviii, 3–4, 5, 13, 22, 25, 29, 58, 64, 65, 67, 71, 72, 73, 77, 80, 81, 82, 95, 97, 98, 105, 108, 114, 120, 122, 125, 129, 131, 134, 165, 167, 168, 169, 170, 171, 172, 173, 174, 182, 189, 190, 211, 216
Barrow, James, of Newton, 115n; James (unid.), 101, 118; John, 26, 96, 105; Mabby, midwife, 67; Capt. Thomas, of Browedge, xxvii, 162; Thomas (unid.), 85, 87, 88, 156; William, 51, 52
Barwick, Edward, of Finsthwaite, carpenter, 16, 72, 73, 100, 104, 106, 170, 172, 173, 182, 200, 225; Henry, of Aynsome, 124, 126, 132, 183, 188, 225
Bateman, Robert, vicar of Colton, 89, 90, 91, 92, 102n
Beck, Isabel, nurse, 55, 67n, 69
Beetham, Westm., 154n
Beirdwell, Mr, dancing master, 70
Benson, Arthur, 177, 149, 225; John, of Tom Crag, 141, 143, 149, 225; Thomas, 12, 14; William, 14
Birkett (Burket) Margaret, servant, xxi, 95, 96, 101, 192; Robert, 161; William, blacksmith, 30; William, writing master, xxvii
Blackstock, E., 98
Bland, Edward, of Backbarrow Co., 18, 215, 225
Blawith, 179
Blendall, John, of Cark, miller, 55, 225
bloomsmithy rents, xvi, xxvi, 19, 20, 139, 140, 179, 204, 205–6
Bolton Head, Cumb., 196
books, 27, 30, 45, 81, 87, 88, 123, 155, 157, 161, 212, 217, 224
Bouth, xiv, 22, 24, 33, 62, 89, 159, 170, 183, 186, 212, 236, 237, 242; fair, xxvi, 56, 166
Bouton, Henry, 44
bracken, 22

256 Index

Bradley, Luke, 99
Braithwaite, Agnes, of Hawkshead, 157; Dorothy, of Town End, 64, 73, 80, 103, 107, 109, 110, 121, 124, 127, 131, 135, 225, 235; Edward, of Hawkshead, 208; George, of Kendal, dyer, 98, 225; George, of Stott Park, xxii, xxvi, 39, 44, 89n, 91, 92, 177, 180, 193, 194, 204, 205, 206, 207, 226; George, of Town End, 17, 20, 64, 66, 95, 103, 107, 108, 109, 110, 111n, 112, 171, 191, 197, 198, 203, 204, 205, 206, 207, 209, 226, 237; Grace, of Town End, 99, 120, 121, 122, 123, 124, 127, 152, 153, 167, 190, 209, 226; John, of Satterhow, 208; John, of Sawrey, 209; Margaret, of Town End, 46, 80, 87, 98, 105, 107, 119, 129, 137n, 168, 179, 172, 191, 202, 206, 211; Thomas, of Town End, 20, 64, 80, 81, 95, 98, 190, 206, 207, 209, 226, 237; William, of Fold, Sawrey, 208; William, of Lane Head, Sawrey, 208; William, of Near Sawrey, 208; William, of Satterhow, 45, 208; William, of Town End, 12, 226; William, borrower, 8, 10, 13, 24, 34, 61, 70, 84, 93, 100; William (unid.), xxi, 192
Brandwood, John and Sarah, of Bolton-le-Moors, 222; children, 183, 186, 222
bricks, see building materials
Brockbank, James, 45; Susan, 17; Mr, 73
Broughton-in-Cartmel, 179; in-Furness, 179
Browedge school, xvi, xxvii, 160n, 220n, 225, 236, 239, 242; Trundlebrow, xxi, 241
Browne, Benjamin, of Troutbeck, 35; George, of Troutbeck, 154n
building materials: bricks, 62, 130; stone, xxi, xxiv, 49, 74, 156, 158, 199; laths, 15, 52, 64, 83, 97, 125, 140; timber, xivn, xxi–xxii, xxiii, 28, 35, 37–9, 40, 41, 42, 43, 44, 46, 48, 52, 53, 54, 62, 66, 70, 73, 75, 78, 83, 96, 123, 126, 155, 157, 162, 198, 216; see also lime, limestone, nails, plaster, slate
bulling, xix–xx, 23, 42, 51, 60, 62, 63, 64, 66, 67, 70, 72, 75, 77, 79, 81, 85, 87, 88, 93, 94, 95, 96, 100, 102, 103, 104, 105, 107, 111, 112, 114, 116, 120, 123, 127, 130, 131, 132–3, 135, 136, 143, 180
Burns (Bornes, Burnes), Edward, of Bouth, butcher, xvi, 15, 19, 48, 49, 71, 192–3, 196, 226–7; Elizabeth, 112; John, 207; Margaret, servant, 71, 73, 108, 177, 194; Thomas, 206
Bury, James, of Ulverston, apothecary, 1, 81, 86, 88

candles, xxviii, 21, 30, 45, 46, 55, 65, 78, 95
Cark-in-Cartmel, xv, xviiii, xxxin, 23
carriers, 21, 28, 61, 191

Cart Lane, xxii, 49, 166
Carter, Agnes, servant, 11, 14, 23, 27
Cartmel, xxvi, 25, 70, 92, 102, 117, 157, 164, 229; Humphrey Head, xxvi, 28n
Cartmel Fell, xiiin, 101, 230, 236; Thorphinsty, 155
Case, John, of Walney, 90, 102, 189, 227
Casson, Ferdinand, 156; Thomas, 114
Caton, 90
Caton, John, of Hatlex, xv
cattle, xiii, xivn, 13, 50, 51, 52, 57, 58, 70n, 71, 92, 102, 166, 167, 171, 172, 211, 212, 228; see also bulling, oxen
Chambers, Lawyer, 43, 90
Chambre, Walter, of Kendal, 115n
Chamney, Francis, of Stock, 9, 10, 15, 58, 109, 227
Chapman, William, of Old Hall, 12, 16, 23, 30, 227; William, apprentice ropemaker, xxix
Chapman House, 204, 205, 228, 233
char, xvii, 36, 97, 187–8, 213
charcoal, xii, xiii, xviii, xix, xx, 14, 24, 26, 28, 29, 30, 32, 33, 43, 46, 59, 64, 65, 68, 73, 74, 75, 77, 78, 81, 82, 84, 98, 107, 111, 155, 158, 159, 162, 168, 172, 182, 189, 191, 216, 220; see also coal
charities, xv, xxvi, 84n, 103, 107, 109, 110, 120, 123–4, 127, 131, 135, 137, 138, 152, 155, 156
Charley Crag, xvii, xxix, 81, 151–2, 160n, 167, 173n, 174n, 202n, 205, 228, 234, 240, 241, 243
christenings, 69, 72, 129
Christian, John, barrister, xxix, xxx, 128n
'Clement Taylor tenement' xiii, xxiv, 156, 162; see also Finsthwaite House
Clifton, Jane, 17
clogs, 41, 57, 102; see also shoes
cloth, xviii, xxvii, xxviii, 3, 6, 19, 20, 21, 23, 25, 26, 34, 41, 42, 45, 52, 54, 56, 59, 63, 65, 70, 71, 74, 75, 78, 79, 81, 86, 88, 93, 94, 98, 106, 119, 133, 134, 157, 159, 160, 162, 165, 169, 192, 202, 204
clothing, xxi, xxvii, 1, 21, 25, 26, 28, 45, 46, 56, 61, 63, 64, 65, 70, 86, 87, 88, 101, 102, 105, 106, 108, 119, 129, 142, 157, 169, 170, 186, 200; see also clogs, shoes
coal, 45, 86, 155; see also charcoal
Cobby House, xiv, xvii, xviii, 207
Cocke, George, of Kendal, 21
cockfighting, xxviii, 42
coffins, see funerals
Coldin, John, of Grange, Manxman, 20
Collinson, William, of Ulverston, tailor, 55, 56, 227

Index

Colton: church, xxv, 15, 22, 24, 29, 90; churchwardens, xxvi, 227, 228, 229, 231, 232, 233, 235, 236, 237, 238, 239, 240, 242; constables, xxvi, 174–9, 225, 229, 231, 233, 235, 236, 237, 238, 239, 240, 242; overseers, xxvi, 108, 160, 225, 227, 233, 235, 236, 237, 238, 239, 240, 242; poor, 103, 108, 109, 112, 137; poor rate, 205; school, 15n, 16n, 19n, 27n; school rate, 14, 19, 29, 137, 138, 139, 140, 187, 206–8; vicar, 84, 227, and see Bateman, Robert; see also assessments
constables, see Colton, and Taylor, Clement IV
Coniston, xxiii, 179, 201
Corker (Corke), John, 15, 178; Richard, 178, 195, 196
Cornthwaite, John, stone merchant, xxiv, 158
Coulton, Christopher, 83
Coupland (Capland), James, of Parkamor, 8, 9, 18, 24, 227; Robert, of Parkamoor, 58, 187, 227
Coward, George, 71; Jane, 138; John, of Plum Green, 35, 37, 46, 61, 66, 68, 75, 94, 104, 141, 216; John, shopkeeper, 88, 92, 96, 98, 140, 187; John, workman, 21, 22, 27, 31, 33, 67, 173, 190, 191; Mary, 155; Samuel, 173; William, of Finsthwaite, butcher and workman, xvi, xx, xxvii–xxviii, 17, 21, 22, 26, 27, 30, 33, 51, 56, 66, 73, 93, 99, 122, 129, 141, 160, 163, 166–7, 170,171–2, 187, 197–8, 211, 212, 216–7, 227–8; William (unid.), 139, 158
Cowperthwaite, John, 111
Cragg(e), John, of Waterside, xvii, xxi, 126, 130, 137, 139, 146, 158, 162, 228
Crank family, of Ulverston, plasterers, xxiii, 201, 202, 203; Henry junior, 66, 201, 219–20, 228; Henry senior, 56, 201, 219–20, 228; Nicholas junior, 96, 219–20; Nicholas senior, 44, 219–20, 228; William junior, 96; William senior, 219
Croasdale, Henry, of Finsthwaite, joiner, 84, 96, 98, 170, 172, 173, 182, 187, 191n, 228
Croft, Dr, 156
Crooklands, Westm., 56
Crosfield, Thomas, 23
Crossfield, Richard, of Seatle, woodmonger, 52, 68, 96, 97, 112, 228
Cunsey forge, xvn, xix, 26, 230, 243

Daffey bottle, 73, 78, 86, 87, 88, 169, 192; see also medicines
Dalton-in-Furness, 179, 182, 221
dancing, xxvii, 27, 33, 70, 73, 75, 161
Danson, Christopher, of Finsthwaite, 152, 153, 228; Edward, of Cobby House, xvii, xviii, xxvii, 2, 3, 4, 5, 10, 11, 12, 13, 15, 17, 24, 31, 32, 44, 47, 57, 59, 62, 63, 64, 65, 71, 74, 75, 77, 78, 79, 80, 81, 82, 220, 228; George, 154; James, of Finsthwaite, xvii, xviii, xx, xxvii, xxix, 2, 3, 5, 7, 10, 11, 25–6, 32, 52, 53, 56, 57, 63, 64, 66, 74, 86, 99, 122, 131, 170, 197, 198–200, 203, 229; Jane, of Finsthwaite, 135, 138; Mary, of Finsthwaite, 217; Thomas, of Cobby House, shoemaker, xvii, xviii, 17, 31, 32, 34, 76, 84, 92, 93, 94, 96, 97, 101, 105, 106, 108, 110, 111, 115, 119, 120, 121, 122, 123, 128, 129, 134, 141, 145, 150–1, 154, 159, 161, 170, 173, 229; William, of Finsthwaite, shoemaker, xxviii, 11, 13, 16, 17, 21, 22, 23, 28, 29, 30, 32, 43, 51, 58, 59, 65, 74, 77, 82, 95, 177, 194, 206, 229; his charity, 135, 152, 229; William, son of James, shoemaker, 155
Denison, William, of Dalton, grocer, and family, 186, 221–3
Denny, Elizabeth, of Newby Bridge, innkeeper, 83, 87, 98, 115n, 157, 158n, 164, 177, 206, 229; Margaret, 42; Thomas, of Newby Bridge, blacksmith, 11, 16, 17, 18, 19, 21, 34, 42, 47, 48, 50, 52, 53, 58, 65, 71, 77, 194, 207, 229, 233
Dixon, Agnes, 107, 166, 167, 172, 209; Christopher, 71, 112; Isabel, servant, 1, 89, 209; James, of Light How and Sinderhill, carpenter, 22, 81, 82, 88, 206, 207; Jennet, 204, 205; John, of Near Sawrey, 209; Thomas, 139, 178, 182, 187; William, 49, 93
Dodgson (Dodson), George, 183; John, lender, 10, 13, 18, 22; John, of Colton, schoolmaster, 15n; Robert, 123; William, pauper, 112
Douglas, Clementina Johannes Sobieski, of Waterside, xvn, 239; James, captain, xvn, 239
drink: beer, xxviii; cider, xviii, 46; punch, xxviii, xxxi, 154; sack, 156; spirits, xxviii, 14, 28, 42, 52, 53, 71, 77, 78–9, 129, 154, 170; wine, 30, 51, 52, 53, 79, 130
Drinkel, George, of Rusland, 147, 148, 178, 229; Myles, of Rusland, 39, 195, 196, 207, 229
Dryden, Henry, deputy registrar, 16n
dyeing, 14, 65, 98, 155

Egton-cum-Newland, 21, 62, 179; Newland forge, 225, 230
Elertson, Henry, 205

fairs, xxvi; see also Bouth, Hawkshead, Kendal, Lancaster
Fallows, Randal, of Far Sawrey, 21, 24, 31, 230

Fell, Agnes, of Town End, 107, 109, 230; Isabel, servant, xxi, 142–3; James, 17, 148, 183, 186; John, 86; Richard, of Town End, xxi, 30, 51, 56, 64, 80, 81, 82, 230, 232; Sarah, of Town End, 80, 82, 188, 203, 209, 230; William, of Town End, 152, 153, 203, 229, 230; Dr, 154

Fenwick, Robert, of Burrow House, 184, 185

Finsthwaite, xii, xiii; bloomsmithy rental, 204; charities, 103, 107, 109, 110, 120–1, 131, 135, 138, 152–3, 155–6, 209; church, xxii, xxiii, xxv, xxvi, xxvii, xxxi, 1, 35, 37–9, 41, 44, 46, 48, 50, 51, 53, 56, 62, 67, 75, 76, 83n, 84, 85, 89, 140, 157, 190, 196, 212, 225, 232, 236, 240; churchwardens, 20, 136n, 157, 225, 231, 232, 233, 239, 240, 242; Colton school rate, 206–8; communion cup, 60; houses, see Chapman House, Charley Crag, Cobby House, Green Cottage, Finsyke, Jolliver Tree, Landing, Plum Green, Sinderhill, Stott Park, Tom Crag, Town End, Waterside; poor, 108, 110, 137n; poor rate, 194, 205; school, xxiii, 27n, 28, 29, 34, 35, 63, 84n, 225, 232, 236, 240, 241; vicars, see Harrison, John, and Simpson, George

Finsthwaite House, xii, xiii, xvi, xxi–xiv, 39, 57, 189–90, 198–9, 200–2, 210, 219–20; see also furniture, windows

Finsyke, xiii, xxi, 167, 225, 241

Fisher, Henry, of Cartmel, chairmaker, 79; Jonathan, of Far Sawrey, 209; Thomas, mercer, 87, 186

flax, 156

Fleming, Sir Daniel, of Rydal, xivn, 28n

Fletcher (Fetcher), John, of Holker, 115n; Mr, 83

fogg, see hay

food: xxvii–xxviii, xxxi; beans, 25, 190; bread, xxvii, 101, 154, 187; butter, xx, 18, 154, 187; cheese, xxviii, 21, 24, 34, 39, 45, 46, 55, 59, 75, 128, 130, 133, 134, 165, 168, 172, 189, 190, 191; cockles, xvi, 25, 26, 191; fish, xviii, xxviii, 16, 18, 29, 83, 129, 165, and see char; fruit, xxviii, 47, 154, 187; geese, 129, 154; ham, 154; meat, xxvii–xxviii, 15, 17, 18, 28, 43, 47, 48, 52, 53, 66, 71, 117, 134, 154, 166, 173, 183, 192–3, 197–8, 211, 212–3, 216–7, 220; milk, 187; peas, 16, 190; potatoes, xxviii, 12, 165, 211; salt, 16, 30, 43, 45, 46, 59; suet, 19; sugar, xxviii, 12, 19, 22, 62, 154; treacle, 78; see also spices

Ford, Richard, ironmaster, xix, 24, 31, 46, 59, 60, 230

funerals, xxxi, 56, 84, 98, 154, 155, 158, 161, 162, 173n, 183, 187, 216

furniture and fittings, xxi, xxiii, xxviii, xxx, 54, 67, 79, 95, 97, 189–90, 202; see also heirlooms

Garman, John, workman, 164, 165, 166, 169, 230; William, workman, 164, 165, 166, 169, 230

Garner, Agnes, of Bordrigg, 208; William, 94

Garnett, Anthony, of Staveley, workman, 139, 146, 147, 148, 155, 158, 230

Garsdale, WR Yorks., 196, 197

Gibson, John, 130; Robert, of Lancaster, lawyer, xxv, 35, 89, 90, 186; Thomas, 146, 147, 148

glass, 66, 77

Goad, James, 78, 230

grain: barley, xxviii, 45, 59, 65, 69, 80, 85, 93, 100, 101, 114, 116, 117, 118, 126, 134, 135, 165; bigg, 45, 130; corn, 23, 186; oats, xvii, 16, 21, 22, 25, 32, 33, 34, 42, 45, 55, 58, 59, 62, 66, 70, 80, 191; rye, 101; wheat, xvii, 18, 26, 46, 68, 166, 168, 169, 172

Grange–over–Sands, xxvii, 20, 43

Grasmere, Westm., xivn

Graythwaite, 93, 94, 236, 237

grazing, xx, 16, 22, 44, 57, 58, 70n, 103, 155

Green Cottage, xvii, 137–8, 139, 225, 237

Greenhow, James, carrier, 191

Greenwood, Jane, 56; James, 196

Grigg, Reginald, of Walker Ground, builder, xxiii, 156, 161, 230

Gurnell, Mary, of Jolliver Tree, 68, 224, 230–1, 239, 241, 242

Guy, James, 39

haberdashery, 26, 78, 87, 102, 154, 157, 159, 160, 162

Hall, Edward & Co., 26n; Thomas, of Cartmel, shopkeeper, xxviii, 45, 61, 62, 65, 73, 76, 212, 231

Harrison, Christopher, 87; John, vicar of Finsthwaite, xxv, xxvi–xxvii, xxixn, xxxn, 50, 60, 67, 75, 84, 85, 87, 90, 91, 95, 96, 99, 106, 108, 114n, 118, 185, 186, 187, 231; entries by, 125, 126; Harrison, John, workman, 149; John (unid.), 160; Jennet, 84; Lawrence, of Stott Park (d. 1732), xxvi, 33, 86, 94, 205, 231; Lawrence, of Stott Park (d. 1765), xx, 130, 136, 180, 231; Margaret, 154; Myles, of Stott Park, xviii, xx, xxvi, 19, 20, 23, 25, 28, 29, 32, 38, 42, 43, 50, 55, 58, 64, 67, 68, 69, 73, 76, 83, 84, 85, 89, 91, 92, 97, 100, 102, 110, 111, 123, 163, 169, 177, 179n, 180, 189, 193, 194, 204, 206, 207, 208, 231–2; Richard, 29, 58; Robert, 173; Roger, mercer, 119

Hathornthwaite, James, and family, 221–3; John, of Sandside, 113, 183, 184, 185, 186, 221–3

Index 259

hay, 20, 105, 106, 117, 168, 188, 191, 203
Haverthwaite, xv, 234; bloomsmithy rental, 204; Colton school rate, 206–8; poor, 108, 109, 120, 137; poor rate, 194, 205
Hawkshead, xiiin, xxvii, 21, 46, 92, 102, 179, 208, 238; fair, xxvi, xxvii, 15, 95; oath at, 208–9
heirlooms, xx, xxx, 35–6, 139
hemp, 63, 99, 168, 172
highways, 65, 66, 68, 164
Hirdson, Richard, of New Close, 14; William, of Oxen Park, 8, 30, 232
Hodgson, Thomas, shopkeeper, 34, 55, 57, 88, 89
Holker, 179; the Frith, xx, 50, 70, 102
Holme, James, proctor, 181, 183, 184, 185; John, workman, xxiii, 62, 67, 102, 148, 201, 210, 232; Thomas, weaver, xxvii, 45, 75, 94; William, 94, 95, 106
horses, xx, xxvi, 10, 58, 59, 61, 104, 141
house of correction, 179
Huddart (Huddarst), Jeremiah, 218
Huddleston, Thomas, of Town End, 141, 232
Hunter, Mr, schoolmaster, 6, 160, 161, 220
Hutchinson, John, of Near Sawrey, 209

ink, 208
iron, xviiin, 11, 111, 220; see also Backbarrow Co., and Cunsey forge

Jackson, Elizabeth, 51; Isaac, of Finsthwaite, poor labourer, 108, 109, 110, 112, 127, 131, 138, 232; John, poor labourer, 108; Roger, servant, xxi, 79, 81, 85, 86, 88, 95, 101, 106, 108, 115, 118, 120, 155, 156, 169, 170, 192, 232
Johnson (Janson, Jonson), Alice, of Town End, 30, 70, 172; John, packman, 21, 63; John, workman, 37; Thomas, of Town End, xvii, 16, 18, 21, 22, 32, 70, 76, 99–100, 102, 104, 110, 117, 121, 123, 139, 141, 159, 168, 170, 172, 182, 232
Jolliver Tree, xxi, xxiv, xxvi, xxixn, 51, 168, 217, 224, 225, 230, 231, 239, 242

Keen, Arthur, collier, 33, 43, 232; Jane, wife of, 112, 232
Kellett, Betty, 186; Dorothy, of Satterthwaite, 181, 232; Edward, of Satterthwaite, woodmonger, xxii, 11, 15, 40, 41, 42, 46, 48, 51, 208, 232; John, 67
Kendal, Westm., xivn, xix, xxiii, xxvi, 21, 28, 30, 61, 93, 95, 130, 136, 157, 182, 183, 184, 185, 186, 192, 197, 225, 240; fair, 30, 31, 57
Kendal, Leonard, 190; Robert, 161
Kilner, Edward, of Ayside, 104; Nathan, of Backbarrow Co., 129n

King, James, naval surgeon, xv; Isabel, wife of, see Taylor, Isabel (b. 1722); Edward, son of, xv; James, of Finsthwaite House, xiin, xv
Kirby (Kurby), Elizabeth, 120, 165, 167, 169; James, poor labourer, 108; Richard, workman, 100, 124, 125, 233
Kirkby Ireleth, 179
Kitchin, Richard, dyer, 106, 233
Knipe, Mr, 185

Lakeside, see Landing
Lambert, Charles, of Lancaster, lawyer, 91, 118, 189; William, of Kendal, 115n
Lancaster, xxv, xxvi, 35, 51, 89, 90, 92, 163, 164, 184, 185, 186; fair, 184; prisoners at, 175, 179
Landing, xii, xiiin, xvii, xxi, xxv, 85n, 115n, 179, 205, 216n, 228, 231
Lang, Christopher, 15
Langram, John, of Coniston, slater, xxiii, 57, 233
lantern, xxviii, 19
laths, see building materials
Law, John, of Ulverston, lawyer, xxixn, xxx, 161; Richard, of Blackburn, 182, 183, 222; Sarah, of Blackburn, 222
Leck, Robert, of Finsthwaite, 153, 165, 166, 217, 233
Leece, 179
Leece, James, of Bouth, tailor, xxvii, 61, 63, 70, 76; James, builder, 202, 233; John, maltster, 47, 48, 62, 65, 69, 75, 100, 101, 233
Leeming, Ralph, workman, 12, 64, 233
letters, 27, 29, 49, 59, 69, 90, 92, 130, 184, 185, 186, 196
Leven, river, xii, xviiin; the Crane, xviiin
Levens, Wcstm., 90
Lickbarrow, Rowland, of Backbarrow, dyer, 155, 233; William, of Backbarrow, dyer, 1, 5, 14, 19, 233
lime, 35, 152, 202; kilns, xxiii, 37, 68, 85, 86, 199
limestone, xxiii, 58, 68, 72, 199
Lindal–in–Furness, xxix, xxx
Liverpool, 43
loans, xvi, xix, 8–9, 10–11, 13, 16, 17, 18, 19, 24–5, 27, 30, 31, 32, 34, 43, 44, 45, 46, 47, 49–50, 58, 60, 61, 63, 66, 69, 70, 71, 72, 73, 75, 76, 77, 78, 79, 63, 84, 92, 93, 94, 96, 97, 98, 99, 100, 101, 102, 105, 106, 114, 116, 117, 118, 119, 132, 134, 135, 141, 159, 162, 163, 188
Lowick, 179
Lowther, Rev., 154

260 Index

Machell (Maychell), George, 207; James, of Haverthwaite, 177; John, of Haverthwaite, ironmaster, 12, 31, 46, 83, 87, 184, 185, 186, 188, 194, 204, 205, 206, 233, 236; William, 54
malt, 45n, 47, 62, 65, 69, 100, 101, 172, 182
manure, 14, 204
Mansriggs, 170
Marr, Christopher, of Speelbank, 9, 11, 13, 34, 47, 58, 71, 83, 98, 233
Marshall, J., 54; Nicholas, 6
Massicks, Thomas, workman, 108, 209, 234; William, of Finsthwaite, collier, 155, 156, 234
medicines, 47, 48, 61, 87, 96, 155, 160, 175, 217; see also Daffey bottle
Miller, Mr, apothecary, 155
Millerson, Thomas, of Ulverston, 10, 22, 27, 29, 69, 234
Milner, Mr, 87
Milnthorpe, Westm., 90, 101
Morris, Emmy, of Sinderhill, 129, 133, 165, 166, 169, 234, 240, 241
Morton, Dr, 160
Muckelt, George, of Kents Bank, woodmonger, 113, 114, 118, 120, 124, 125, 126, 128n, 167, 171, 234

nails, xxxii, 51, 61, 88, 89, 140
Newby (Nuby), Edward, 20, 204, 205, 207; Eleanor, servant, xxi, 119; John, waller, 200; Peter, 93, 190; Richard, of Haverthwaite, swillmaker, xviii, 12, 18, 30, 50, 62, 78, 112, 177, 206, 208, 234, 242
Newby Bridge, xii, xivn, xvin, xviii, xx, 8n, 23, 42, 46, 56, 85n, 115n, 157n, 158, 161, 184, 185, 229, 235, 236
Newland, see Egton–cum–Newland
newspapers, 130, 218–9
Nibthwaite, xxiii, 230; Daniel of, 138; George of, xxiii, 201; poor, 108, 137; poor rate, 205
Nicholson, William, of Hannakin, 208
Noble, Matthew, of Egton, ropemaker, xxxn, 234
Nook House, 239, 240
Nusam, Joseph, 130

Old Hutton, Westm., xv; Blease Hall, xvn
Ormandy (Ormady), Jane, servant, xxi, 28, 41, 63, 64, 77, 79, 81, 86, 88, 102n, 234; William, 178
Orpin, Mary, xxixn
Osmotherley, 179
Over Kellet, Westm., xxii, 49, 112
overseers of the poor, see Colton, and Taylor, Clement IV

oxen, xx, 12, 14; see also cattle
Oxford, xvi, 6, 16, 28, 44, 61

packmen, 21n
paint, 50, 159
paper, 46, 55, 123, 172, 173
parchment, 172
Park, Alan, of Haverthwaite, 194; Edward, workman, 12, 16, 19, 23, 33, 200, 203, 235; George, workman, 148; Jacob, of Finsthwaite, workman, xxi, 33, 44, 50, 56, 59, 67, 74, 82, 84, 85, 86, 97, 105, 111, 120, 163, 200, 201, 202, 203, 234–5; Leonard, workman, 201; William, workman, 12, 23, 33, 56, 61, 65, 163, 235
peat, xxix, 59, 99, 100, 188, 198, 199, 202, 203, 204, 237
Pedder, Elizabeth, of Finsthwaite House, xiin; Rev. James, vicar of Garstang, xiin
Pennington, 179
Pennington, Benjamin, weaver, 133, 134, 235; Garnet, of Cowridding, 8, 9, 235; Paul, of Low Longmire, 98, 101, 106, 235; William, of Bandrakehead, 29
Penny, Joseph, of Haverthwaite, 15, 177, 194, 196; Richard, 29; William, of Penny Bridge, 103; Mr, senior, 184, 185
Penny Bridge, xviii, 65; Co., xvn, xix
Pepper, Thomas, of Newby Bridge, blacksmith, 12, 105, 137, 155, 187, 235
Pirt (Pert), John, of Dunnerdale, xvn; – (unid.), workman, 201
Plain Furness, manorial court, xxix
plaster, xxii; hair for, 49, 50, 51, 87, 93, 95, 157
Plum Green, xii, xiiin, 35, 36, 115, 216n, 226, 227, 233, 239
Pool (Pull), Joseph, 170, 173
poor, in Colton, 103, 108, 112; prisoners, 175, 179; see also assessments
Postlethwaite, John, 196; Richard, of Abbots Reading, 12, 14, 20, 46, 177, 194, 206, 207, 235
Preston, 185, 186, 196
Preston, Christopher, of Holker, xivn; John, 68; Roger, 22
privy, xxiv, 57
Prudence (Prudah, Prudey), Agnes, of Town End, 103, 235; John, of Town End, carpenter, 106, 107, 120, 122, 146, 167, 170, 171, 172, 235; Sarah, of Town End, 103, 235

Quarter Sessions, xxvi, 162–3, 163–4
Queen Anne's Bounty, xxv, 35, 83, 84n, 99, 196

railings, xxiii, xxiv, 157
Rawlinson, Abraham, of Rusland Hall, xviii, xx, 42, 60, 62, 64, 67, 69, 136, 143, 178, 195, 196, 205, 207, 235, 236; James, 137, 139, 158; John, of Haverthwaite, 206; John, of Haverthwaite, smith, 206; John (unid.), 187, 194; Richard, of Haverthwaite, 177; Stephen, 206; Thomas, of Low Graythwaite, 11, 236; William, of Low Graythwaite, ironmaster, xviii, 31, 33, 46, 72, 93, 94, 100, 127, 131, 132, 135, 184, 185, 223n, 236; Mr (unid.), 139
recipes, 26, 48, 208
Redhead (Readhead), Elizabeth, poor woman, 112; Margaret, poor woman, 112
rents, xvi, 2–3, 4–5, 6, 7, 10, 14, 15, 25, 26, 31–2, 36, 44, 48, 52–3, 57, 58, 59, 63, 65, 68, 71, 74–5, 76–7, 79, 82, 92, 94, 99–100, 101, 104, 105, 110, 111, 115, 117, 119, 120, 121, 123, 128, 134, 141, 143, 144, 154–6, 149–52, 159, 220
Ridgway, Robert, 216
Rigg (Rigge), Edward, of Rusland Hall, 23, 72, 103, 187, 236; George, 111; James, tailor, 161; James (unid.), 29, 156; Rebecca, 112; Richard, of Force Mill, xvin, 8, 10, 17, 27, 43, 50, 73, 93, 236; Robert, 11, 25, 28, 32, 33, 194, 206, 209; Thomas, 109, 195, 215; Mr, apothecary, 160
Robinson, Agnes, of Waterside, xiv, xxixn; Ann, of Newby Bridge, 113, 114; Christopher, of Waterside, joiner, xiv; Elizabeth, of Arnside, 208; George, 76, 96; Isabel, of Waterside, see Taylor, Isabel; John, of Arnside, 208; John, of Bouth, xiv–xv, xxixn; John, of Newby Bridge, xx, 111, 112, 113, 114, 116, 120, 123, 236; John (unid.), 15n, 171, 206; Mary, of Waterside, xiv; Richard, of Waterside, xv, xvii, xxiii, xxvi, xxix, xxx, xxxin, 4, 11, 13, 14, 15, 17, 21, 22, 27, 32, 34, 35, 38, 43, 44, 45, 50, 51, 53, 66, 70n, 85, 89, 90, 91, 92, 117, 122, 129, 155n, 157, 167, 171, 177, 182, 185, 194, 204, 205, 206, 207, 208, 217n, 236, 238; his charity, 152; Samuel, workman, 12, 44, 177, 194, 206; Thomas, 120; William, of Bouth, xivn, 44, 45, 46, 53, 61
Rook How, 177n, 178, 195, 196, 221
Roskell, Robert, schoolmaster, 1, 25, 220, 236
Rowlandson, James, 9, 236; James, schoolmaster, 1, 220, 236
Rownson, Esther, poor woman, 108; James, 16, 22, 24, 45, 50, 57, 186; John, of Bouth, 15n, 22; William, of Bouth, shopkeeper, xxviii, 11, 12, 19, 22, 24, 30, 38, 39, 50, 61, 63, 66, 78, 81, 85, 87, 88, 103, 106, 154, 155, 236–7; — (unid.), tailor, 63
Rusland: bloomsmithy rental, 204; Hall, xviii, xx, 72, 75, 77, 136, 235, 236; Heights, xviii; Hulleter, 63, 64, 66, 67; Pool, xiiin, 1n, 203n; poor, 108, 109, 120, 137; poor rate, 194–5, 196–7, 205; school rate, 206–8
Russell, Charles, poor labourer, 112; John, of Force Forge, 137n, 167, 168, 178, 195, 196, 237

saddles, 55, 94
salving, xviii, xx, 2, 5, 23n, 198
Samson, Henry, 215
Sandys, Adam, of Bouth, 16n; Myles, of Graythwaite, xxvi, 90, 99, 163, 184, 185, 223n, 237
Satterthwaite, John, merchant, xviii, 120, 122, 124, 125, 126, 132, 134, 167, 169, 170, 171, 174, 237; Thomas, of Thwaite Moss, 178, 195, 196, 208; William, of Hawkshead, mercer, 56, 63, 106, 119, 237; William (unid.), 160, 161
Sawrey, John, xxiii, 201, 204; Margaret, of Green Cottage, 70n, 99, 101, 105, 106, 107, 137, 177, 194, 206, 237; Myles, of Coniston, 209; Peter, 133; Robert, of Green Cottage, xvii, 2, 3, 5, 10, 12, 13, 14, 20, 25, 28, 204, 205, 207, 237
Scales, John, of Grizedale, xvin, 8, 9, 11, 24, 79, 93, 106, 238; John, of Thwaite Moss, xiv, 178, 195, 207; John (unid.), 45; Robert, of Thwaite Head, 23, 30, 33, 81, 87, 96, 97, 102, 103, 105, 107, 178, 195, 196, 207, 238; Samuel, seaman, 128n
Scotson, Thomas, of Abbot Park, 8, 238
Sedgwick, Westm., 196
Sedon, John, of Deane, 183, 186, 223
seeds, xxviii, 62
Senhouse, Humphrey, of Netherhall, Cumb., xxviii
Sergeant, Mr, dancing master, 161
servants, xx, and see Birkett, Margaret; Burns, Margaret; Carter, Agnes; Dixon, Isabel; Fell, Isabel; Jackson, Roger; Newby, Eleanor; Ormandy, Jane; Singleton, Mary; Taylor, William; Thompson, Thomas
services, see tenants
sheep, xivn, xvn, xvi, xviii, xx–xxi, xxx, 2, 3, 5, 6, 9, 16, 18, 23, 35–6, 63, 75, 94, 100, 139, 140, 141, 166, 167, 171–2, 181, 199, 211, 212–16; see also heirlooms, salving
sheriff, under–, xxvi, 55, 162–3
Shippard, Robert, of Natland, Westm., 46, 47, 60, 69, 83
shipping, xix, 128n, 161, 225
ships: *The Jane*, xixn, 160; *The Globe*, 126, 128n

shoes, xviii, 22, 65, 74, 82, 92, 97, 105, 110, 115, 123, 126, 127, 134, 141, 145, 151, 155, 159, 161; and see clogs
Shuttleworth, Mr, dancing master, 27
Simondson, Mr, apothecary, 155
Simpson, George, vicar of Finsthwaite, xvn, xxvii, xxxi, 154, 156, 217, 238, 239, 242; entries by, 152–3, 217; Richard, of Haverthwaite, 177, 178, 194, 206; Richard of High Cragg, 194
Sinderhill, 115n, 119n, 171, 207, 225, 234, 239, 240
Singleton, Mary, servant, 101, 102, 105, 106, 169, 170, 238
Skelding, Jonas, of Haverthwaite, 140, 177, 187, 194, 207
Slaidburn, WR Yorks., 196
slate, xxiii, 39, 57, 58, 65, 152, 201
Soulby (Sealby, Soaby, Solaby), Elizabeth, of Finsthwaite, poor woman, 107, 109, 110, 121, 123, 124, 131, 135, 138, 152, 153, 238
Soame, William, of London, silversmith, 60
soap, 45, 63, 170
Spence, William, of Ellerside, 177, 206
spices, 26, 34, 36, 46, 55, 108, 188, 191
Stamper, George, of Roger Ridding, 162, 238
Stewardson, Henry, 173; John, borrower, 10, 13, 24, 31, 44, 58
stone, see building materials
Stott Park, xii, xiiin, xviii, xx, xxvi, 35, 37, 225, 228, 229, 231, 233, 242
Stout, Leonard, of Lancaster, xxixn, 128, 238; Rebecca, of Lancaster, xxixn, 238
Strickland, Anthony, of Kendal, plumber, xxiii, 118; Reginald, 195, 196, 197; Robert, of Sike, 196; Thomas, of Iconthwaite, charity, 103, 109, 127, 131, 137, 138, 209, 238; Thomas, of Light How, 178, 188, 195, 196, 207, 208; Thomas (unid.), 76, 102, 187, 208; widow, of Sike, 178, 195; William, of Sike, 195, 196; William, of Whitestock, 178, 195, 196, 207
Swanson, William, borrower, 8
Swarthmoor, 184

tar, 23, 29, 43, 83, 85, 102
taxes, see assessments
Taylor, Adam, of Hawkshead, 44, 49, 55, 59, 238
Taylor, Agnes (fl. 1645), xiii; Agnes (d. 1700), see Robinson, Agnes; Agnes (b. 1717), xiii, xxxin, 24, 25, 26, 60, 67, 70, 73, 75, 215n
Taylor, Benjamin, of Hardcragg, xxvii, 1, 238–9, 241, 242; Benjamin, of Nibthwaite, 18, 49
Taylor, Christopher, of Jolliver Tree, 69n, 242; Sarah, wife of, 69n, 230, 239, 241, 242; Christopher, of Plum Green, xix, xxvi, 10, 22, 37, 87, 89, 91, 92, 94, 105, 177, 194, 204, 206, 207, 238, 239
Taylor, Clement I, xiii; Clement II, xiii; Clement III, xiii–xiv; Clement IV, xii–xxxi, 204, 206, 207, 208; as churchwarden, xxvi, 20; as constable, xxvi, 174–9; as overseer, xxvi, 20, 108, 112; as tax collector, xxvi, 20; as under-sheriff, xxvi, 55, 56, 61, 162–3, 163–4; in rate and rent lists, 177, 194, 204, 205–6; politics, xxvi; will, xxix–xxxi, 154; Clement V, xiii, xvii, xxvii, xxix, xxx, xxxi, 45, 60, 67, 70, 75, 99, 106, 108, 128n, 170; Clement of Hardcragg, xxviin, 10, 13, 16, 23, 58, 59, 239, 241; Clement, of Roger Ridding, 178, 195, 207
Taylor, Cuthbert (fl. 1600), 128n
Taylor, Edward I, xiii; Edward II, xiii; Edward III, xiv, xvi, xix, 8n, 205; Elizabeth, wife of, xiv, 63, 69, 161, 204, 224; Edward IV, xv, xix, xxivn, xxvii, xxx, 18n, 42n, 137n, 156, 157, 158n, 159, 160, 161, 162; entries by, 121, 140–1, 142, 143, 144, 145, 146–7, 148, 152, 156, 217, 218, 220; Edward (1691–1770), xiv, xv–xvi, xvii, xxx, 12, 18, 24, 25, 30, 34, 42, 66, 69, 75, 78, 88, 92, 113, 114, 135, 151, 154, 182, 183, 184, 185, 186, 187, 194, 221–3, 239; Emma, wife of, xv, 118, 187; daughters, xv, 69n; entry by, 145; Edward, of Craikside, 11, 239, 241; his charity, 107, 110, 123–4, 131, 135, 138, 152; Edward (unid.), 2, 4
Taylor, Elizabeth (b. 1630), xv; Elizabeth, of Nibthwaite, 112; Elizabeth (b. 1715), xv, xxvii, 24, 25, 26, 27, 28n, 29, 61, 73
Taylor, Elkanah, of Greetyside, 128, 240
Taylor, George, of Chapman House, 89, 177, 180, 194, 195, 206, 207, 240; George, of Finsyke, 11, 73, 85, 89, 91, 92, 106, 138, 177, 194, 204, 205, 206, 207, 240; George, of Rusland, 194
Taylor, Henry, of Finsthwaite, 108, 138, 152, 153, 156, 173, 187, 202, 217, 239, 240, 241; Elizabeth, wife of, 138; Henry, of Landing, xvii, xxv, 34, 35–6, 50, 54, 59, 60, 76, 78, 84, 89, 92, 115, 118, 119n, 177, 179, 180, 194, 206, 216n, 227, 240; Margaret, mother of, 37
Taylor, Isabel, wife of Clement IV, xiv, xviin, xix, xxi, xxiii–xxiv, xxvii, xxixn, xxx, 42, 55, 62, 77, 79, 137n; entries by 135, 136, 142–3, 145–6, 149–50, 151, 152, 153–8, 181; Isabel (b. 1722), xv, xxxin, 75, 99, 101, 106
Taylor, James, of Nibthwaite, xxiii, 201; James, of Tom Crag, xvii, xxii, 12, 16, 19, 20, 23, 33, 44, 56, 58, 61, 62, 63, 65, 73, 74, 201, 202, 203, 204, 205, 207, 240

Index

Taylor, Jane, of Charley Crag, xvii, xxix, 11, 16, 17, 18, 20, 23, 29, 70n, 202n, 207, 240, 241, 243; John, husband of, xvii, 202, 240; John, son of, of Dublin, 10, 17, 240, 241
Taylor, John, of Charley Crag, 69, 95, 98, 101, 173, 187, 190, 191, 194, 206; John, of Cobby House, tanner, xiv; John, of Espford, 24, 31, 46, 47, 60, 83; John, of Jolliver Tree (d. 1724), 16, 18, 204, 208, 241, 242; John, of Plum Green and Landing, 204, 205, 207, 216; John, of Rusland, 195, 196, 208; John (unid.), 4, 12, 13, 14
Taylor, Margaret, of Finsthwaite, xix, 10, 13, 14, 16, 24, 25, 30, 32, 46, 49, 60, 66, 72, 84, 219, 239, 241, 242
Taylor, Mary (b. 1727), xv, xxivn, 67n, 69, 101, 106, 136
Taylor, Matthew, of Town End, 149, 151, 173, 174, 241
Taylor, Myles, miller, 32, 34, 42, 45, 59, 66, 103, 190, 241
Taylor, Peter, of Charley Crag, xvii, xxi, xxiii, 33, 44, 50, 63, 64, 67–8, 78, 84, 122, 123, 128, 129, 131, 133, 134, 156, 163, 165, 166, 167, 169, 170, 171, 172, 173, 174, 182, 187, 200, 202, 239, 240, 241; Anne, wife of, 128, 129, 163, 165, 166, 172, 209, 241; Elizabeth, daughter of, 129n; Peter, of Waterside, smith, xiv; Peter (unid.), 178
Taylor, Richard, of Finsyke, 27, 28, 45, 61, 239, 241; Alice, wife of, 23, 111, 112, 173n, 241; Elizabeth, daughter of, 99, 106, 107, 109, 110, 121, 124, 127, 187, 239, 240, 241; Emmy, daughter of, see Morris; Richard, of Waterside, xiiin, xiv, xxixn, 236
Taylor, Robert, of Crosslands, 178, 194, 196, 207, 209; Robert, of High Stott Park, 17, 37, 76, 79, 84, 85, 89, 91, 92, 139, 140, 177, 189, 194, 204, 205, 206, 207, 208, 238, 240, 242; Robert (unid.), 195
Taylor, Roger, of High Stott Park, xiin
Taylor, Rowland, of Thwaite Moss, 17, 115, 178, 187, 242
Taylor, Rownson, waller, 50, 51, 200, 201, 202, 203, 212, 219–20
Taylor, Thomas, workman, 64
Taylor, Rev. William, xiv, xvi, xix, xxvii, 1, 6, 8n, 16, 21, 25, 26, 44, 61, 79, 92, 102, 113n, 160n, 185, 186, 187, 188, 191, 207, 213, 218, 220n, 242; William, servant, xxi, 10, 11, 17, 19, 23, 28, 30, 33, 41, 59, 239, 241, 242; William (b. 1634), xiii; William (unid.), 195
tenants, services by, xviii, 3–4, 5–6, 15, 25–6, 29, 32, 52, 65, 67–8, 71, 74, 77–8, 82, 86, 92, 93, 100, 101, 104, 105, 106, 110, 111, 115, 119, 123, 128, 134, 141, 145–6, 149–51, 159, 198–200; see also rents
Thompson, Thomas, servant, xxi, 142
timber: sales of, xviii, 10, 15, 23, 38–9, 49, 51–2, 53–4, 96, 107, 112, 112, 114, 118, 124, 125, 126, 154, 164, 174, 225; for wheels, 19, 31; see also building materials
tobacco, 62, 81, 168, 172
Tom Crag, xvii, 19n, 62, 140–1, 143, 160, 203, 225, 240
tools, xivn, 18, 70, 129, 237
Torver, 179
Towers, George, of Coniston, 208; James, xix, 27, 57, 58, 63n; Samuel, workman, 210; —, tailor, 61
Town End, xii, xvii, xxi, 63, 64, 65, 77, 81, 107, 150, 168, 169, 203, 225, 226, 229, 233, 235, 237
Townson, —, fishman, 18, 29
trees, xviii, xxviii, 17, 21, 24
Troutbeck, Westm., 35, 39, 154n
Turner (Torner), John, 9, 10, 12, 14, 29, 102, 178, 196; Mr, 123; widow, 112
Twisaday, James, of Thwaite Moss, 19, 22, 31, 33, 44, 47, 242
Tyson, Daniel, wool dealer, 17

Ulverston, xix, xxiii, xv, 21, 22, 23, 25, 27, 28, 33, 35, 62, 64, 89, 104, 128, 129, 164, 175, 176, 179, 183, 185, 186, 191, 221, 227, 228
Urswick, 179

vagrants, 174

wages, of midwife, 67; of nurse, 55, 69; of servants, xxi, 11, 23, 27, 28, 33, 41, 59, 64, 77, 79, 86, 88, 95, 101–2, 105, 196, 115, 119, 141–2, 169, 170; of workmen, xxi xxiii, 29, 44, 61, 62, 65, 67, 82, 84, 97, 98, 100, 105, 107, 116, 129, 135, 156, 158, 159, 164–5, 168, 173, 190, 200–2, 203, 211
Wainhouse, Rowland, of Cartmel, mercer, 12, 25, 26, 28, 29, 61, 242
Wainman (Wayman), Thomas, of Finsthwaite, 18, 22, 243
Walker, Edward, fuller, 19, 26, 70, 78, 177, 194, 243; Isabel, of Elinghearth, 108, 112; James, of Elinghearth, 2, 5, 64, 68, 75, 78, 93, 177, 194, 200, 201, 204, 243; James (unid.), 194; John, house–carpenter, xxiii, xxxi, 9, 11, 13, 24, 34, 35, 36, 37, 38, 43, 44, 45, 48, 54, 57, 66, 67, 70, 76, 93, 95, 97, 116, 117, 118, 132, 134, 135, 169, 189–90, 201, 202, 210; John, tailor, 119; John (unid.), 69, 164, 165, 177; Margaret, 108, 207; Myles, of Haverthwaite,

Walker, Edward, *continued*
    177, 184, 206; Thomas, 22, 178, 180, 206; William, 17, 18, 34, 35, 96, 101, 187, 220; William, of Dale Park, 209
walls, 9–10, 33, 44, 50, 65, 73–4, 158, 200
Warton, 154n
Waterside, xiv, xv, xvii, xxi, xxiv, xxix, xxx, 136, 144, 151, 156, 162, 167, 180, 203, 236, 237, 239, 241
Wells, Samuel, workman, 65
Wilkinson, John, of Bouth, smith, 67, 243; John, wool dealer, 94
Williamson, Alice, of Staveley, 155n
Wilson, Anthony, of High Wray, xix, 31, 46, 54, 74, 105, 243; Edmund, of Near Sawrey, grocer, xxviii, 16, 21, 24, 30, 34, 45, 46, 55, 59, 243; James, 35; John, wool dealer, 30; John, smith, 108, 178, 196, 207; John (unid.), 63, 67, 201, 210, 178, 195, 196, 207; Jonathan, 112, 138, 195; Mary, of Near Sawrey, 209; Robert, 178, 195, 196, 207; Rowland, of Crosslands, 178, 195, 196, 208; Thomas, workman, 154; William, 11, 30; Colonel, of Kendal, 182, 183, 184, 185, 186
windows, 66, 77
wood, see timber
Woodburn, William, of Charley Crag, xvii, xx, 3, 4, 6–7, 10, 29, 31, 61, 68, 81, 82, 124, 243; Agnes, daughter of, 13, 51; Jane, wife of, 7, 13, 15, 36, 43, 48, 58, 61, 63, 68, 81, 82, 96, 97, 103, 107, 109, 110, 121, 122, 124, 125, 127, 131, 135, 138, 152, 153, 167, 172, 182, 202–3, 209, 240, 243; Margaret, 122; Robert, 148
wool, xx, xxvii, 11, 17, 22, 28, 77, 79, 80, 83, 94, 105, 106, 169; cards, 19, 89
Wright, John, 16, 46